THE Beading ANSWER BOOK

Solutions to Every Problem You'll Ever Face

Answers to Every Question You'll Ever Ask

KAREN MORRIS

Storey Publishing

The mission of Storey Publishing is to serve our customers by publishing practical information that encourages personal independence in harmony with the environment.

Edited by Deborah Balmuth and Nancy D. Wood
Art direction and book design by Mary Winkelman Velgos
Text production by Jennifer Jepson Smith

Cover photographs by John Polak Photography
Illustrations by © Gayle Isabelle Ford

Indexed by Nancy D. Wood

Printed in China by R.R. Donnelley
10 9 8 7 6 5 4 3

LIBRARY OF CONGRESS CATALOGING-IN-PUBLICATION DATA

Morris, Karen.
  The beading answer book : solutions to every problem you'll ever face :
answers to every question you'll ever ask / Karen Morris.
    p. cm.
  Includes index.
  ISBN 978-1-60342-034-1 (pbk. : alk. paper)
  1. Beadwork—Miscellanea. I. Title.
TT860.M6687 2008
745.58'2—dc22
                                        2008017997

To all my beading students:
thank you for letting me know what you
wanted/needed to learn.

Contents

Introduction

Whether you've been beading for a while or you're entirely new to the craft, you've doubtless got lots of questions that need answers. But finding those answers can almost require becoming a full-time sleuth, searching through piles of books, class handouts, and magazine articles — at least it did until now. The book you're now holding conveniently provides answers to all the key beading questions you're likely to have while you're learning, from the essentials of stringing to how to get started with special techniques such as bead crochet. So tuck this little beading bible into your bag and keep it handy. It will serve as a faithful companion and guide while you travel the often topsy-turvy road to beading knowledge.

The students in my classes are always bursting with questions. I have gathered more than 300 of the most urgent questions together in this book, and answered them as if we were sitting together in a private class. But unlike information given in a class, these answers will be available to you anytime, anywhere, day or night.

If you're new to beading, you may look at the sheer quantity of information contained in these pages and say, "Good grief, what are they talking about?" It's true; beading can seem overwhelming at first. But once you've taken the first few steps, I'll bet, if you're like me, that you'll just want to learn more; and little by little, the information will fit together and make sense.

One great thing about the diversity of beadwork is that we are all beginners at some aspect of beading! What we love is the process of discovery and adventure. Beads are like puzzle pieces — tiny particles of color and light that can be arranged and configured in an infinite variety of pleasing ways.

Many of us spend our days working with numbers and spreadsheets, or words and contracts, or difficult people (feel free to toss in a couple of toddlers and piles of laundry here). I invite you to step away from all that for a moment, and try bringing some light and color into your life. Just a few minutes of working with your beads, even if you're only organizing them, can cleanse your mind of prior thoughts (what was it that I was worrying about?) and refresh your outlook, like a form of meditation.

Please join us.

CHAPTER 1

Getting Started

What Is It About Beads?

Q **What does the word "beading" actually mean? And what are some of the different ways to use beads?**

A "Beading" is a general term that refers to making or embellishing something with beads. And the word "bead" is a broad category that includes any small decorative object that has a hole in it or has been pierced to form a hole for stringing. Beads then can include drilled seeds, shells, pearls, and stones, as well as beads made of glass, wood, and plastic.

You can string a group of beads to create a necklace or bracelet; weave beads together with a needle and thread to make everything from jewelry to sculpture to tapestries; sew beads to embellish a garment or other fabric; and even knit and crochet with beads.

....

Q **Why do people make such a big deal about beads?**

A Throughout history, people have decorated their bodies with beads, so much so that beads help date the earliest existence of human life on the planet. The use of beads is thought to indicate a certain level of cultural complexity and development, and beads are among the oldest human art forms. Several beads made from Nassarius shells are thought to be the earliest known forms of jewelry. Until

Nassarius shell bead

BASIC BEADING STYLES

strung necklace

bead-crocheted rope bracelet

bead-knitted bracelet

bead-woven earring

beaded picot edge

recently, the earliest beads were assumed to date to 38,000 years ago, but newer discoveries in Algeria and Israel may push the date back to 75,000 or even 100,000 years ago.

Q **Why is beading irresistible? I find myself very attracted to beads, their colors and patterns, and to the idea of wearing them.**

A If you're attracted to beads, you're in good company. Just about every culture for thousands of years has incorporated beads into their clothing, rituals, and religions. From protecting newborn babies from evil spirits to celebrating weddings to anointing a king, beads have been there. If you'd like to learn more, I suggest that you watch the DVD series *World on a String* by Diana Friedberg. (*See* Resources.) After watching, you'll wonder why everyone you know isn't into beading! (What's wrong with them? Do they have any idea what they're missing?)

. . . .

Q **I saw a "beaded" sculpture made entirely from pencil points woven together. Why does this piece qualify as beading?**

A The definition of a bead includes just about any small object with a hole in it. If the pencil points have holes drilled in them so they can be strung together, then technically, each pencil point is a bead. Dramatic beaded jewelry and sculpture can be made from traditional, expected materials such as glass beads and chunks of turquoise, or from surprising, refreshing materials such as drilled pencil points, metal washers, nuts, mesh hardware cloth, and clear plastic tubing cut into bead lengths. Once you start to tune in and notice beading, the diversity will delight and inspire you. For more on these unexpected beading materials, check out the work of Jennifer Maestre and Ingrid Goldbloom Bloch. (*See* Resources.)

. . . .

Q **A lot of beadwork I've seen is made with teeny-tiny beads. I don't think I can work with them! Can I still enjoy beading?**

A The tiny beads you refer to are called seed beads. You may already know whether you enjoy working with tiny objects. If you don't, or you're not sure if you'll have the patience, start with larger 6° seed beads, 4mm squares and drops, and 4mm to 6mm and larger Czech glass and semi-precious stone. *(See page 51.)* When it comes to bead sizes, it's important to remember that the larger the number, the smaller the bead. So, 6° are the larger, easy-to-see seed beads and 15° are the really small ones.

After you've become familiar with some of the techniques, and are using good magnification and adequate light, you might consider trying smaller beads. But aside from broadening your beading options, there's no reason why you have to use the small beads. There's a lifetime worth of projects you can make using larger beads.

SEE ALSO: Magnification/Lighting, page 130.

Q **Is beading an expensive hobby?**

A If beads weren't so darn addictive, I would say it's one of the most affordable hobbies! You don't need an expensive sewing machine, for example, or really any machinery at all beyond a needle, thread, and a couple of hand tools. Nearly everything you purchase for beading goes into the finished product. So, no, beading doesn't have to be an expensive hobby. That is, unless you decide you immediately must have every single type of bead in every color made.

Q I'd like to experiment with beading without spending a lot of money. Since I'm just learning, doesn't it make sense to use the cheaper seed beads I've seen in dime stores or children's kits?

A It's fine to start with small quantities, but in my opinion, it's always better not to scrimp on quality. The quality of your materials affects the outcome of any project you decide to make. If you're going to put your time and ideas into a piece, I think it makes sense to use good-quality beads, supplies, and findings. This doesn't mean that you have to purchase the most expensive of everything, but you'll find, for example, that sterling silver and gold-filled clasps tend to be smoother and better made than many similar findings made of base metal. And they often cost just a little more.

Although the inexpensive beads in some shops may look like a bargain, they will actually cost more than you think when you factor in the waste. These beads may be okay for a more organic piece, or for a lamp base that you want to cover with glue and beads. But they're often uneven in size, and may have sharp or irregular holes. To find beads that look smooth and uniform enough for a strung or woven beaded piece, you'll spend time culling or separating out the defective beads, and end up throwing beads away. Be sure to calculate this waste into the cost of your project.

I suggest that you choose beautiful materials in colors you love, that will make you proud every time you see or wear the piece. Good-quality beads and materials are more important than a fancy or complicated design. One way to save money on beading supplies is to consider buying good-quality beads and jewelry at tag sales and thrift stores. You can take these pieces apart and recycle the beads and findings into your own new and exciting projects.

*strand of irregular
seed beads*

*strand of high-quality
seed beads*

Basic Knots

Q **Do I need to learn a lot of fancy knots to do beading?**

A You don't need to know a lot of knots to do beautiful beadwork. There are just a few essential knots, and you probably already know some of them from Girl Scouts. Check out the next four pages for a look at the basic knots and when you'll use them.

BASIC KNOTS YOU NEED TO KNOW
....

Whether you want to tie knots between beads, are ready to finish off
a stretch bracelet, or need to knot when adding thread into a woven
piece, there are just a few basic knots you'll need to know.

Overhand knot. One of the most basic knots, often used to start or end
a thread and as a component of other knots. Create a loop, bring the
working end through the loop, and pull both ends to tighten and complete the knot. When using an overhand knot to join two or more ends:
Bring the ends together, make a loop, and then pass both ends through
the loop (a). For extra security, tighten the first knot and tie a second
overhand knot just next to it (b).

Double overhand knot. Used in the same instance as the single overhand knot, but it is more secure. Create a loop, bring the working end
through the loop as in the overhand knot, pass the end through the loop
again, and pull both ends to tighten and complete the knot.

Square knot. Another knot used for joining and ending threads, as it is
basically two overhand knots tied in opposite directions. It can also be
used to add a new thread in the middle of a piece when you come to
the end of the first thread and your project is still unfinished. Pass the
right end over the left and around it. Then pass the left end over the
right and around it. Pull the ends tight.

Surgeon's knot. Similar to the square knot in its use for beginning and
ending threads, but it is more secure. On the first overhand knot, wrap
the right end around twice. Complete as for the square knot.

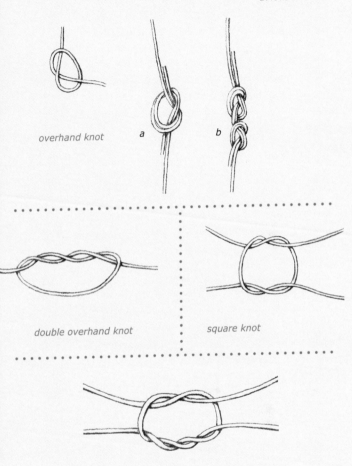

overhand knot

a

b

double overhand knot

square knot

surgeon's knot

17

BASIC KNOTS YOU NEED TO KNOW (continued)

Slip knot. Used for starting bead crochet. Create a loop, lay one end of the thread behind the loop and pull a small second loop of thread through the first loop. Tighten to form a slip knot. The end can slide to adjust the size of the second loop.

Figure-eight knot. Can be used for knotting flexible beading wire without kinking. Create a bend and lay the lower, shorter end over the other to make a loop. Pass the short end behind the other end and then pass it through the first loop.

Lark's head knot. Often used in macramé and to join stringing material to a wire or cord. Fold the stringing material in half, lay this fold on top of the cord, and bend it behind the cord (a). Bring the ends through the loop and pull to tighten (b).

Sliding knot. Often used to create an adjustable closure on thin leather cord. Allow about 12" of cord on either end. Lay right and left ends together, facing in opposite directions. Fold right end back about 3". Wrap it around itself and the left end three times. Pass the right end through the wraps and pull tight. Turn the piece and repeat with the other end. Slide knots away from each other to shorten the loop and toward each other to open it.

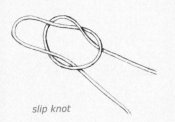

slip knot

figure-eight knot

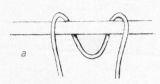

lark's head knot

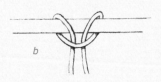

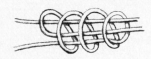

sliding knot

19

How to Buy Beads

Q **Where's a good place to buy beads?**

A I suggest that you always shop first at your local bead store, if you're lucky enough to have one. Selecting bead shapes, seeing the way they reflect light, and choosing color combinations is so much easier when you can actually touch and arrange the beads. I recently had to buy a certain type of bead online. Because my work is all about color, I had a very difficult time selecting an interesting four-color combination using only the small flat squares on my computer screen. I couldn't even move the color squares around. In fact, the task was nearly impossible. So for me, buying online only works when I already know exactly what I want.

· ·

Q **The prices in bead stores are higher than the same products online, so why shouldn't I purchase my supplies online?**

A Companies that sell beads online are able to operate from a pared-down warehouse with relatively low overhead. They also may sell beads in larger quantities, which helps to keep prices down.

A retail store has higher overhead costs for rent, décor, and utilities, plus it pays employees to keep the store open six or seven days a week, assist customers, and answer questions. Your local retail store can give you personal service, advice, and guidance. You can see and touch the beads before you buy them, and see how they work with other beads. This usually results in fewer buying mistakes and disappointments.

As in other things, you get what you pay for. If you love the advice, help, camaraderie, and instant gratification of your local bead store, you'll need to make your purchases there to help keep them in business.

. . . .

Q **In my local beading shop, why do two different beads of the same size and shape have such different prices?**

A Sometimes, two similar beads may have different prices because one arrived recently, while the other has been hanging in the store for a number of years. But more often, the variance between prices is a result of different colors, finishes, or treatments used to make the beads. *(See a list of finishes on page 43.)* Transparent and plain opaque beads tend to be a bit less expensive, although certain colors are more difficult or costly to make. Those with matte finishes, lusters, and metallic coatings are progressively more expensive. The most expensive beads are made with 22- to 24-karat gold.

. . . .

Q **If I pay more for beads, does that mean they will last longer?**

A Not necessarily. Sometimes, the most expensive beads, like the gorgeous gold-plated ones, are relatively fragile, and the coating may eventually wear off from repeated exposure to skin acids. My opinion? Either way, they're worth it for the rich and beautiful effect they provide.

Many of the less expensive glass beads are made in India and China. Although these beads may last as long as other glass beads, you'll need to discard more of the beads because of their irregular shape. In general, more expensive Japanese and European beads tend to be smoother, more uniform (far less waste), and of higher quality than the less expensive beads made in China or India.

BEADING QUANTITIES

Cent (C) = 100 pieces

Gross (GR) = a dozen dozen, or 144 pieces

Kilogram (kg) = 2.2 pounds

Gram (g) = 1/1000 kg, or 0.035 ounce

Ounce (avoirdupois) = 28.35 grams

Ounce (troy) = 31.10 grams; used in weighing wire and other metals

Mass (MA) = 1,200 pieces

Mille (MI) = 1,000 pieces

Millimeter (mm) = $\frac{1}{25}$"

Piece (PC) = one

Hank = 6 to 12 strands, each usually 18" to 20"

Q When buying beads for a project, I'm frustrated because the packaging for different beads varies so much. My pattern may call for 200 beads, but they're sold by the gram or tube or ounce. How do I know how many beads I'm getting?

A Seed beads are generally sold in 1-ounce packages, in tubes or small zip bags by the gram, or on strands in hanks. There's little standardization between types of packaging, so it's helpful to be able to figure out the numbers yourself. The Seed Bead Size/Quantity Guide on pages 48–49 shows approximately how many beads of each size, lined up hole to hole, measure 1", and how many beads are contained in a gram, in an ounce, and in a standard 12-strand hank.

It's important to realize that these counts are approximate. Beads of the same size from various manufacturers in different countries can be slightly different sizes and shapes, and may have larger or smaller holes (which can drastically affect the weight of the bead). Even beads of different colors and finishes from a single manufacturer can vary slightly in size and weight. Using this information and a calculator, you can usually get a fairly accurate idea of how many beads you're buying. It's always best to purchase extra beads, so you don't run out of the color or dye lot.

MAKING YOUR OWN BEADS

We have so many beads available from all over the world, but what if we'd like to make our own? Here are just a few ideas to get you started.

▶ **Recycled jewelry beads.** Turn a vintage Bakelite pin, shoe clip, or other decorative object into a bead. One way is to add wire loops around each end of the pin or clip and string it as a focal bead on a necklace.

▶ **Lampwork beads.** Many beaders become attracted to working with glass and decide to make their own glass beads. Take a class to explore this creative art form.

▶ **Felted beads.** Beads made from wool roving or wool yarn can be embellished with seed beads.

▶ **Fiber or ribbon beads.** Create beautiful beads using yarn, ribbon, and other fibers by wrapping them around wire to create a hole, and securing ends with glue or stitching.

▶ **Paper beads.** Cut and roll paper to form bead shapes, seal with shellac, and drill a hole if necessary.

▶ **Shell or coin beads.** Simply drill a hole to change a small solid object into a bead.

▶ **Polymer clay beads.** Shape beads from clay and bake to make them permanent.

▶ **Precious metal clay beads.** Shape beads and/or findings from PMC and fire to create metal beads or findings.

▶ **Beaded beads.** Use off-loom weaving techniques from chapter 8 to create an infinite variety of beaded beads.

How Do I Learn Beading?

Q The bead store feels overwhelming. I look around, buy one or two things, and dash out. How am I ever going to make anything?

A First, allow yourself enough time at the bead store to browse. Take a few deep breaths as you walk around and look closely at the beads. Sit and leaf through a couple of books or magazines to see what sort of beaded designs attract you. Reading about the techniques and how a piece is made can give you an idea of what you'd like to learn first. Go with what attracts you. Really, it's up to you.

Second, if you're attracted to certain beads, it's okay to buy them before you know what you're going to make. Beginners sometimes worry that they're spending money on beads but don't have a clear goal. If you see a color or shape that attracts you, buy it and take it home. This is the beginning of your bead collection, or "stash." The beads you like will start to "get friendly" with each other, and you'll begin to have ideas about how you want to combine them.

. . . .

Q What's an easy way to jump in and get started with beading?

A Stringing beads on wire or cord is an easy way to start, and you'll find a lot more about this type of beading in chapter 5. If you're looking for some immediate gratification, try making a bracelet by stringing beads on stretch cord. Since the cord stretches to slide over your hand, you don't even need to add a clasp. The style possibilities are endless.

SEE ALSO: Stretch Cord, page 178.

Q Once I get my feet wet, how do I pick up skills?

A When you're first learning to bead, it's important not to become overwhelmed by the abundance of bead choices and techniques. Yes, there are many, but the best path is to master one technique at a time. You have years to learn and gently progress from one technique to the next. Pay attention to what attracts you, and follow that direction.

I would venture a guess that there's not a single beading expert who knows and practices every beading technique. There are just too many choices. So, you are not alone! We are all beginners at something.

Take advantage of the classes offered by your local bead store or adult education program. Beading with a group can be relaxing and fun, and you'll gain confidence and learn from observing the bead choices and ideas of the other students, as well as from the teacher's samples and suggestions.

Once you take a class, continue making more of that item until you feel comfortable with the technique from start to finish. In fact, I tell my students to keep making that bracelet until they're sick of it! Then when you're ready to move on to another class, you'll be building on your knowledge. After a few classes, you'll start to feel like a pro.

Notes to Yourself

A notebook can help you keep track of the details of your beading experiments, such as the beads, colors, and techniques used. It's also helpful to include other important information: Did you like the result? If you have any false starts or a small sample piece, tape it right onto the page, and write what you did or did not like about it. Keeping a notebook will help you remember what you've made and what worked well, especially if you will be selling or giving pieces away as gifts. These notes will refresh your memory and lead to ideas for future projects. You'll be building on your knowledge, instead of starting all over again every time.

Q **How do I retain the information I learn in beading class? I understand the instructions when the teacher is explaining them, but it's hard to go back to it later.**

A If you really want to build a solid foundation of beading and jewelry-making knowledge, I suggest that you begin to keep a notebook of the things you make and the techniques you learn. Jot down the name of the technique, notes about what you made, the date, and details on the beads and colors you used. If you learned the project in a class, include the class handout in a plastic sleeve. If it's from a magazine or book, add the title and page number so you can find the pattern again, or photocopy the instructions and place them in a plastic sleeve with notes.

After taking a few classes, you'll start to notice similarities between projects and techniques, and you'll reach the point where you won't need to take a class for every new design. Carefully read through the instructions in beading magazines to see if you understand the steps. When you notice that the instructions don't seem too alien, you may be ready to attempt the project on your own.

Working with Color

Q **When I shop, I always seem to go for the same colors and color families. Won't this make my work boring?**

A Not necessarily! This is one way to develop your own color sense and preferences. If you continue to buy beads you like, you'll find that they start to work together, and a combination or new design idea may begin to develop. When shopping, buy beads that are calling out to you (You know what I mean, don't you?), even if you're not sure how you'll use them. When you get home, experiment and play with your beads.

One thing I love to do is design a piece around many different shades of the same color. Maybe these two shades of green don't look good together when they're alone, but combined with a few other greens, it can become interesting, like the many greens in a garden. A variety of shades of the same color can create texture and depth in a piece. Choose another color, possibly one from the opposite side of the color wheel, to use as an accent color, to provide balance. For example, if I'm combining several shades of green, I might use copper or persimmon red as an accent color.

COLOR WHEELS

If you search "color wheel" on Google Images, you'll find many beautiful examples of color wheels to work with and interesting ideas to try. If you don't have Internet access, look for color wheels in art and design books.

Also, you don't need to make your color combinations too pretty. If everything matches in a too-tidy way, it can give the feeling that there's no motion, nothing to look at. Adding some "wrong" colors can create tension in the piece and make it more interesting. Try using "rude" shades of yellow, chartreuse, or orange to give a piece a shot of energy, wake it up, and give it some life.

Q I feel as if I don't have a good eye for color. How can I make things that I'm going to like?

A Every time I teach a class, I hear someone say, "I don't have a good color sense." But your color sense is like a muscle that hasn't been exercised for a while. When you start to use it, it may feel a little rusty, but then it will start to develop and grow. As it gets stronger, you will become more confident about what you like and don't like, and more courageous and willing to explore new ideas and take risks.

To come up with interesting colors for the next project, jot down color combinations that attract you. Notice colors you like in people's clothing and jewelry, in books and magazines, in home décor, and even in art and nature. Play with a variety of beads to see how different colors might look together in smaller proportions.

· ·

Q **How can I learn more about color?**

A I suggest that you keep color ideas in a file folder for inspiration. Tear out magazine ads with color combinations you find exciting or surprising. Nonbeading magazines are a great source of ideas for color. When you see a full-page ad in a recent magazine, you can be sure that the company spent thousands of dollars making sure the colors in the ad are fresh, appealing, and very current. Plan a beading project using the colors in the ad. You can even bring the ad to the bead store to match colors. Estimate the proportions of the colors in the ad, so you can use them similarly in your piece. The best part is that you already know that the color combination works, and you like it!

It's important to realize, too, that the beads in early pieces you make are not ruined or finished. This is one happy distinction between beading and sewing. Let's face it — a treasured piece of expensive fabric becomes nearly useless if you don't like the jacket you sewed, or it doesn't fit. But if you don't completely love one of your finished jewelry pieces, remember that you can wear it for a while and then cut it apart, improve the design, and make it again, or save the beads to use in an entirely different piece. Be willing to take a risk, make a mistake, and experiment!

Planning a Design

Q **How do I plan a design for a necklace?**

A For a first project, I suggest sticking with a simple two-color design. You can't go wrong with black and ivory or black and white. If you wear black often, you may find that you enjoy wearing this simple design all the time. To add a little more variety, choose two different bead shapes in each color. Try out some sample designs. *(See* Playing with Design Ideas *on the next page.)*

Remember that you're not making a piece yet. This is a safe, playful part of the design process. If the samples you make don't compel you to move forward, set them aside until the next morning. Waking up and taking a fresh look at the options usually helps you make choices or come up with a new idea. Then you can move on with a plan for the piece.

Now imagine adding a third or fourth color. As you can see, there are infinite options for patterning. And a necklace

PLAYING WITH DESIGN IDEAS

Try out different design ideas and combinations by stringing 1" or 2" of each idea on the end of your beading wire to see what looks good and what you prefer. Laying out larger beads on a bead board *(see page 103)* is another good way to experiment with design, color, and placement before you start to construct a piece. These illustrations show a few suggestions to get you started. Use A for the first bead or color, B for the second, C for the third, and so on. Using letters is a quick way to note a stringing sequence or design idea. Writing down the sequence and taping the design samples into your notebook can help you jump-start the process the next time you're working on a new project.

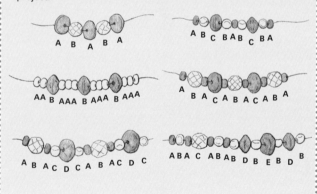

A B A B A

A B C B A B C B A

AA B AAA B AAA B AAA

A B A C A B A C A B A

A B A C D C A B A C D C

A B A C A B A B D B E B D B

doesn't have to be the same design all along its length. You can use larger beads at the center front, or you can space the large beads closer together at the front, gradually adding more small beads as you approach the back. Or you can alternate two or more different sequences around the necklace.

SEE ALSO: Bead Board, page 103.

Q **Why do I need patterns? Can't I just combine beads randomly?**

A Of course, not all your pieces have to be arranged in neat, orderly patterns. It's just a safe place to start. Beaders jokingly refer to that illusive design called "random" as the most difficult pattern there is, because it can be tricky to create balance and harmony in a random design. If you feel comfortable with the idea of working randomly, though, it's fine to start there.

There's also the possibility of compromise; for instance, creating a necklace with planned patterns, then adding a wilder tassel with a random design.

Q **I want to make a necklace using a unique strand of beads that I bought, but I'm worried that I don't have enough of them. What should I do?**

A The answer to this dilemma leads directly from the previous two questions. By thinking of a new piece as a combination of several different beads, you're freed from worrying whether you have enough of one special type of bead. Work with what you have, and let that limitation help to shape the outcome.

· ·

Q I have trouble planning a jewelry project when looking at a whole bunch of the beads or a big ounce bag of seed beads. How do these quantities in the store translate into a wearable piece?

A You're right, the proportions of a whole hank or bag of beads are very different than they will look in your finished piece. That's why you want to string up a few of the beads before you make too many decisions. If the bead color looks too bright in the package, remember that you'll be combining one small particle of that color at a time in your piece. Colors become much more subtle when the proportions change, so don't rule out colors that seem a bit too bright in the larger quantity.

You can't get very far with your design while the beads are still in the bag or on the big hank. You have to cut a strand, dump some of each bead out on a mat, and start playing with color combinations. And then trust your instincts; go with what you like and discard ideas that aren't as appealing. In this way, you will start to strengthen and trust your own color sense and develop your own unique style of beading.

· ·

Q **I have a strand of beautiful beads, but don't know what else to put with them. What do you suggest?**

A Variety makes a piece interesting, which is one reason it's good to have some beads at home to help you get started. If you play with bead combinations and colors at home first, you'll already have a few ideas about the new piece before you're standing in the bead store, surrounded by so many bead choices.

Be willing to ask for help. Most bead store employees are happy to give you their opinions about what may look good with your strand of beads, and many of them are very experienced beaders and even teachers. Even though you may not always agree with their ideas (remember that there is no "right" answer!), these ideas can help to push you in the direction of what you envision for this piece. At each store visit, only buy the beads that you're sure about, and take your time to let the design unfold.

When you start working on the project, you don't need to know what the final piece will look like. It's a process. You'll just head in that direction and make decisions all along the way. Pretend that it's a road map, and you're deciding which way to go. Like this idea? Yes! So include it. Like that idea? Not really! So change it.

Beading TLC

Q How should I care for my beads?

A There are a few simple rules to follow that will extend the life of your beads and the jewelry made with them.

▶ Never allow your beads to get wet. I'm always surprised to learn that some people take showers wearing their beaded jewelry.

▶ Avoid sunlight, especially during storage, which can fade some colors.

▶ Put on your jewelry after applying any creams or hairspray, since skin acids, creams, and cosmetics can cause colors to change and coatings to gradually wear off. After wearing, gently wipe jewelry with a soft cloth before putting it away, especially if your skin became clammy or sweaty during wear.

▶ Store each piece of sterling silver jewelry in a plastic ziplock bag with the excess air pressed out, which will help to reduce tarnishing.

CHAPTER 2

All About Beads

A World of Choices

Q **What are beads made of?**

A Since any small object with a hole in it can be considered a bead, this term obviously includes a huge variety of items, from tiny shells to elaborately layered handmade glass. Although glass is one of the most common materials for beads, you'll also find beautiful beads made of wood, ivory, pearls, seashell, coral, crystal, plastic, polymer clay, precious metal clay, porcelain, fiber, seeds, teeth, ostrich shell, amber, bone, horn, tusk, metals, paper, cloisonné (enamel or powdered glass over metal), and all types of gemstones.

The world offers a staggering array of beads. Some are so beautiful that a single bead or strand can stand alone, while other smaller beads are designed as building blocks for patterns that can be simple or intricate, woven or strung. In time, you will learn your way around the expansive possibilities of bead types, shapes, and sizes.

===

What Are Seed Beads?

Q **Why are smaller beads referred to as seed beads?**

A The generic term "seed" simply refers to the size of the beads, meaning that they are tiny. Early beads were made from actual seeds and other plant materials. When small beads began to be handmade from glass, the name "seed" remained.

Because they're small, seed beads lend themselves to intricate designs, texture, and types of work that combine color and pattern. Seed beads are frequently used for loom and off-loom weaving. They also work well as spacers between larger beads in a strung design, as embroidered embellishment on fabric, and in crochet designs with thread or wire.

. . . .

Q **How are seed beads made?**

A Traditionally, the techniques for making these beads have been kept secret. However, we do have some basic information about early drawn glass or seed bead production:

▶ A glob of molten glass was dipped onto the end of a metal blowpipe.

▶ A second rod called a punty (short for puntile) was attached to the other end of the glob.

▶ Air was blown into the pipe to create the hole.

▶ Two people, one holding the pipe and the other holding the punty, ran in opposite directions (some say on horseback), quickly pulling the molten glass into a hollow rod up to 300 feet long.

▶ The cooled rods were chopped or sliced into bead lengths.

▶ The beads were refired or tumbled with hot sand to round them and smooth the rough edges without melting the holes closed.

▶ The beads were sifted to sort them into different sizes.

▶ The beads were reheated in a kiln to give them a glossy finish.

Similar methods are employed today, using more automated machinery — at least in some parts of the world. Japanese seed bead production is probably the most highly mechanized, using high-tech processes and cutting tools. Chemical formulas for different colors of glass are extremely sensitive and must be mixed with absolute accuracy. These formulas, and most bead manufacturing techniques, are still closely guarded secrets. To produce the modern beads:

▶ A compressed air device blows molten glass through a hole, with the shape of the hole creating the different shapes of beads.

▶ Specialized cutting machines are used to cut the long glass tubes into bead lengths.

▶ A huge variety of coatings, linings, glazes, dyes, mattes, and lusters are added to create the hundreds of colors and finishes.

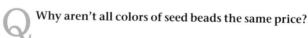

Q Why aren't all colors of seed beads the same price?

A The price of beads reflects the cost of the chemicals, processes, and ingredients used to produce them. For

Secret Formulas

Beads have been made from glass for more than 5,000 years, and the details of seed bead production (also called drawn glass) have remained closely guarded secrets. In Venice, Italy, drawn glass has been made primarily on the island of Murano since the thirteenth century. Bead makers and glass workers were highly skilled and respected members of society, but their glass and bead-making secrets had to remain on the island. Legend has it that if a bead maker tried to leave the island of Murano, he and his family were killed.

example, gold must be added to the glass formula to produce many of the deep red colors. The wide range of seed bead prices also reflects the huge variety of linings, coatings, and finish combinations applied to the beads after the glass is formed. Some finishes are created with costly metals, while others require multiple additional finishing steps. It continues to be a frustrating fact of life that the most amazing and beautiful seed beads seem to be the most expensive ones.

Charlottes are seed beads that have a single facet cut into each bead, to add sparkle. These are usually Czech beads, and they are often called "the most brilliant of all seed beads." The higher cost for cut beads arises from the additional labor required to grind or cut the facet on each bead, which is a separate step after the bead has been formed.

SPEAKING THE BEADING LANGUAGE

TYPES

▶ **Charlotte (1X).** Seed bead with one ground facet, creating subtle sparkle

▶ **Two-cut (2X).** Seed bead with two ground facets

▶ **Three-cut (3X).** Seed bead with three ground facets, creating all-over sparkle

▶ **Aiko.** Japanese cylinder bead available in size 10° (really closer in size to 10½°); brand name by Toho

▶ **Bugle.** Narrow glass bead in a tube shape; can be smooth, hex-cut, or twisted

▶ **Cabochon (cab).** Smooth, domed stone, often opaque; usually oval with a flat bottom; technically not a bead because it has no hole, but often used in beaded jewelry as a wire-wrapped pendant or glued to a surface with beads stitched around it; sized by millimeters (mm)

▶ **Delica.** Japanese cylinder seed bead available in three sizes (11°, 10°, and 8°); brand name by Miyuki

▶ **Druk.** Smooth, round pressed-glass bead; sized by millimeters (mm)

▶ **Fire-polished (FP).** Pressed glass bead with facets

▶ **Hex-cut.** Thin-walled cylinder seed or bugle bead with six sides

▶ **Pendant.** Stone, glass, or metal piece with a top hole only

▶ **Rondelle.** Relatively thin bead used as a spacer between two beads

▶ **Swarovski.** Leading Austrian manufacturer of faceted crystal beads; often used incorrectly as a generic term; and sized by millimeters (mm)

FINISHES

Beads are available in a staggering array of colors and finishes, with new variations continually being developed. They may be made from glass that's transparent, translucent or opalescent, or opaque. Some of the more common finishes include:

▶ **Aurora borealis (AB) or iridescent.** Rainbow finish on outside of bead or inside hole

▶ **Bronze or gunmetal.** Metallic luster glaze

▶ **Ceylon (CY).** Pearlized or luster coating on an opalescent bead

▶ **Galvanized.** Silver or dyed plating on surface of the bead

▶ **Inside color.** Dyed color inside the bead hole

▶ **Iris (IR).** Iridescent metallic coating

▶ **Lined (LI).** Transparent or opalescent bead with metallic silver, gold, or copper, or an opaque color, lining the hole

▶ **Luster/lustre (LU).** Glossy coating, often clear or gold, on an opaque or opalescent bead

▶ **Matte.** Frosted or dull finish

▶ **Opal.** Milky or opalescent glass

▶ **Opaque (OP).** Solid color; no light passes through

▶ **Rocaille.** Transparent seed bead with a silver lining

▶ **Satin.** Matted color with a luster finish

▶ **Semimatte.** Partially frosted or dulled finish

▶ **Silk.** White color with satin finish

▶ **Special plating.** 24-karat gold, palladium, copper, or nickel plated on the bead or inside the hole

▶ **Surface-dyed.** Dyes are used to create color on surface of the bead

▶ **Transparent (TR).** Allows light to pass through

Delica Beads

Q **What's the difference between a seed bead and a Delica?**

A Delica is a brand name of the Japanese company Miyuki; the generic term is Japanese cylinder bead. Seed beads have a spherical or ovoid shape, while Delicas have a cylindrical shape with a thin glass wall and relatively large hole. Technically, though, a Delica is still considered a seed bead, because it is small. These cylinder-shaped seed beads are relatively new and have become increasingly popular in the last decade.

Japanese Delica

Japanese seed bead

(enlarged view)

Q **Can I weave with Delica beads?**

A Cylinder seed beads are uniform in shape and size, so they work beautifully for woven bead pieces. They fit neatly together like small tiles to give the work a flat, smooth texture. Manufacturers of Japanese cylinder beads make them in a mind-boggling array of colors and finishes, so they're wonderful for shading and subtle color combinations. Miyuki, for instance, currently makes nearly 900 different types of beads in both Delica and 11° seed beads. (*See* Resources.)

Although you can also weave with round seed beads, cylinder beads give a very different result. I usually explain the difference to my students this way: A piece woven with round seed beads resembles a cobblestone street (bumpy), while one woven with cylinder beads resembles a brick street (flat).

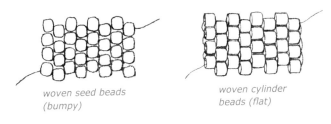

woven seed beads (bumpy)

woven cylinder beads (flat)

Q **Are cylinder beads available in many sizes?**

A There are now several sizes available from two or three Japanese manufacturers: 11° (which is actually narrower than a round 11° seed bead, but about the same length), 10°, and 8°. The brand names include:

▶ Delica (from Miyuki) in all three sizes

▶ Magnifica (available through Mill Hill) in size 11°

▶ Treasure, formerly called Antique, (made by Toho) in size 11°

▶ Aiko (also made by Toho) in size 10° (although their actual size is slightly larger than size 11°)

Q **What are the long skinny beads called?**

A The longer beads that look like slender rods are bugles. Bugles are available in a variety of sizes, based on length, from short #1 bugles (3mm long) to 30mm-long bugles. Bugles are available in straight and twisted styles. Czech bugles tend to be thicker than Japanese ones. The shorter 3mm and 6mm Japanese bugles are about the same width as an 11° Delica.

#1 = 3mm   #2 = 6mm   #3 = 12mm   twisted bugle

Bead Sizes

Q **I find the seed bead sizes so confusing. What does the tiny zero after the bead size mean?**

A When speaking, we tend to refer to seed bead sizes by numbers, such as size 11, 8, or 6. But in writing, we still use the official size names. For example, 11° (also written as 11/0) is an abbreviation for "11-aught." Aught refers to the number of seed beads that will fit in a standard unit of measurement. This is the reason smaller beads have a higher size number. Seed beads have been manufactured for many centuries, and these antiquated size names date from a long-ago era.

Q **I bought a bag of 15° seed beads, and they seem larger than my 13° seed beads. Why is that?**

A Bead sizes and shapes are not an exact science; the sizing and terminology has evolved over many centuries. Seed beads made in different countries can be slightly different sizes and shapes, even though they may be labeled the same size. The sizes of the holes may also differ greatly. For example, a 15° Japanese seed bead is about the same size as a 13° Czech seed bead, except that the Japanese bead has a much larger hole. In general, Japanese seed beads are more uniform in size, shape, and finish, and have larger holes than Czech seed beads of the same size. The larger hole offers two advantages: a single bead weighs less so you get more beads per gram, and you can make more passes through the bead when working woven stitches that require multiple passes.

Even two manufacturers in the same country can make beads of slightly different sizes and shapes. Seed beads made by Matsuno in Japan are slightly more chunky or square than a Japanese Miyuki seed bead of the same size. Also, the Matsuno beads often have square holes, which can alter the appearance of the bead, especially if it's silver-lined.

Czech seed beads tend to be a bit shorter from hole to hole (more like a doughnut shape) and more irregular in size and shape. Czech seed beads are sold on strands, usually 20" long, and grouped in a hank. A hank of 11° seed beads usually contains 12 strands. Fancier cut beads like charlottes, two-cuts, and three-cuts may be grouped in 10-strand hanks, while larger 8° and 6° seed beads are sold in six-strand hanks.

SEED BEAD SIZE/QUANTITY GUIDE

Note: All quantities are approximate.

Bead name	Diameter	# per inch
11° Czech	2mm	19
11° Japanese	2mm	19
11° Japanese cylinder (Delica, Magnifica)	1.8mm	19
10° Japanese cylinder (Aiko)	1.9mm	19
10° Japanese cylinder (Delica)	2.1mm	15
8° Japanese cylinder (Delica)	3mm	9
13° Czech	1.5mm	24
15° Japanese	1.5mm	24
10° Czech	2.2mm	17
8° Czech	3mm	14
8° Japanese	3mm	12
6° Czech	4mm	9.5
6° Japanese	4mm	8.5
3.4mm Japanese drops	3.4mm	13
3mm Japanese cubes	3mm	8.5
4mm Japanese cubes	4mm	6.4

# per gram	# per ounce	# per hank
125	3,544	4,800 in 12-strand, 20" hank
110	3,120	—
200	5,670	—
212	6,000	—
104	3,062	—
33	850	—
250	7,088	3,456 in 12-strand, 12" hank
250	7,088	—
100	2,835	4,080 in 12-strand, 20" hank
45	1,275	1,800 in 6-strand, 20" hank
40	1,106	—
16	454	1140 in 6-strand, 20" hank
12	340	—
20	567	—
21	595	—
12	303	—

Q **My local bead store sells a range of seed bead sizes, but the smallest they sell is 15°. Where can I get the really tiny seed beads?**

A Actually, the smallest seed beads, such as 18° to 24°, haven't been manufactured for nearly 100 years. If you do find any in these sizes, they most likely will be vintage beads and extremely rare; hanks will usually be shorter with fewer strands. With a limited and diminishing supply, not all colors are available in these small sizes. There are a few shops that specialize in tiny and antique seed beads and purchase them all over the world whenever possible. (*See* Resources.)

To work with the tiniest seed beads, which can measure less than 1mm and have equally miniscule holes, you'll need to use extra-thin needles (such as size 15) and thread *(see page 111)*.

. . . .

Q **Why would I want beads with larger holes?**

A When you're weaving with beads, you will often need to pass through each bead several times. A bead with a larger hole is more versatile and helps to prevent the dreaded condition of bead holes packed full of thread, when you still need to pass through the hole again.

Also, when stringing, it can be helpful to have a few beads with larger holes to use at each end of a necklace, next to the clasp, so the flexible beading wire will easily fit through the beads twice.

. . . .

Q **Which beads have larger holes?**

A These include, in order of descending hole size: pony beads (craft beads shaped like a huge seed bead, with really large holes), wooden beads, faceted roller beads, some handmade lampwork beads, 4mm and 3mm Japanese square beads, and 6° and 8° seed beads. Four mm Japanese squares and 6° seed beads can fit on 1mm and .5mm leather and synthetic leather cord, while 3mm Japanese squares and 8° seed beads fit on .5mm cord only.

SEE ALSO: Leather Cord, page 199.

Czech Glass Beads

Q **How are Czech glass beads made? I'm confused by all the different shapes and sizes.**

A Since bead manufacturers around the world tend to be secretive about the methods and equipment they use, we don't know all the details. But in general, Czech pressed glass beads are produced in the Czech Republic from large rods of colored glass. The molten glass is pressed into molds of various shapes and sizes, with a needle forming the hole.

Each of the huge variety of shapes is described by a name or a couple of names, which you'll start to recognize as you shop in bead stores. Twenty-eight of the more readily available shapes are shown on page 52 with their popular names.

COMMON SHAPES FOR CZECH GLASS BEADS

druk (round)

oval

rondelle or wafer

square

donut

fringe or dagger

faceted rondelle

drop

fire-polished (faceted round)

coin

cathedral window

heart

star

trumpet flower

daisy

leaf

leaf dagger

tube

table-cut

lozenge

faceted drop

faceted roller

bicone

nugget

flying saucer

petal drop

fluted rondelle

fruit

52

Other shapes not shown include various types of fruit and animals such as elephants, owls, cats, and fish. Each shape is made in sizes from 2mm to 30mm, with the most commonly available sizes ranging from 3mm to 10mm.

. . . .

Q **How are the Czech beads sold?**

A Most types of nonseed beads are measured in millimeters by their length and diameter. *(See* Measuring Bead Size *on the next page.)* Czech glass beads are packaged at the factories on strands of varying lengths, with a specified number of beads on each strand, usually 25, 50, or 100 beads. The strands are grouped into hanks of 12 to 24 strands. In wholesale quantities, Czech glass beads are sold by the mass, which contains 1,200 beads (for example, 24 strands of 50 beads). Some retail bead stores sell Czech glass beads by the strand, while others sell beads individually. The strand generally offers a better price per bead.

Most modern 10° and 11° Czech seed bead strands are 20" long, and grouped in 12-strand hanks. As the seed beads become larger or more costly, the length or number of strands may be reduced. For example:

▶ Seed beads with facets cut on them, such as charlottes (one-cuts), two-cuts, and three-cuts (tri-cuts), may be grouped into 10-strand hanks.

▶ 8° and 6° seed beads are often grouped into six-strand hanks.

▶ Relatively rare 13° charlottes are strung on shorter 12" strands and grouped into 12-strand hanks.

▶ Strand lengths and hanks of vintage seed beads vary, but tend to be smaller and shorter.

Czech seed beads are sometimes repackaged into tubes or bags and sold by the gram. Purchasing them by the full hank is usually a better value.

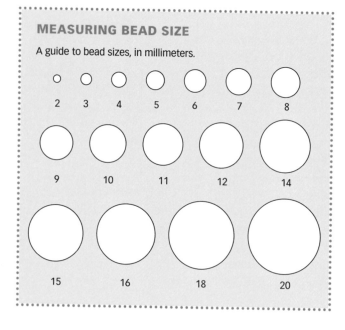

MEASURING BEAD SIZE

A guide to bead sizes, in millimeters.

2　3　4　5　6　7　8

9　10　11　12　14

15　16　18　20

Q Whenever I shop for Czech glass beads, it seems that the styles and colors have changed since the last time I looked. Why can't I find the same beads that I admired before?

A Czech glass bead selections do change frequently. Czech bead producers manufacture beads to order and constantly innovate to produce new and interesting colors, combinations, and finishes. Czech factories, some of which are small cottage industries, make a certain type of bead in large quantities, and then move on to produce a different bead.

The good news is that there's a constant flow of new bead shapes, fashions, and color combinations. But the factories don't always go back and reproduce a previous shape or color, unless they receive large orders for it. So if you see a bead you love, it's a good idea to buy it on the spot, rather than risk never finding it again.

If it's any comfort to you, the beads coming from the Czech Republic always seem to be getting better and more interesting! The current crop of beauties includes opal glass, luster finishes, opaque and metallic linings, and gemstone beads (which often have three or more types or colors of glass combined in each individual bead so they resemble gemstones). So if you can't find a plain color of glass in the bead, size, and shape you want, consider substituting one of the new beads for an updated look.

Q **What's the difference between Swarovski crystal and Czech fire-polished beads?**

A Swarovski is an Austrian manufacturer of faceted crystal beads in a huge variety of colors and shapes. Sometimes, the trademarked name is incorrectly used generically to refer to crystal beads made by another manufacturer or even to cut glass beads.

The difference between crystal and glass is that crystal has a high lead content with other minerals that give the bead incredible clarity and sparkle. To achieve this quality, Swarovski crystal contains approximately 32 percent lead.

Swarovski beads are made in a variety of shapes (including the four below) and cut in very precise designs with up to 100 sharp-edge facets on each bead.

round

bicone

teardrop

cube

Fire-polished beads (FP) are glass beads made in the Czech Republic, with machine-cut facets that have been glazed or fire-polished in a hot oven so they're slightly rounded. A crystal bead tends to be more expensive than an equivalent-sized bead in glass. People often call Czech FP "crystals" because the facets sparkle, but this is technically incorrect.

Wound Glass

Q What is a "wound glass" bead?

A While seed beads are produced in large quantities using drawn glass techniques, wound glass beads are created individually by melting glass over a flame and then winding the molten glass on a metal rod or wire called a mandrel. Each wound bead is more time-consuming to make and therefore more expensive than a seed bead.

Venetian Glass

Wound glass bead production became a hugely successful industry in Venice during the 1600s, with more than 100,000 bead types and designs being produced in Venice and Murano, Italy, alone. Examples of popular wound and drawn glass bead designs included floral sprays, millefiori ("thousand flowers"), combed designs, eye beads, and chevron beads. These bead styles are still being produced in Italy today. To give you an idea of the magnitude of the Italian bead industry: During the 1880s, Venice shipped 6 million pounds of beads every year to the United States.

chevron bead

eye bead

millefiori bead

feathered or combed bead

Lampwork Glass Beads

Q I've seen some expensive beads at shows that are one-of-a-kind, called lampwork beads. What does this mean?

A The terms "lampwork" and "flamework" describe a type of bead production similar to wound glass. These handmade glass beads are made from rods of glass that have been torch-melted, wrapped on a mandrel or steel rod (coated in a clay slip called bead release), shaped with graphite, brass, and steel tools, and layered and decorated with other colors. After the bead is formed, it's annealed in a kiln. Annealing, which is the process of bringing the whole bead to a high temperature (just before its melting point) and then cooling it very slowly over many hours, makes the bead stronger and helps prevent cracking.

Even though modern lampwork artists work with sophisticated torches that combine propane or natural gas with pure oxygen to make a hotter burning flame, the name dates from a time when glass was melted over an oil lamp to make beads. These wound glass beads were one of the earliest types of beads made from glass.

Q Who makes lampwork beads today?

A There's a thriving international community of lampwork artists who are creating original and imaginative beads in a multitude of different styles. These handmade beads can be perfect as a focal bead on a necklace or bracelet.

By educating yourself about what to look for in a quality bead, you can shop for beads knowledgeably and find bargains from new artists. Become a discriminating shopper. Here's what to look for:

▶ No sharp edges or rough spots
▶ Smoothly dimpled or indented holes
▶ A balanced, symmetrical bead

Choose color combinations that speak to you, so you'll enjoy wearing the bead. It can be great fun to purchase a unique lampwork bead, and then design a piece that incorporates it.

lampwork glass bead

Q Why are lampwork beads so expensive?

A When you purchase a lampwork or handmade bead, you're basically buying an original work of art. Each bead is made by hand from sticks of glass, melted, layered, and shaped using a wide variety of simple to elaborate techniques. Lampwork artists often incorporate many colors of glass, gold and silver leaf, fuming with precious metals, wire mesh, and other materials into their beads and may spend an hour or more making a single bead.

Of course, some lampwork beads are more beautiful and intricate than others. Beads by nationally recognized artists are collectible objects that will appreciate in value. Collecting lampwork beads is one way you can develop an affordable, pocket-sized art collection.

. . . .

Q **I just bought a lampwork bead that I love, but now what do I do with it? I don't think I'm ready yet to make it into a major piece of jewelry.**

A One way you can use a lampwork bead is as a focal point of the design for a major necklace. But you may not be ready to make a new necklace every time you purchase a bead. Sometimes it can take months of owning a bead to figure out exactly how you'd like to use it.

Meanwhile, you want to enjoy it! You don't have to leave the bead languishing in a dish or a drawer. I like to wear a single beautiful lampwork bead on a long sterling silver chain, so I can admire it during the day. A 2mm snake chain often has a narrow eye end that easily fits through the hole of many lampwork beads.

With this type of chain, you can keep a dish of favorite beads in your dressing area and change the one on your chain every day to suit your mood or the color of your jacket. Using and wearing the bead will help you become friendly with its colors and design, which can make it easier to plan and create a piece of jewelry that incorporates the bead.

Other Bead Materials

Q What kinds of beads are made of metal?

A Metal beads include spacers, plain and scalloped round and oval beads, and handmade decorative beads, such as the wide variety of shapes and sizes from Bali, Thailand, Turkey, and India. Many of these handmade silver beads have been oxidized to bring out the intricate stamped, carved, soldered, or filigree designs, with dark areas remaining in the crevices and polished silver on the higher surfaces. Most of these decorative beads are made of sterling silver, which contains 92.5 percent (or .925) silver. The remaining 7.5 percent is usually copper.

silver filigree bead

Plain sterling silver, gold-filled, gold, copper, and brass beads in various sizes, from 2mm to 10mm and larger, are available in round and oval shapes and flattened spacers, and are often used to accent other beads. The smaller sizes also work beautifully in crocheted ropes, either made up in all-silver or all-gold or designed in patterns with Swarovski crystals, small semiprecious stones, or seed beads.

These metal beads are available in both seamless and seamed styles. The seamless type is more durable, especially when used in bead crochet. Even when strung, seamed metal beads may eventually pry open along the seam and fall off the piece.

Q What are wood beads used for?

A Natural and dyed wooden beads are available in a variety of shapes and sizes, such as oval, round, drum (like a cylinder), and disk (like a rondelle). They tend to have large holes and a more rustic look.

Wooden beads are often used to string on leather, to make men's jewelry, and for kids' projects. They also work well as a base for bead weaving, to create beaded beads and other designs using peyote stitch or another of the off-loom weaving stitches shown in chapter 8. *(See pages 254–255).*

oval   round   square   drum   disk

. . . .

Q How can I tell whether the pearls I'm buying are good quality?

A There are a lot of inexpensive pearls on the market today, which is a great benefit to beaders who love the beauty and luster of pearls.

Cultured pearls are grown inside an oyster or mussel, either in saltwater or freshwater. Saltwater pearls are started from a small shell bead or nucleus that's inserted into the mollusk. The mollusk coats this irritant with nacre, which forms around the nucleus in layers, creating the luster of the pearl. Most freshwater pearls don't begin with a nucleus, so they are made of nacre all the way through. They also tend to be more irregular in shape.

Pearls grow naturally in a variety of colors, including white, silver, cream, subtle shades of pink and green, and even black. Most pearls have been cleaned, polished, and often treated to increase their luster and beauty. Many have been dyed or irradiated to produce more dramatic colors.

To determine the quality of pearls you're thinking of buying, hold up the strand, bend the strand, and examine the pearls for:

▶ A rich luster
▶ Uniformity of shape, size, and color
▶ Smooth holes
▶ Even layers of nacre

If you need pearls that are very uniform in color, size, and shape, another option is synthetic pearls such as Swarovski crystal pearls. Built around a crystal core, these are perfectly shaped and available in 25 or more colors and seven sizes from 4mm to 12mm round.

Choosing Colors That Last

Q **Why are some beads dyed? Does this matter to me?**

A Yes, it's a good idea to consider the durability of the beads you are planning to use in a project. A dyed finish tends to be less stable than colors that are integrated as part of the glass.

The fact is, though, that some colors are nearly impossible to achieve in glass. Pinks and purples are the color families that seem to be the most difficult to create. For this reason, bead manufacturers sometimes dye beads so they can offer a more complete selection of colors, as well as brighter shades of some difficult colors.

LASTING COLOR

The Web site for Miyuki beads (*see* Resources) includes a 19-page Delica Color & Durability chart that offers guidelines for which bead finishes are affected by sun, friction, skin acids, and dry cleaning. This information applies to other seed beads manufactured by Miyuki, as well.

There are other types of bead finishes that also can be less stable. The silver, gold, copper, or color linings in some beads may wear off, especially when exposed to moisture. Galvanized finishes, which means the glass bead has been bonded with a metal coating on the outside, can wear off, usually after repeated exposure to skin acids. Bead manufacturers are currently working to develop more durable versions of these finishes.

Q Is it a problem to use dyed beads?

A The stability of a bead's color does matter, but it doesn't mean that you have to avoid dyed and galvanized beads completely. Just use them wisely. If you've used dyed beads in a piece, limit its exposure to sunlight and moisture, both of which can cause dyed colors of glass to fade or rub off. Some colors and finishes tend to rub off when exposed to skin acids, and certain people have more acidic skin chemistry that seems to cause fragile bead finishes to wear more quickly.

A final factor to consider is this: How will the bead look when it has faded or some of the color or finish has rubbed off? If you still like the appearance of the bead, then the color's stability becomes less of a problem.

Q **Some of the seed beads at my local bead store have warnings that the color might fade or rub off. I also checked the Miyuki Delica Color & Durability chart and found that some of my favorite beads have durability problems. Should I avoid these colors?**

A The warning you mention usually indicates one of the following factors, that a bead:

▶ Has been dyed to achieve the color
▶ Has a galvanized finish
▶ Is otherwise less stable than other bead colors and finishes

Some of the most gorgeous (and costly) beads are those finished with 24-karat gold. And many of the dyed beads fall into the pink and purple range. Are you willing to give up all those beautiful colors?

In my experience, various beads marked with such warnings are not all fragile to the same degree or in the same way. In fact, there are vast differences. While doing peyote stitch with one dyed Delica, I noticed that the color started to rub off just from touching and stitching with it. Beneath the dye was a lighter shade of the same color, so I didn't find the change objectionable. Another bead in a pink shade became just a shade lighter after being worn for an entire year. In other words, the change was not very noticeable.

. . . .

Q How do I know which dyed beads are low-risk?

A When deciding whether to use a dyed or less stable bead, think about these issues:

▶ **How much will the bead touch the skin?** If you alternate the less stable bead between larger beads, the larger beads will lift it away from the skin, so there will be little skin contact with the more fragile bead.

▶ **How much sunlight will the bead be exposed to?** To reduce exposure, store your beads and finished jewelry in a drawer or other location protected from direct or bright sunlight.

▶ **Isn't it more important to wear and enjoy your beaded work than to fret about its longevity?** After all, we're working with glass, not diamonds. By the time a piece wears out, you may be tired of it anyway. Or you may love the way it looks after it changes, much like a treasured antique. Or if you still adore the piece, and it's looking a bit shabby, consider making it again. Beaded jewelry is for fun. Wear and enjoy it.

Lasting Pleasure

Personally, I love playing with color so much that I don't want to give up a color just because it may be dyed. I feel that it's okay if some colors and finishes change after being worn for a long time. If you really love something, and it finally fades or wears out, you can always make it again.

A good example is a peyote stitch flat bracelet that I wove from seven colors of special 24-karat gold-plated Delicas. These are some of the most expensive seed beads available, but because they are plated with pure gold, I knew the gold would eventually start to wear off. The bracelet fitted snugly on my wrist, looked great with everything, and I loved it.

After wearing it nearly every day for two years, I noticed that the gold was starting to wear off on the inside where it touched my skin, and that the glass inside was black. I also noticed that the plated finish on the matte gold beads seems to be a lot more durable than the finish on the shiny beads, for some reason.

Still, even where it has become worn, the bracelet looks like something ancient and rare, like an artifact that was buried in the ground. Someday, if it becomes too worn out, I may make it again. Meanwhile, I've worn it hundreds of times, and it has given me so much pleasure.

Q **I made a piece of jewelry a couple of years ago, and some of the colors no longer look the same. Why?**

A As we've been discussing, some glass colors and finishes are more stable than others. There are three factors that tend to cause wear in beads:

▶ Exposure to sunlight

▶ Exposure to skin acids and cosmetics

▶ Exposure to water and/or dry cleaning chemicals

Always consider the use and placement of a bead and its durability when creating a design. You don't have to worry about skin contact if you're making a wall or sculptural piece, which won't be touched often.

Is It for Real?

Q **I've heard that a lot of gemstone beads are "fake." I hate to be fooled. Any advice?**

A You're right that a lot of semiprecious stone beads currently being sold as "natural" have been dyed, reconstituted, or are even synthetic. Heat treatment to improve color and clarity of gemstones is a generally acceptable practice, and beads should include a label to that effect, but rarely do. It's been reported that:

▶ Most of the hematite now sold as genuine is synthetic or man-made.

▶ Stones sold as onyx are nearly always dyed or chemically treated to create the black color.

▶ Most amethyst has been color-enhanced by dyeing or is man-made.

▶ Much of the turquoise on the market has been dyed, ground and reshaped, or is synthetic.

What can be done? There is a movement afoot for more accurate reporting and labeling of stone beads available for purchase. But you'll notice that many bead sellers simply don't want to talk about the problem.

To become an educated consumer, read up on the topic. Ask questions whenever you shop for stone beads. Above all, decide whether it's important that your stones are genuine, or whether it's the natural *look* that you want. Do your home-work, ask questions, and be aware of what you are purchasing. If the price seems too good to be true, it probably is.

. . . .

Q Is carnelian a natural stone?

A A natural carnelian is a type of quartz that includes iron. Most carnelian sold today, however, has been color-enhanced. Heating it causes the stone to deepen its naturally reddish color. Probably the most popular color for carnelian is a rich, rusty red, but it's also available in flesh tones and reddish-brown. A lot of beautiful carnelian beads are made in India.

TELLING THE TRUTH

A simulated gemstone is a bead that looks like semiprecious stone but is actually made of glass, ceramic, acrylic, plastic, or other man-made material. A reconstituted gemstone may look like an irregular nugget of pure turquoise, but the term refers to a bead that's made of small pieces of gemstone mixed with resin to hold it together. Merchants often pass these beads off as genuine semiprecious stone, with no explanation.

If you take a look at the Fire Mountain catalog or Web site (*see* Resources), it's refreshing to see a company selling beads that look like semiprecious stone, yet clearly labeling them as natural, stabilized, dyed, reconstituted, or simulated gemstones.

Q **Why is amber so light in weight?**

A Although it's often considered a gemstone, amber is neither a stone nor a mineral. The reason amber feels so light is that it is fossilized tree resin, with the most expensive specimens including insect parts or whole insects. Most amber ranges in age from 30 million to 90 million years old. Amber also has a warm feel that's very different from that of stone beads. Exercise caution when purchasing amber, however. Amber is often melted down and reformed to include a fly or other insect, and a lot of fake amber is made of plastic.

Q I got a really good buy on some semiprecious beads at a bead show. But now that I'm trying to string them, I'm running into problems, like my wire won't always go through them. What's wrong?

A Although it makes sense to shop for good prices, beware of unusually inexpensive semiprecious stone beads. These beads often have uneven holes, so the strand will never hang correctly, or they may have sharp holes or jagged spots inside that can cut your thread and even saw through or snap beading wire.

large hole on one end; small hole on the other

To save time and reduce production costs, beads may be drilled from one end only, resulting in a bead with a large hole on one end and a tiny hole on the other. This type of bead can be tricky to string. Especially avoid using this type of bead for knotting. If you try to knot between these beads using the largest silk thread that will fit comfortably inside the smaller hole, the knot will disappear inside the larger hole.

uneven holes that don't meet at the center

A different but equally annoying problem can happen if the bead is drilled poorly from both ends. It takes skill and adequate tools to drill from both ends so the holes meet precisely at the center. And if the holes do not meet exactly, there may be a very sharp edge of stone at the center of the bead, which can cut or snap the stringing material. This problem is especially difficult because you can't see these uneven spots; they're hidden inside the bead.

You'll start to notice the problem when attempting to string these beads, as the wire will enter the hole easily, but then it will run into a block or jog inside the bead. Whenever possible, use heavy .024-diameter, 49-strand wire with larger stone beads or those with larger, sharp or uneven holes, and allow plenty of ease for the beads to move without overstressing the wire.

Q **How can I tell when bead holes are low quality?**

A To protect yourself from buying beads with poorly drilled holes, become a picky shopper. Check the quality of a strand of semiprecious stones by holding it up both horizontally and vertically to notice whether the beads lie in a straight line. Hold the strand in a curve, as it will be worn. This is how they will line up when used in a piece of jewelry, too. Move the beads apart and check the condition of the holes. You want beads that lie in a straight line with smooth, centered holes.

If you unknowingly purchase some very uneven or poorly drilled beads, try mixing them with other beads. In a busier design, their lack of symmetry will be less noticeable.

Birthstones

Q Which semiprecious and precious stones represent the birthstone for each month of the year?

A Birthstones have been given and worn since ancient times. Some choices were based on astrology, and the stones had mystical significance. The chart below shows the list of stones in general use in the United States since the early 1900s. Some of the alternates were adopted to offer a less expensive option to the precious or semiprecious stones.

CLASSIC BIRTHSTONES

Month	Birthstone	Alternate
January	garnet	rose quartz
February	amethyst	onyx
March	aquamarine	bloodstone
April	diamond	quartz crystal
May	emerald	chrysoprase
June	pearl	alexandrite, moonstone
July	ruby	jade
August	peridot	adventurine
September	sapphire	lapis lazuli
October	opal	pink tourmaline
November	yellow topaz	citrine, turquoise
December	blue topaz	blue zircon, tanzanite

Gemstones and Healing

Q I've heard that gemstones can help with healing. How are they used by healers?

A Some energy healers use crystal formations and other natural stones as part of a treatment. They may place stones under the treatment table or strike them to create tones. Other ways to gain benefits are to wear the stone in a necklace, sleep with it under your pillow, or place it over an injured area or on a chakra. *Chakras* are seven energy centers found along the spine from the tailbone to the head. They have been recognized in yoga and Eastern philosophy and medicine for thousands of years.

For those of us steeped in Western medicine, it seems easy to dismiss the idea of stones aiding in the healing process. But when you consider that these practices have been developed over centuries of systematic experimentation and use, you may decide that the topic merits another look.

CHAKRA STONES

First chakra	dark red	bloodstone, garnet, or obsidian
Second chakra	orange	amber or carnelian
Third chakra	yellow	amber, citrine, or topaz
Fourth chakra	green	emerald, jade, or moss agate
Fifth chakra	blue	amazonite, aquamarine, or blue topaz
Sixth chakra	indigo	lapis, azurite, or sapphire
Seventh chakra	purple	amethyst or moonstone

CHAPTER 3

Findings

Beading Essentials

Q **At the bead store I hear people talking about findings, but I'm not sure what this word actually means. What are they?**

A The term "finding" refers to all the metal components that are used in making beaded jewelry, such as clasps, metal beads, bead tips and clamshells, jump rings and split rings, French coil, bead caps and cones, ear wires, headpins, and eyepins. The metal may be sterling silver, fine silver, gold in various qualities from 10- to 24-karat, gold-filled, gold vermeil, niobium, or base metal including copper, pewter, surgical steel, or brass, which may be electroplated with a thin layer of silver, gold, copper, or other finishes.

There are literally thousands of different findings manufactured for use in jewelry, so it can be tricky to find exactly what you want — especially if you plan to wear the piece tonight. Because availability varies, get into the habit of buying beautiful clasps and other findings when you see them, building a collection of good-quality metal components to choose from so you don't have to wait, or stop and go shopping, in order to finish a piece you're making. Since the prices of silver and gold seem to always be increasing, you'll be glad that you built a collection at last year's prices.

You'll find more information on how to use findings such as clasps, crimps, bead caps and cones, bead tips, and clamshells in chapters 5 and 6.

EXAMPLES OF FINDINGS

Besides clasps and ear wires, findings include:

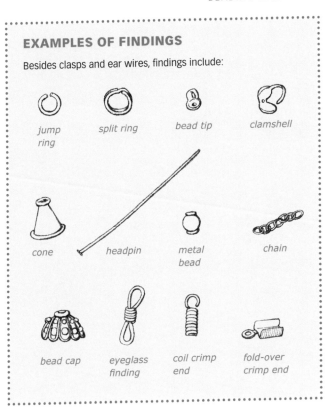

jump
ring

split ring

bead tip

clamshell

cone

headpin

metal
bead

chain

bead cap

eyeglass
finding

coil crimp
end

fold-over
crimp end

Clasps

Q **What types of clasps work well for jewelry?**

A The drawings below show some of the basic, tried-and-true clasp styles. Many of the styles are used in combination with a split ring, jump ring, or soldered jump ring on the other end (to fasten into). The hook-and-eye and S-clasp styles are usually sold as a set with soldered rings. Each type of clasp is available in a variety of simple or decorative designs to complement the style of the jewelry.

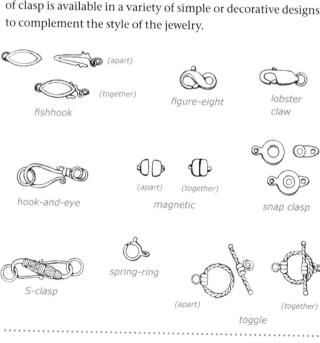

(apart)

(together)

fishhook

figure-eight

lobster claw

hook-and-eye

(apart) *(together)*

magnetic

snap clasp

S-clasp

spring-ring

(apart)

(together)

toggle

Q What kind of clasp do I use if I want more than one strand of beads?

A The drawings below show some of my favorite multi-strand clasp styles for bracelets and necklaces. In general, multistrand clasp options include:

▶ Some types of toggle clasps (two- or three-strand and multistrand with holes)

▶ Box clasps (filigree and other styles are available in one-, two-, and three-strand styles)

▶ Multistrand hook-and-eye clasps (from two to six holes)

▶ Sliding tube clasps (with bar or two, three, four, and five rings)

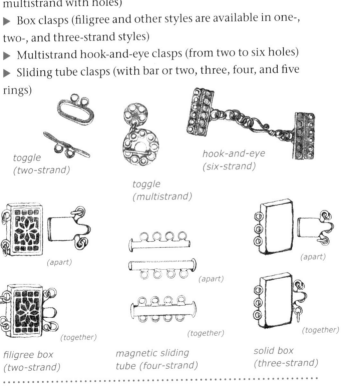

toggle
(two-strand)

toggle
(multistrand)

hook-and-eye
(six-strand)

(apart)

(apart)

(apart)

(together)

(together)

(together)

filigree box
(two-strand)

magnetic sliding
tube (four-strand)

solid box
(three-strand)

Q How do I know which bracelet clasp to buy?

A I apply several rules when selecting a clasp for a bracelet. An ideal clasp should be:

▶ Easy to fasten with one hand (unless you don't mind carrying your bracelet to work and asking the first person you see to fasten it for you)

▶ Secure, so you don't lose the bracelet

▶ Interesting to look at and harmonious with the style of the piece, or hidden or nearly invisible in the design

▶ Relatively short to avoid showing a large patch of the arm or a gap between bracelet ends

In general, I prefer sterling silver and gold-filled findings over base metal for quality, value, and durability. An exception to this rule is the snap clasp, which is secure, solidly made, and available in eight different plated finishes, including copper, gunmetal, gold-plate, silver-plate, antique gold, antique silver, antique brass, and pewter.

Each type of clasp can be the best choice for a certain style of necklace or bracelet. For example, small spring-rings and lobster claws work well on delicate necklaces that need an unobtrusive clasp. Balance the size and style of the clasp with the size, weight, and style of the jewelry piece.

Another factor in selecting a clasp is personal preference. You may choose a certain clasp style because it was used on your all-time favorite bracelet. Because it has become familiar and easy for you to fasten, it's an ideal choice for you.

Q I love making bracelets for friends and family members, but find that many older women have difficulty fastening a clasp with one hand. Is there a clasp that's easier to fasten?

A The snap clasp discussed in the previous question is especially easy to fasten with one hand. It's an ideal choice when making bracelets for those who have difficulty maneuvering other clasps.

. . . .

Q What are the advantages and disadvantages of using magnetic clasps on bracelets?

A Magnetic clasps can provide a real benefit to someone who has arthritis or otherwise has difficulty fastening bracelets with one hand or necklaces behind the head, but these easy-fastening clasps also have several drawbacks. A magnetic clasp may come apart rather easily as well, especially if you tend to pile several grocery bags onto each wrist (as I do). A favorite bracelet may fall off in the parking lot unnoticed and be lost forever.

Remember: Magnets attach to other metals. If you like to wear several bracelets together on one wrist, the magnetic clasps tend to glom together so the bracelets will not hang evenly. And if you work near a metal cash register or other metal equipment, the magnetic clasp can drive you crazy as it sticks to every metal object in sight. At the end of a workday, you may find your bracelet now includes every paperclip and staple that crossed its path. A magnetic clasp also may damage a watch worn on the same wrist.

My feeling is that magnetic clasps are a wonderful invention for some people and a not-so-good solution for others. They work better for necklaces than for bracelets, as necklaces receive less tugging in day-to-day wear, and we tend to be more aware of a falling necklace than a falling bracelet. Be aware that not all magnetic clasps are of equal strength. Test the clasp by prying it open with your fingers, and choose the strongest magnetic clasps you can find.

SAFETY CHAIN

One solution to the falling bracelet problem is to add a 2" safety chain to each bracelet that has a magnetic clasp. Leave the safety chain fastened all the time. It provides enough length to slide the bracelet over the hand and can help prevent a bracelet from being lost.

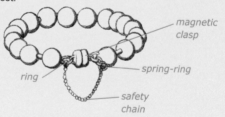

magnetic clasp

ring

spring-ring

safety chain

Q **Do you feel that toggle clasps are secure?**

A I find toggle clasps to be a very secure style, although I have seen inferior or defective toggles in which the post is too short for the diameter of the ring. A too-short post can result in a clasp that comes apart easily. The post must be long enough so it has to be lifted, pointed, and inserted through the hole in the ring; it can't be so short that it wanders through the hole on its own.

I have heard one person say that a well-designed toggle clasp wriggled open and she nearly lost a bracelet. This has never happened to me, possibly because I wear my bracelets rather closely fitted to my wrist. A toggle on a looser, bangle-style bracelet may possibly be pushed open when an arm is inserted into a coat sleeve, for example. If you prefer to wear your bracelets loose, you may want to consider toggle clasps with caution.

Q **I saw some little silver findings shaped like a horse-shoe. What are these used for?**

A Called a wire guard or wire protector, the little U-shaped tube is a relatively new finding designed to extend the life of your jewelry. It cradles and protects the flexible beading wire where it connects to the clasp, and also forces you to leave a larger loop between the crushed crimp and the clasp or ring. In function, it resembles French coil *(see page 211),* except that its shape is rigid. Currently, wire guards are available in sterling silver, gold-filled, silver-plated, and gold-plated.

To use a wire guard, string it onto the beading wire just before or after you string the clasp, and before going back through the crimp and beads. The wire guard also ensures that the clasp can move freely. The ones I've seen will work with beading wire that is .021" or thinner, but larger sizes may become available.

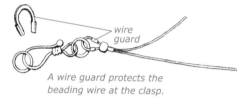

A wire guard protects the beading wire at the clasp.

Findings for Earrings

Q **I'd like to make earrings. What different types of ear wires can I use?**

A There are a number of different styles of findings available for earrings. Like other findings, they can be made of high-quality precious metals or inexpensive plated metals or surgical steel. These days, pierced ears are so prevalent that pierced-ear findings are much easier to find than findings for ears that are not pierced.

Q **What are the pierced earring options?**

A Styles for pierced earring findings include these *(see illustrations on page 86):*

▶ **French ear wires** are popular J-shaped wire findings that may include a decorative coil and/or ball above the hanging ring. Small rubber stoppers are available in several styles and can be placed on the pointed end of the French ear wire when worn, to help prevent earring loss. One current fashion is for a larger, open hook shape, while Bali versions of the French ear wire can include delicate hooks made of twisted wire.

▶ **Posts** may have a metal ball on a straight wire that's inserted through the hole in the ear, usually with a ring below the ball for hanging a wire, chain, or headpin with beads. Decorative versions of the post may have a Bali bead or other metal design in place of the ball.

▶ **Lever-backs** are one of my favorite styles. They're slender and practically disappear when worn, plus the spring-hinged back opens and closes so the earring is more secure during wear.

▶ **Hoops** are another popular pierced earring style. Beads can be strung directly onto the hoop or hung off the hoop using headpins. Or a design can be worked in wire or thread around the hoop. Depending on the type of hoop, the embellished piece can be worn directly through the hole in the ear or suspended from another earring finding.

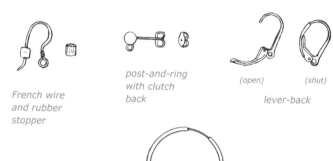

French wire
and rubber
stopper

post-and-ring
with clutch
back

(open)   (shut)

lever-back

hoop

....

Q What can I use to make earrings if I'm allergic to
metal?

A About 10 percent of the population is allergic to metal,
usually nickel. Some are highly allergic, while others
have a mild reaction over repeated exposure. For people with
metal allergies, some practical alternatives include better-
quality gold and silver, surgical steel, and niobium findings.
(See page 218.)

....

Q **How do I know which findings to use for my earring design?**

A The style you choose depends on several factors, including personal preference, comfort, security, and the height of the loop. Some styles cause the decorative part of the earring to hang closer to the earlobe, while others create a greater drop from the ear, so think about where you want your design to be positioned.

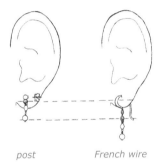

post   French wire

The dangle on a post earring hangs closer to the ear than on a French wire and other styles.

. . . .

Q **I'd like to make earrings for my mother, but she doesn't have pierced ears. What are my options?**

A For someone who does not have pierced earlobes, there are two basic styles available: clip-on and screw-back earring findings. Both styles may include a ring for hanging beads, or have a flat area where you can glue on a bead, button, stone, or woven bead design.

. . . .

Q What is niobium? I've seen it in bright colors. Is it a type of steel?

A Niobium isn't made from steel and is an entirely different, relatively rare metal. It's a wonderful alternative if you or someone you make jewelry for has an allergic reaction to other metal types, such as nickel. Niobium is a strong, gray metal that takes on a bluish tone when exposed to room-temperature air. It's often anodized with oxides to create a range of beautiful colors without dyes.

In other industries, niobium is used in superalloys to make parts for jet engines and rockets. It's also used in welding and in medical devices, such as pacemakers. Because niobium is hypoallergenic, it works great for earring findings. You also can purchase niobium wire and make your own jewelry components.

Bead Caps

Q I bought some interesting filigree bead caps, but am not sure how to use them. Any suggestions?

A Bead caps are often used to enhance a design by framing and highlighting certain beads. You can use two bead caps, one on each side of a bead, for a balanced look when stringing, or just one bead cap for an unbalanced design, such as a tassel or the dangle on an earring.

Filigree bead caps are great because the open design shows more of the bead being framed. So the bead cap doesn't hide the beauty of your bead, make sure the diameter of the bead is at least 2mm larger than the diameter of the bead cap. Some thin filigree bead caps can even be shaped carefully to echo the contours of an irregular bead.

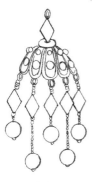

using holes in a filigree bead cap

using crossbar inside a specially designed bead cap

Q **Aren't there special caps for making tassels?**

A Some specialized bead caps are designed to sit at the head of a tassel and may have crossbars soldered inside so it's easy to join the strands of a tassel to the cap. *(See illustration above.)* Others are perforated with holes around the edge of the cap, which is a perfect place to join jump rings or wire loops to create tassels made of beads or a combination of chain and beads.

You'll also find cones with spring mechanisms that fit inside, which make it easier to join several strands of a necklace into the cone without using a separate piece of wire. To use this type of cone, you'll crimp or tie each strand to the spring mechanism, and then clip the spring inside the cone, where it's engineered to spring open and grip a ledge inside the cone.

. . . .

Q **Cones and bead caps seem pretty similar. When should I use one versus the other?**

A You're right that cones and bead caps have similar shapes, and they can sometimes be used interchangeably. In general, a bead cap is rounded to echo the shape of a bead, while a cone is a taller, tapered cylinder that's open on both ends, designed to hide the joining of two or more strands. Cones are usually placed at each end of a multistrand necklace, where it connects to the clasp. Both findings are sold in a wide variety of diameters for different needs, and cones are available in a variety of heights as well.

Because of the wide variety of bead caps and cones manufactured, it can be difficult to find just the right size and shape when you need it. Many beaders buy and collect various sizes of beautiful findings when they see them (some would call it hoarding), so they'll have choices available while working out a new design.

As far as using the two interchangeably: If you have two or three strands of beads to join together at the ends of a necklace and the join will be fairly neat, you may be able to bring the strands into a bead cap of the correct size, instead of using a cone. A bead cap of the right diameter also can be used to finish off each end of a crocheted rope, if it will be joined to a clasp. Conversely, if you want to accent a single bead or create a tassel for an earring dangle, you may be able to use a decorative cone in place of a bead cap. So if you wonder whether a finding might work for a different purpose, it's definitely worth a try.

SEE ALSO: For more on multistrand work, see chapter 6.

Working with Silver

Q **What's so special about Bali silver? The beads and clasps are beautiful, but seem really expensive.**

A Sterling silver beads made in Bali are relatively expensive because they are made by hand, and they have a distinctive look that's very desirable in many current jewelry designs. Often, the bead or clasp has an intricate raised design composed of scrolls, swirls, granulation, dots, or filigree. The finished bead is usually oxidized (or intentionally tarnished) and then polished, so the deep crevices are dark, and the high spots are polished, to emphasize the design.

Thai Silver

Thai Hill Tribes silver is made by the Karen Hill Tribes in northern Thailand using traditional methods passed down through generations. This silver is similar to the sterling silver from Bali, with a few important differences. Thai Hill Tribes silver is typically 95 to 98 percent pure silver, which gives it a whiter, lighter color than sterling (due to less copper in the mix of metals), and reduces tarnishing. Because the purer silver is softer, designs tend to be rustic and simple, often including stamped designs of stylized flowers or geometrics. They may also be shaped into natural forms, such as leaves, fish, seashells, and dragonflies, with isolated areas of oxidation.

Since Bali silver is usually sold by weight, filigree pieces may be the best value because they weigh less than an equivalent solid piece. One of the most beautiful Bali clasp designs has a powerful magnet hidden inside the halves of an intricate bead. When in use, the clasp completely disappears into the bracelet or necklace, looking like one of the beads.

SEE ALSO: Other Bead Materials, page 61.

Q It's annoying when silver tarnishes. How do I polish tarnished silver in a finished piece of jewelry?

A Over time, most silver will eventually darken or tarnish, which is caused by chemicals in the air, such as sulfur. Tarnishing occurs more quickly in a humid environment.

If we were talking about a silver fork, you would use a good silver polish to remove the tarnish and then would wash the piece in hot soapy water. But for many pieces of jewelry, it's not a good idea to get the beads, thread, and other components of the piece wet, even with plain water, and it is difficult to dry thoroughly. I recommend polishing the dry silver gently with a polishing cloth to remove the tarnish and restore the shine. This type of cloth can also be used on other metals, including copper, brass, and gold.

Since exposure to air, sunlight, and moisture speeds tarnishing, you can reduce tarnishing by storing jewelry with silver components in airtight ziplock bags. One piece per bag will help to reduce scratching caused by two pieces knocking against one another. Some people even recommend using double ziplock bags to further reduce exposure to air.

There's a new sterling silver alloy available called Argentium Silver, that contains a small amount of germanium. The result is a sterling silver that remains virtually tarnish free. Hopefully more findings will be produced using this new alloy (*see* Resources).

Working with Gold

Q **What does it mean when gold is identified as 14-, 18-, or 24-karat? How do these numbers affect the cost of the piece?**

A Because pure gold is expensive, the difference in price usually reflects the amount of gold contained in the finished piece. Karated gold is gold all the way through. But since pure gold is 24-karat, a finding or piece of jewelry marked 14-karat contains 14 parts of pure gold mixed with 10 parts of other metals, such as silver or copper. Likewise, 18-karat gold has 18 parts of gold combined with six parts of other metals. The minimum gold karat weight sold in the United States is 10-karat gold.

All solid-gold pieces should be marked with the karat content. You can't really see the other metals, but the higher the karat number, the better quality the gold. The main way you can tell the difference between lower- and higher-quality gold is by its color. Gold at 18 karats and higher has a very rich yellow color, while 14-karat gold and lower has a less brilliant, slightly orange tone brought on by the additional copper content.

Q **Why are metals added to the gold? Is it just to save money?**

A Just as with sterling silver, the addition of other metals makes the gold harder and more durable. Both sterling silver and 14-karat gold can be fashioned into thinner pieces than either fine silver or 22-karat gold, and the pieces will be more resistant to bending and wear.

Most beaders don't choose 14-karat gold findings because they are expensive. But if you're making a very special piece of jewelry, it may be worth the investment. When I beaded a complex woven band for my real gold watch, I decided to use a gold clasp to maintain the integrity of the entire piece.

Local bead stores often don't stock 14-karat gold findings. You can find them at local jewelry stores, where they may have to be ordered for you, or online at various suppliers. (*See* Resources.)

....

Q **What does it mean when a finding is gold-filled?**

A Gold-filled findings are much less expensive than solid gold, but they are still considered to be good-quality findings. A gold-filled piece has a solid outer layer of gold bonded to an inner piece made of base metal, such as brass. Gold must make up at least ¹⁄₂₀ the weight of the piece to qualify as gold-filled.

....

Q **What is the difference between gold-filled and gold-plated?**

A Gold-filled jewelry components are generally more expensive and more finely made than gold-plated ones.

Gold-plated findings are made with a thin layer of 10-karat or higher gold electroplated to base metal. The thin layer of gold can wear off more quickly than the thicker layer on a gold-filled piece. Not all, but most, gold- and silver-plated findings are manufactured using rougher techniques that can include stamping and sharp edges. Examine each piece closely, and you'll see why it's usually worth the extra cost to use sterling silver and gold-filled findings in your jewelry pieces.

. . . .

Q **What about vermeil? Isn't that gold too?**

A Yes, vermeil (pronounced vehr-MAY) is another excellent alternative if you'd like to include affordable but high-quality gold-colored findings in your jewelry.

Vermeil is a French term that is used to describe findings made of sterling silver that have been plated with gold. To qualify for the title, the gold needs to be at least 10-karat and 1.5 micrometers thick, but many high-quality vermeil findings are plated with a thicker layer of 14- to 22-karat gold. Vermeil findings with a satin finish are especially beautiful. And if the gold layer ever begins to wear off, you know that the piece inside still has the quality of solid sterling silver.

CHAPTER 4

Organizing Tricks and Tools

Handling and Storage

Q I've purchased quite a few beads that I'd like to use, but have trouble seeing what I have and finding a certain bead that I want. Do you have any tips on organization?

A My favorite storage system for smaller beads, from seed beads to pearls to strands of Czech glass, is a system of transparent plastic boxes with six or more different sizes of clear flip-top rectangular tubes. Individual tube sizes range from 1" to 3¾" high.

Inside the 4" × 6" × 1½" clear plastic storage boxes, you can organize the small tubes containing your beads by color, shape, or size. It's easy to search through the boxes to find a bead you want, or just hold the box up to a window to gaze at the beautiful colors or see how much you have of each bead. I find that browsing through the beads and organizing them is a good way to begin when designing a new project. This system is also wonderful because it's modular. You can add additional boxes as your bead collection expands, so you never outgrow it.

As with anything, your choice of container for storing your beads is really just that — a personal choice. What works best depends on the size and quantity of the beads you have. Besides the clear, rectangular storage boxes, here are some other options:

▶ A portable plastic storage box with individual compartments and snap lids (a drawback: it can be hard to remove beads from compartments without dumping them all out)

▶ For larger quantities of beads: clear, round containers that either have individual snap lids or screw together in a stacking system (available in several sizes)

▶ A fishing or make-up tackle box or plastic shoe box, all of which easily stack on a shelf (useful for larger beads)

The main idea is not so much the system you choose but, rather, the simple idea that keeping things organized will help to free your mind of clutter and encourage creativity.

Regardless of how you store and organize your beads, keep them out of direct sunlight in a safe, dry place that is easily accessible. Moisture can damage bead finishes and is certainly not good for metal findings. Safety is also key, especially in homes where there are children. Beads are a choking hazard for small children, so it is better to store them out of the reach of little hands.

Small boxes and tubes fit neatly into a larger box.

A Sweet Idea

The rectangular tubes used for bead storage are often referred to as "tic-tac boxes" — after the plastic candy boxes that inspired them. The story I've heard is that teens were saving Tic-Tac candy boxes to use for storing their beads, and someone got the idea to produce the boxes specifically for bead storage. I don't know whether it's true, but it makes a good tale (and was a great business idea).

Q **How can I remember which beads I have?**

A My local bead store uses a system of stick-on labels that includes useful information for identifying the bead, such as the color number, bead size, manufacturer, and price. Carefully peel off these labels (if you do it slowly, they won't rip) and transfer them to the flip-top tubes. That way, if you need to buy more of a particular bead, you'll have all the information at hand.

If the container your beads came in doesn't use this labeling, adopt your own. Record the bead's color, size, manufacturer, price, and any code numbers on a white address label sticker for your own tracking purposes.

Q How do I store larger beads that are still on strings?

A You can store strands of beads, such as semiprecious stones or pearls (especially if you don't have a lot of storage space) by hanging them on a wall on a man's tie rack. It's easy to see what you have and experiment with color combinations. If you artfully arrange the strands, you can start enjoying them on your wall long before you use them in a piece of jewelry. Tie and coat racks with wooden pegs are a great way to display and store finished necklaces and bracelets, as well.

Q I see people working with their beads in little ceramic or plastic dishes. They seem so slippery, and I think I have too many colors to use a separate dish for each one.

A Some people love to bead from dishes. These are sometimes referred to as "honey pots," any variety of single round glass or plastic dishes or the 50-cent metal triangular dishes. Another dish option is what's called a "bead sorting dish," generally a larger ceramic dish with a circular section in the middle and several other sections fanning out around the center circle (like those used by watercolor artists).

For me, though, the vertical sides of dishes tend to get in the way of my needle, and the beads slide around too much. I prefer picking up beads from a nonslippery fabric surface, such as a piece of Vellux fabric (used to make lightweight

PICKING UP BEADS

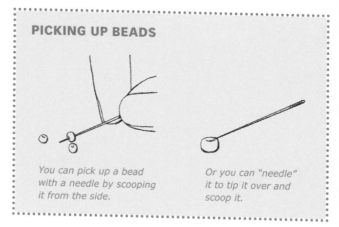

You can pick up a bead with a needle by scooping it from the side.

Or you can "needle" it to tip it over and scoop it.

blankets). Other fabric options include a placemat-sized piece of faux suede, felt, velvet, or a terrycloth towel (my last choice because the needle can catch easily in the terry loops).

Rather than having a separate dish for each bead color, you can just dump out a little pile of each color or type of bead onto the fabric surface. When you're finished working, it's easy to scoop up each bead pile with a metal triangle dish *(see page 125)* and use the corner to dump the beads back into their flip-top storage box, without needing to remove the lid.

Preference for a beading surface is again a personal choice. There's no right or wrong way! Be sure to try different methods, and then use the one that works best for you.

Q What is a bead board?

A A bead board is a design tool with a soft, flocked surface that is used for testing bead and color arrangements. The bead board surface has grooves and inch markings to help you plan a piece at its desired length. Use it to lay out beads, see what looks good together, get an idea of length, and make color and design decisions before you start stringing the piece together.

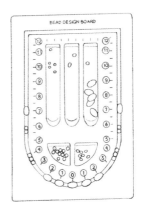

Use a bead board to plan and lay out a stringing design.

Q I hate it when I'm beading along, enjoying myself, and then I see a mistake I made several rows back. How can I catch my mistakes sooner?

A One of my friends, who is also a wonderful and patient beading instructor, always tells her students to "stop and admire your work." In other words, pause often and look at your work to see whether everything looks correct. If a pattern or sequence doesn't look or feel quite right, chances are it's not! You want to catch any mistake quickly, so you won't have to do much ripping to fix it. If you make a habit of stopping frequently and checking over your work, you'll feel confident about cruising ahead.

Beading On-the-Go

Q I'm always bringing my beadwork with me to appointments, my kids' baseball games, or on car trips. Sometimes, it seems that I'm leaving a trail of beads behind me. Do you have any suggestions to make my work more portable?

A It's great to keep your hands busy. You accomplish something creative with those empty minutes and realize that you don't even mind waiting at the doctor's office. Bringing your beads with you works best if you choose a project that's easy to take out and put away quickly. You also need to organize your supplies accordingly.

POST-IT!

Keep up with small beads by tipping out a small amount at a time onto the adhesive strip of a sticky note. Don't laugh! The beads stay put and the adhesive leaves no sticky residue.

You don't want to lug a big plastic suitcase with half your beading stash in it. By the time you get everything out and set up, it'll be time to put it away. I like to carry my beadwork in a hard plastic sandwich keeper. It's the perfect size for a small beading project and will easily hold your beading supplies. You can keep a portable project ready to go at all times.

The perfect project for on-the-go beading, especially if you have only 10 or 15 minutes free at a time, is a crocheted rope bracelet *(see page 327)*. Because the beads are prestrung, you don't have to worry about picking up individual beads, or dropping the

TRAVEL TIP

A great gadget to store and carry your bead crochet projects is a plastic eyeglass case. Unbreakable and water resistant, they're available at drugstores, department stores, and your local eyeglass shop.

ones in your lap when the hygienist calls your name. When it's time to stop beading, all you have to do is place a safety pin in the last stitch crocheted, so it won't unravel in your bag.

Beading Needles

Q **I'm confused about sizes of beading needles and wire. What do the numbers mean?**

A It may help you to remember that seed beads, beading needles, and wire all follow the same rule: the higher the number, the smaller the bead, needle, or wire. So 26-gauge wire is smaller than 22-gauge; a size 12 needle is smaller than a size 10; and an 11° seed bead is smaller than an 8°.

Q **Why are beading needles so hard to thread?**

A In order to fit through a bead as many times as possible, the eye of a beading needle (unlike that of a regular sewing needle) is designed to be very narrow. The same goes for the shorter needles called sharps; the eye is nearly as narrow as the shaft. When sewing on regular woven or knit fabric, a needle can push the fibers aside to make more room for the eye. But glass beads have a finite amount of space inside, and for some stitches, you'll pass through the same bead a number of times. When adding a new thread, you'll make even more passes through beads. To accomplish these stitches, you need a needle with a slender eye.

Beading needles are available in various sizes, from 10 (the largest) to 15 (the smallest). In general, you want to use the largest needle that works for your project, because it's stronger and easier to thread. Always keep a few smaller needles on hand, though, in case you reach a tight spot.

Be assured that when you can't pass through a bead, it's due less to the thread you're using than to the width of the needle. You can use a chain nose pliers to gently ease the needle through a tight bead, but it's always better to stop and change needles than to risk breaking a bead by forcing the needle through it. There's a sickening little "pop" when one of your beautiful seed beads breaks as you try to pass the needle through it one more time. Trust me, you don't want that to happen.

THREADING A NEEDLE

Teachers often joke that learning to thread the needle is the hardest part of beading. Sadly, there is some truth to this joke! Here are a few tips to make the job easier:

1. Stretch the thread between your hands to flatten the thread and remove stretch, and then use a sharp scissors to make a clean, angled cut on the end of the thread.

2. Moisten the tip of the thread (usually by licking it). You can also try moistening the eye of the needle.

3. Flatten the thread tip. Some people do so between their teeth; I prefer to use my thumb and index finger.

4. Hold the thread between the thumb and index fingertip of your dominant hand with only a small amount of thread visible (about ⅛") and the flat side vertical.

5. Hold the needle with the other hand so the eye is turned toward you, and you can see into the eye.

6. Slide the tip of the thread into the eye of the needle. Or slide the needle onto the thread. Try it both ways and see which works better for you. A white background helps.

You may find beading needles a little easier to thread than sharps, because the longer needle also has a slightly longer eye. If you do find threading needles difficult to master, though, there's an ultrafine needle-threading tool available that works with needles up to size 13 and thin threads. Most regular needle threaders are too large to use in the thin eye of a beading needle.

Keep practicing, and it will get easier!

Q Why is my needle sometimes easier to thread from one side than from the other?

A It's a trade secret that needles have two different sides. The eye of the needle is created by stamping a hole through the needle shaft. Even in the best English-made steel needles, this results in a hole that is smoother on one side than the other. So, if you're having trouble threading a needle, flip it over and try the other side. If you've been working with waxed thread, check the eye to see whether it may be clogged with wax. If so, use the point of a second needle to gently clear out the wax before attempting to rethread.

Q When would I use a beading needle instead of a sharp of the same size?

A A sharp is similar to a beading needle, only shorter. There are times when you need a long needle: when picking up a number of beads at a time to work fringe, or when passing the needle all the way across a wide bracelet. But when picking up one or two beads at a time as for most off-loom woven beadwork, either needle works fine; it's a matter of preference.

I use a sharp whenever possible. When making a piece that requires thousands of stitches, I can't help but think that passing that extra 1" of metal through each and every stitch must add up to miles of extra work.

sharp   *beading needle*

Q I've seen large-eyed needles at the store. What are they used for?

A A large-eyed needle has a long eye that extends down the center of the needle, with a blunt point at each end. Available in a couple of lengths, from 2¼" to 4½", the elongated eye makes these types of needles very easy to thread. Gently push a fingernail into the eye vertically to separate the wires and insert the thread.

Some beaders, especially those who dislike threading beading needles, adore the large-eyed needles, which are marketed in a couple of different brand names (*see* Resources), and use them whenever possible. I love these needles for certain jobs, such as stringing beads for bead-crochet ropes. The thread is too thick to fit through a beading needle, but the larger eyes can accommodate large thread in their long flexible opening.

But for many beading jobs, large-eyed needles aren't the best choice. They're too thick for a lot of bead weaving and bend too easily for some types of work. Note that you will need to treat your large-eyed needles more carefully than you would a regular steel needle. The eye in these needles is held together with a soldered join and can break if you yank on it too hard.

large-eyed needle

Q **I'm trying to string beads on thread for crocheting a rope — but the bead holes are too small for the large-eyed needle, and my thread is too thick to fit through a beading needle. Do you have any other ideas?**

A Try using a twisted wire needle, which has a large collapsible eye, or a dental floss threader. The eye of a twisted wire needle can accommodate thicker thread and flattens when you pull it through the first bead. If you have difficulty rethreading it after the eye has collapsed, use the blunt end of a tapestry needle to gently push the eye open again. Handled carefully, a twisted wire needle can be reused many times.

Or you can try this trick, which works anytime you need to string beads on a thicker thread with a thinner needle:

1. Take a short length of thin beading thread, thread it through the eye of a regular beading needle (size 10 or 12), and tie the ends in an overhand knot. *(See page 16.)*

2. Insert the larger crochet thread (or other thread) through the loop and string beads on the needle, sliding them over the thread loop and onto the crochet thread.

3. Leave the tied-on loop in place on the needle so you can use it repeatedly.

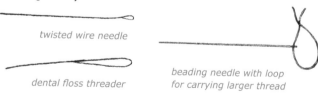

twisted wire needle

dental floss threader

beading needle with loop for carrying larger thread

Beading Threads

Q **Why are there so many different kinds of beading thread? How do I know which thread to choose?**

A It's true that we bead lovers have more thread types to choose from than ever before. In the early 1980s, when the current resurgence of interest in beading was just getting under way, there was only one type of thread available: Nymo. It was sold in two colors: black and white.

These days, stores sell many types of thread in a variety of sizes and strengths. Each one has slightly different properties and tends to be used for a different type of beadwork. Beading threads are used primarily in projects that incorporate off-loom weaving, loom weaving, and bead embroidery. By contrast, flexible beading wire works better for most stringing projects (such as bracelets and necklaces).

Today, most beading threads fall into two categories: nylon and gel-spun polyethylene. *(See chart on the next page.)*

For some projects, we may want a thread that matches the bead color, because it's going to show a bit between beads. At other times, we want the strongest, thinnest, smoothest thread available. And sometimes, we just use whatever is lying around. This is how we develop our thread preferences, by trying them all to find out what tangles least for the way we wield a needle, and what works best for a given project.

THREADS: MULTIPLE CHOICE

Nymo, a parallel multifilament nylon thread originally made for sewing leather, was one of the earliest and is still one of the most popular bead-weaving threads. You'll find a lot of beaders who still wouldn't consider using anything else. I tend to use the finer sizes of Nymo when I need an extremely thin thread. Here are some of its characteristics:

▶ Comes in sizes ranging from 000 (the thinnest) to 0 and A to FF (the largest)

▶ Made in 18 colors in sizes B and D

▶ Tends to fray, making it less desirable for projects where a very long thread is required (as in weaving, where the goal is to avoid adding thread often)

Silamide, a two-ply twisted nylon thread, is prewaxed tailoring thread that's also been used for bead weaving for many years. Like Nymo, it has a group of devotees who use it exclusively. Interestingly, the Nymo people seem to cluster on the East Coast, while the Silamide lovers tend to gather on the West Coast. Here's the lowdown:

▶ Available in size A

▶ Made in 26 colors

▶ Has a tendency to fray and stretch

C-Lon is a parallel multifilament nylon created just for beading, and it's particularly good for bead weaving. Here are its properties:

▶ Comes in two thread weights, AA and D, as well as a cord weight

▶ Made in 36 brilliant colors

▶ Resists fraying and stretching better than Nymo and Silamide

Illusion cord, also known as monofilament nylon fishing line, is the only nonstretch beading thread that's completely clear, which makes it great for floating or illusion necklace styles *(see page 168),* but it's not recommended for regular bead weaving. Check out the details:

▶ Comes in various weights

▶ Breaks more easily than beading thread

▶ Tends to become yellow and brittle with age

PowerPro and **FireLine,** both made from gel-spun polyethylene, are high-tech fishing lines. Both are prewaxed, strong, and flexible with a soft hand. Because they're so strong, these two threads can be difficult to cut with regular scissors, which tend to chew them without cutting. Surprisingly, the best scissors for cutting them cleanly are small, blunt Fiskars scissors made for children. Being hard to cut makes these threads ideal for use with crystals, which can have sharp edges that cut other threads. They knot easily, resist fraying, have near-zero stretch, and are available in very limited colors.

PowerPro is braided (similar in construction to plied or twisted thread made with four plies). Some other details include:

▶ Available in six weights from .004 (5-pound test) to .011 (30-pound test)

▶ Made in three colors: moss green, neon yellow, and white

▶ Can be more difficult to thread because of its rounded shape, but both .006 PowerPro and .006 FireLine fit through a size 12 beading needle

FireLine also has a braided construction, but feels thinner and smoother, and I find it easier to thread than PowerPro. Details include:

▶ Manufactured in a range of weights from .006 (4-pound test) to .012 (10-pound test)

▶ Available in smoke grey and crystal (translucent white)

Q What weight of thread is best for beading?

A There are no hard-and-fast rules about which weights of thread to use. The decision depends not only on the hole size of the beads you're using, but also on the stitch you're weaving, and how many times you need to pass through each bead. Consider these tips:

▶ Use a relatively large thread when you want the piece to be stiff.

▶ Use a D-weight thread, waxed and doubled, when weaving with 6° seed beads.

▶ Use the same thread as a single strand when weaving with 8° and 11° beads.

Each beader's thread preferences tend to be based on the type of work they do, the threads recommended by teachers and/or favorite books, and their own past experiences with threads. (See Threads: Multiple Choice on pages 112–113.)

New beading materials are constantly becoming available, so be sure to experiment with new offerings to find your favorites. It's probably better not to be blindly loyal to a single brand of thread. For one type of work, you may choose a thread for strength; for another piece, a perfect color match may be the overriding concern.

Q I bought a bobbin of Nymo thread and really liked it, so I bought a large cone of it. The thread on the cone doesn't seem the same. What's up with that?

A The two threads are not the same, and there's a simple explanation. Nymo thread originated in the sewing industry, where it is used for sewing leather. The cone serves as the upper thread on a powerful sewing machine, and the bobbin is used for the lower thread. To form the machine stitch correctly, these two threads are not the same; the upper one is heavier. So if you like the bobbins, stick with bobbins. If you want a slightly heavier weight, try the cones or spools.

Q Why can't I use the same string my beads come on to make a necklace?

A When you purchase a strand of beads, it's generally strung on either cotton cord or stiff nylon monofilament. Both methods are meant to be temporary. The cotton cord will rot and break over time, and the monofilament will not give a fluid drape to your finished piece. They're both designed to be replaced with better materials when you're ready to create a piece. These days, the material of choice for stringing projects (necklaces and bracelets) is flexible beading wire. *(See chapter 7.)*

Using Beeswax

Q **When is it necessary to wax the thread?**

A When weaving with beads, waxing your thread is a matter of preference. Some beaders always use wax, while others rarely do. But I can help you make an educated decision. A few reasons to wax:

▶ Helps reduce thread tangling

▶ Coats the thread to strengthen it

▶ Discourages fraying and splitting

▶ Creates a beaded fabric that's relatively firm and tight and that holds its shape

▶ Helps the strands of thread inside each bead stick to each other, resulting in less slipping of thread and a firmer weave

And a couple of reasons not to wax:

▶ Makes the thread a bit fatter, so bead holes fill up with thread more quickly. (Pay attention if your pattern requires many passes or suggests not waxing for this reason.)

▶ Tends to make the thread a bit dirty or to pick up dirt

▶ May plug the needle hole when you use too much. (One solution is to iron the waxed thread between two sheets of absorbent brown paper before you start stitching. This is a technique used in couture sewing, but too fussy for my beadwork.)

Q **What kind of beeswax should I buy?**

A Pure beeswax for beading and sewing is usually sold in a small block or flat, round button, sometimes enclosed in a plastic case to keep it clean.

Another option is synthetic beeswax, sold in a small cup, which many beaders prefer over regular beeswax because it's softer, stickier, and spreads more evenly than natural beeswax. Once I tried it, the synthetic form quickly became my favorite choice for bead weaving.

Q **What's the difference between treating thread with Thread Heaven versus beeswax?**

A Thread Heaven is a thread conditioner with a synthetic formula designed to reduce static electricity and lubricate the thread, which helps keep thread from tangling. It's packaged in a little blue box that lasts for years. Although applied to thread in the same way as beeswax, Thread Heaven is less sticky than beeswax, so it doesn't build up and clog your needle, but it also doesn't assist in beading more tightly the way beeswax does.

I generally prefer beeswax over Thread Heaven, but many other beaders love it. Which product you choose depends on the type of work you're doing. Try Thread Heaven if you're having trouble with static electricity and tangling. Use real or synthetic beeswax if you want to work firmly, for example when bead weaving a vessel or other structure that needs enough body to stand up. Use the tools that help you succeed and reduce the hassles you encounter.

. . . .

Q How do I use these products to wax or condition my thread?

A The goal is not to carve the thread into the wax, but to deposit a light, even coating of wax on the thread. Here's how to condition your thread:

1. Cut a workable length of thread, which will be between 1 and 5 yards, depending on your project and skill level.

2. Use a thumb to hold the thread length lightly but firmly on the top surface of the wax or thread conditioner.

3. Draw the thread across the wax with the other hand, repeating three or four times.

4. Turn the thread length and wax the other end of the thread, as in steps 2 and 3.

coating a thread with wax

Threading Tips

Q **What length of thread should I work with?**

A My quick answer: As long as you can tolerate! I like to work with a long thread so I don't have to stop and add thread often. Adding thread can take time, especially when you're weaving tightly on an intricate piece.

But if you're a beginner or find that your thread tangles easily, start by using a shorter thread. This will give you more practice at tying secure knots, and you can build up to longer lengths of thread after you've had a little more experience.

I usually suggest that beginners start with about 1 yard of working thread, plus whatever amount they want to leave as a tail (which may be used for adding a clasp or working an extra row later). Another alternative is to cut a 2- to 2½-yard length of thread, and wrap half of it into a small ziplock bag. Begin work at the center of your piece or design. When you've finished working with the first half of the thread, you have another fresh thread ready to work in the other direction, without stopping to add thread.

Q **Sometimes I get a knot in my beading thread, or even in a fine metal chain. Do you know any tricks for untying knots?**

A I do have a trick for untying knots that seems to always work. First, recognize that the only difference between a tangle and a knot is that when a tangle is pulled tight, it becomes a knot. You can loosen a knot back to a tangle using two needles or pins. Here's how:

1. Insert one needle into the center of the knot (avoid splitting the thread if possible).

2. Use the second needle to "tease" around the knot, lift, and loosen it.

3. Pull the threads of the loosened knot apart and you'll have a manageable tangle that you can gently undo with your fingers.

4. Wax the thread again to help reduce future tangling, and continue beading.

teasing out a knot

. . . .

Q I'm weaving a project with 13° Czech seed beads. How do I get through these beads several times?

A You're not only working with very small beads, but the Czech beads also have relatively tiny holes. For this work, you'll need a thin thread such as Nymo 0 with a size 13 needle. (*See* Threads: Multiple Choice *on pages 112–113.*)

If you run into tight spots where the needle won't fit, such as when adding a new thread, switch temporarily to an even smaller size 15 needle. These needles are more expensive, harder to thread, and break rather easily, so I suggest reserving them for emergency tight spots.

THREAD STORAGE

There are several ways to keep track of your beading thread. You want to be able to put your hands on it quickly, so find the method that works best for you. Here are some ideas:

▶ **Small plastic boxes** designed for sewing machine bobbins work nicely for bobbins of beading thread, too.

▶ **Plastic tubes,** like those in which C-Lon beading thread is delivered to bead stores, are just the right size for a dozen bobbins of thread. When buying several bobbins of C-Lon, ask your local bead store if you can have an empty tube to use for storing and transporting your thread.

▶ **4" binder rings** from a stationery store (one for each size of thread) can be used to organize a large collection of beading thread bobbins. String the bobbins on the ring, organized by color if you like. Then add a tag, cut from thick paper or cardstock, with the thread size, or string on a letter bead. This method has an advantage: You can reel off and cut a length of thread without removing it from the ring.

▶ **Ball chain lengths** can be used the same way as the binder rings, with one for each thread size, organized by color.

thread bobbins organized on a binder ring

Q **What the heck is a stopper bead? Do I really have to use one?**

A Yes and no. The purpose of a stopper bead is to prevent beads from falling off the end of the thread at the beginning of a weaving project before you have a chance to get a couple of rows completed. It's a helpful thing.

You add a stopper bead by stringing it and then passing through it once again (or even twice) in the same direction, without piercing the previous wrap of thread. The bead is able to slide along the thread but still provides a little tension.

Instructions often say to use a larger or contrasting bead for the stopper bead, but I usually just use the first regular bead of my row. This way, I don't have to locate a different type of bead, and I don't have to bother removing it later. When it's no longer needed for tension (usually after the first few rows are completed, but there's no hurry), just remove the extra wrap(s) of thread around the first bead.

Once you become comfortable with starting a piece of bead weaving, you may find that you don't always need a stopper bead. Use your own judgment.

Q **Instructions often warn not to split the thread, but I don't really know what this means. Will something bad happen if I do?**

A Yes, what's the big deal about splitting thread? Frequently beading instructions tell you not to split your thread, without telling you why not, or how to avoid it.

First, the why: When you insert the needle through a bead and split or pierce through the thread that's already inside the bead, it:

▶ Weakens the thread

▶ Makes it difficult or impossible to tighten or loosen the thread later, if needed

Now, how to avoid splitting the thread: When you insert your needle into a bead, lift up gently on the needle to create some "air space" at the top of the bead hole and slide your needle into that space. Creating a space helps you to avoid piercing other strands of thread that are already inside the bead hole.

REDUCE SPLITTING

Some expert beaders snip off the sharp tip of their needles, so they're working with a blunt needle, rather than a sharp point. Using a blunt needle can help to reduce splitting, because the tip won't pierce the thread so easily. If the snipped-off end seems rough, you can smooth it by dragging the tip several times across a jeweler's file or emery board.

Q **I often see instructions to leave a thread tail at the beginning of the work, but I never know how much to leave. Why should it be 4"?**

A When instructions say to leave a 4" tail, be aware that 4" is the *least* amount of thread to leave at the beginning of a piece of work, as it is just enough thread to weave in the tail after the piece is completed. If you think you might want to add a clasp, or work an extra row or two, or you just aren't sure what you want to do yet when beginning a piece, please consider leaving additional thread. Thread is cheap. You can always cut it off if you don't need it.

I recommend leaving at least 12" to 18" of thread as a tail, so you don't have to add on a new thread later just to complete a small bit of sewing. If a longer tail of thread gets in your way when you're starting the piece, wrap it up and put it into a small ziplock bag. It will stay clean and unknotted until you need it.

Basic Tools

Q Do I have to buy a lot of tools to start beading? What are the most important things I need to get started?

A One of the great things about beading is that you really don't need a lot of tools and supplies to get started. I know that most new beaders would prefer to spend their money purchasing beautiful beads, rather than spending it on all the peripheral supplies. Some basic items you'll need right away, while others can be added gradually as you refine your techniques or branch off into different types of beading. Here are the basics to get you started:

▶ **Scissors.** Choose a small, sharp pair with pointed tips. They're great for clean-angled cuts on thread, which makes it easier to thread the eye of a thin beading needle, and also for closely trimming excess threads from your work. To keep the edges sharp, avoid using these scissors for paper or any other cutting.

▶ **Pliers.** For stringing, begin by buying **crimping pliers** to fasten crimps. For wirework and general jewelry making, purchase **round nose pliers** for making wire loops, and **chain nose pliers** (or **flat nose pliers**) for bending wire at right angles, opening rings, and grasping onto harder-to-reach areas. *(See* Pliers and Cutters *on pages 128–129.)*

▶ **Wire cutters/flush cutters.** For cutting regular wire, it's okay to start with a basic side cutter, but the preferred style is a flush cutter, which leaves a smoother, more even cut end on the wire. If you'd prefer to buy just one tool for cutting flexible beading wire as well as regular wire, get the flush cutter called a Softflex cutter. All of these cutter styles are shaped like a set of pliers.

▶ **Bead sorting dish.** The most inexpensive is the very handy 50-cent **triangle tray** for sorting and scooping up beads. Other sorting dishes are available in larger ceramic, plastic, or metal versions.

A triangle tray is handy for either sorting or scooping up beads.

▶ **Flat, flocked beading surface.** Various fabrics work well for beading because beads perch on top of the fibers and are easy to pick up with a needle; also, the needle doesn't easily snag in the fabric. You can customize a piece of felt, suede, faux suede, Vellux, fleece, or other fabric to fit your beading tray. (*See* Resources.) For larger projects, try beading on cookie sheets, which can be stacked and stashed on top of the fridge when you need to quickly clear the table for dinner. Cut a smaller piece of fabric to take on the plane or for those portable projects.

▶ **Ruler/tape measure.** Retractable tape measures are the most portable, but a regular ruler works just as well for measuring wire or thread lengths, bead sizes, and more. (A **bead gauge,** also called a caliper, is a measuring tool that can be helpful for more experienced beaders.)

▶ **Fine-point permanent marker.** Use it to mark wire for cutting, or to make indication marks on pliers so all your loops come out the right size.

SEE ALSO: Stringing Tools, page 157, and Wire Tools, page 224.

Q Do I need any special scissors for beading?

A Besides the sharp-pointed pair that's so helpful for closely trimming threads from your work, you'll also need a pair of kids' scissors to cut strong, "uncuttable" polyethylene threads. For some reason, the blades on these scissors align just perfectly for cutting these tough threads.

Q When I use hand tools on metal, especially sterling silver, my tools leave scratch marks. How can I prevent these dings and scratches?

A The goal is not to crush the wire with the tool, but to grasp and hold it gently so it can be bent or shaped. To prevent scratches on sterling, you can use a piece of soft cloth between the metal and the pliers. If you need to use electrical pliers in a pinch, wrap the ridged jaws of the pliers with masking tape.

Liquid rubber products are also available, which you can use to coat the tips of pliers. Such products dry smooth and soft to prevent scratching or scarring, and the rubbery texture makes it easier to grip wire and other metal findings. Available in a variety of colors, liquid rubber is easy to peel off and reapply when needed. Look for these products in beading stores; in jewelry-making or beading catalogs; online at jewelry-making, beading, or auction Web sites; and in hardware stores.

As you practice and do more wirework, you'll learn to use your tools more gently so they don't mar the wire.

SEE ALSO: Wire Tools, page 224.

PLIERS AND CUTTERS
....

Round nose pliers have two smooth, tapered, cone-shaped tips that are used to make loops of different sizes, usually at the end of a wire, or on a headpin or eyepin. This is probably the most important tool for doing wirework. If you're able to purchase one good German hand tool, make it this one. Round nose pliers are available in a variety of sizes. My favorite pair has long tips that offer a lot of options for loop sizes, from tiny to large.

Chain nose pliers have smooth, flat, tapered tips that are good for getting into small places. Use them for opening and closing jump rings, gripping wire firmly but gently, attaching bead tips and other findings, breaking out an extra bead, and pulling the needle through a tight spot. (Be careful not to force it, however, or you may break the bead.) Chain nose pliers are also available with bent tips. Pliers with very long, tapered tips are sometimes called needle nose pliers.

Flat nose pliers are similar to chain nose pliers but with wider, squared-off jaws. These also have smooth jaws and are good for making clean square bends, but are less versatile for many types of wirework because they don't fit into tight spaces.

Crimping pliers have a unique two-section jaw that allows you to securely attach a crimp bead in any stringing project by first crimping the bead around the wires (first jaw section) and then folding the crimp bead onto itself (second jaw section).

Flush cutters/diagonal wire cutters can be used for cutting regular, soft, and half-hard metal wire. The backs of the blades meet smoothly so they create a straight cut, while the fronts of the blades make an angled cut. For smoother work, always place the straight cut on the wire end that will be visible in your piece. If necessary, flip the tool and cut again so both ends are smooth. To cut flexible beading wire as discussed in chapter 5 *(see page 157),* use the Softflex flush cutter, which can also be used for cutting regular wire. Don't *ever* use either of these flush cutters on memory wire, which is hardened steel and will ruin the cutters.

Memory wire cutters are the appropriate cutters to use on memory wire, which is made from hardened steel and requires a heavy-duty cutter that basically snaps the wire rather than cuts it. You can also use a pair of cutters designed for piano wire.

round nose pliers

chain nose pliers

flat nose pliers

crimping pliers

flush cutters

memory wire cutters

Q I prefer to use split rings because the double wrap is more secure than an open jump ring. But when I open these little rings with a fingernail, I tend to launch the ring across the room and lose it. Is there an easier way?

A I agree that the fingernail "tool" is convenient because it's attached to the arm, but I lose far fewer split rings if I use a pair of split ring pliers or tweezers. Made just for this job, the tool has a small "L" on one jaw that presses one side of the split ring open and holds it in that position while you attach the clasp or other finding. Switch to chain nose pliers and rotate the ring until the object is completely inserted. This method results in fewer lost rings.

Small-diameter split rings are more challenging to use than larger ones. It takes practice to insert a clasp or other ring into the split ring without distorting its shape. Especially with smaller split rings, take care to open them as little as possible.

split ring pliers

SEE ALSO: *Beading Essentials, page 76; Examples of Findings, page 77; and Wire Findings, page 222.*

Q How can I learn to work with smaller beads, if I can't really see them?

A You're touching on the most important beading tools of all: magnification and light. If you can't see the beads clearly, you won't be able to follow the stitch or execute the design.

The problem is that many beaders do not realize that they're not seeing the beads well. Regular prescription glasses that are perfect for reading and driving may not provide the magnification needed for beading. Remember that your doctor's goal is to correct your distance or close-up vision, but for beading, we really want to see those tiny beads a little larger than life-size. For that reason, it's helpful to have a pair of stronger reading glasses on hand.

Magnification. If you'd like to wear your prescription glasses plus obtain some additional magnification, you have several options:

▶ A magnifier that's built into a lamp

▶ A magnifier that hangs around your neck and sits on your chest, like those used by embroiderers

▶ Clip-on reading glasses that fasten to the front of your regular glasses and flip up out of the way

▶ A headband-style set with a tilt-up magnifier (*see* Resources)

Each of these styles is available in a variety of magnification strengths.

Lighting. Good light is another essential "tool" that you need. Here are some pointers:

▶ Choose a powerful localized light.

▶ Full-spectrum light is easy on the eyes and helps when selecting colors. Because it simulates natural sunlight, you can see colors accurately, even at night.

▶ A portable-style lamp is easy to bring to wherever you'll be working and will concentrate the light just where you need it. It's also great for taking to classes (so you don't have to share a light with others).

▶ Floor lamps, as well as lamp styles that clip onto tables, are available, and some models include a magnifier inside a lighted ring.

Other Useful Items

Q Before I crimp and finish off a necklace or bracelet, I like to try it on to check the length and make sure that I like the design and bead arrangement. How can I try on and play with the piece without dropping the beads on the floor?

A Yes, this is tricky. In my stringing classes, I can count on at least one person dropping their carefully arranged efforts on the floor before the piece is completed. There's an easy solution to this problem.

First, never rely on your fingers to hold the wire. Wire can be slippery and hard to control. Before you walk around with the piece to examine it in the mirror or test the length, or anytime you're not quite ready to crimp and finish the piece, be sure to secure each end to prevent accidents. One easy method is to fold a strip of invisible tape around the wire. This works well if you plan to finish the piece fairly soon. (If you wait too long, you may find a sticky residue from the tape on your wire.)

Other helpful tools are available. For years, beaders have used a hemostat (a tool used in surgery) or an electrical clip at each end, but each has its drawbacks. The hemostat is heavy and clunky, and the electrical clip has sharp teeth that can cut through the protective nylon coating on the beading wire.

There's another nifty gadget that offers the perfect solution, called a stopper clip. (*See* Resources.) It has coils of smooth wire that safely grip your beading wire without cutting into it, causing kinking, or leaving a residue. This little spring device is so secure that you can place one on each end of the piece and then walk around with it, try it on, or transport it in your bag without worrying about losing beads. It won't come off until you squeeze the ends to release it. And it's so small that you can stash a pair in your beading kit so you'll always have them handy. It's one of those inexpensive accessories that you don't want to live without.

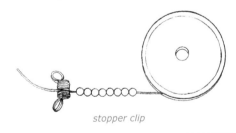

stopper clip

Q What is a bead spinner?

A A bead spinner is a handy tool to help you string solid-color or randomly mixed seed beads more quickly. The spinner is basically a small bowl with a spindle or post at the center. Here's how it works:

1. Fill the bowl with the beads you want to string.

2. Hold a curved needle in the puddle of beads and rotate the post to spin the bowl. As if by magic, the beads whose holes are pointing in the right direction will jump onto the needle.

3. Collect a couple of inches of beads, slide the beads down the needle and onto your thread, and begin again.

When you first try using a bead spinner, experiment a bit to get the angle of the needle right for picking up the most beads. It doesn't take long to become proficient in using this helpful tool. Bead spinners are available at local bead stores and online. (*See* Resources.)

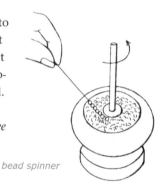

bead spinner

Q Is there an easy way to make bead holes larger?

A For removing glue on a few beads in a restringing job or widening the holes in a couple of pearls, it can be very helpful to have a set of bead reamers or broaches. The steel reamers are graduated in width and have five cutting surfaces along the length of each tool. The tiny sizes are fragile and break easily, so use them with care.

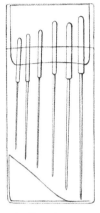

set of bead reamers

I must include a few words of caution. The reamers work best on softer materials such as pearl, amber, and sterling silver beads. Don't try to use them on hard bead materials such as glass or hard stone, or you will quickly dull the cutting blades. And don't plan on reaming out uneven holes on an entire strand of beads! This is not a fun or an easy job, and it's the reason we attempt to purchase beads with well-made holes in the first place. *(See page 72.)*

For serious hole drilling, you'll need a more professional setup, such as a drill with a flexible shaft and diamond drill bits in various sizes. *(See* Resources.*)* Some materials must be drilled underwater, so they don't overheat. If you have a friendly local jeweler, you may be able to pay him or her to drill out a couple of troublesome bead holes for you.

Q My friend makes wedding dresses, and worries about keeping her hands clean so she doesn't stain the dress. Does this problem come up in beading?

A You bet it does, and for the same reasons. Whenever you're working on something white or light-colored, especially a fiber-related piece such as knotting pearls or bead embroidery, it's essential to keep your hands clean and dry. Just a bit of sweaty hand grunge transferred to the silk cord, beading thread, or background fabric can give a ground-in dingy effect that won't go away with washing or cleaning. So, wash your hands or keep a small pack of baby wipes or instant hand cleaner in your beading bag to use before starting to work on a light-colored project.

. . . .

Q I love matte beads, and can't always find them in the colors I want. What do you suggest?

A As bead lovers, we are lucky that beads today are available in more colors, finishes, and options than ever before. But if you can't find a certain glass bead that you want in a matte finish, or you already own some shiny beads that you wish were matte, there is an easy way to matte the beads yourself. Liquid, nonacid etching products allow you to matte any glass object by immersing it in etching solution for 15 minutes or so. Etching solutions are relatively expensive but reusable, so a jar lasts a long time. You can probably buy or order some from your local bead store, or it's available from various online suppliers. (*See* Resources.)

CHAPTER 5

Stringing Basics

On a "String"

Q What are some ways of stringing beads?

A Stringing means to place beads on a "string" — usually flexible beading wire, leather cord, or strong thread — so they can be worn or hung. This is probably the oldest way of wearing or displaying beads, and it is a great place to start doing beadwork. There are as many different ways to arrange beads on a string as there are beaders. For example:

▶ One bead can hang alone at the center of a wire or cord.

▶ The beads may all be alike.

▶ Beads can be alternated with different types, colors, or sizes of beads.

▶ The beads may be all the same color and material but graduated in size, so the strand becomes narrower as it approaches the clasp.

▶ Use a variety of beads to create an intricate pattern.

▶ Beads may be strung in a random design.

▶ Two or more strands of beads may be joined at the clasp.

Using easy stringing techniques, a beginning beading student can make beautiful, wearable, and expressive necklaces, wrist and ankle bracelets, eyeglass leashes, purse handles, and even home decorating projects, such as curtain tiebacks and strands to catch light at a window. If you enjoy this type of beading, it's a natural progression to continue into other, more complicated beadwork, such as weaving and crochet.

SEE ALSO: Playing with Design Ideas, page 32.

Q **Is thread the only material used to string beads?**

A I recommend stringing on flexible beading wire instead of thread. I do a lot of beading repairs related to beads strung on thread. Either the thread itself has stretched, broken, or frayed, or there's a broken bead tip or clamshell where the thread joins the clasp. So why not make your pieces stronger from the beginning? I try to steer new beaders away from thread to stronger, more long-lasting stringing methods.

> ## CHOOSING WIRE
>
> Stringing on flexible beading wire is the most reliable and permanent method for stringing beads. Choose one of the good-quality brands, and generally avoid beading wire that includes less than 21 strands of stainless steel.

Q **I strung a necklace on coated wire and now it's all curled and twisted. I like to use the wire with fewer strands because it's less expensive. What did I do wrong?**

A Not all coated wires are created equal. You may be using an older-style wire called tigertail, which is relatively stiff. It's usually made from only three to seven strands of steel and can curl, kink, and break where it's bent.

The new, high-tech flexible beading wires are made of many strands of tiny micro stainless steel, so they have an extremely soft drape and are strong and flexible. To maintain drape, strength, and flexibility, choose good-quality flexible beading wire with 21 to 49 strands of cabled stainless steel, depending on the size of your bead holes. (*See* Resources.)

Stringing your own beads is an investment of time and energy, and the result can last a long time. It doesn't make sense to economize on the wire. Avoid headaches and use the good stuff.

· ·

Q **How do I decide which size of beading wire to use? There are so many choices.**

A In general, you want to use the largest size of wire that fits comfortably through the holes in your beads. The larger wire makes a piece stronger. Also, if the necklace happens to break, the beads won't fly easily off the larger wire, thus minimizing the chance of losing beads.

If you're using the largest beading wire that fits comfortably through your beads, you may find that the wire will not fit twice through the beads next to the crimp. In that case, reserve a few beads with larger holes to use at each end next to the clasp, or use 8° or 6° seed beads, which have larger holes, in a coordinating color. Another elegant choice is 3mm or 4mm hollow sterling silver or gold-filled beads, which look especially nice with pearls or a dressier piece.

· ·

WIRE WEIGHTS

Flexible beading wire comes in a wide range of sizes so you can choose the one that works best for your project.

▶ For small seed beads and pearls, which tend to have small holes, try a fine weight (.014 or .015) with 19 to 21 strands.

▶ For any beads that are large, are heavy, or have sharp edges or large holes, or for pieces that will receive a large amount of movement, friction, and frequent wear, such as watchbands and bracelets, use a heavy wire (.024) with 49 strands.

▶ For most everything else, choose a medium-weight wire (.018 or .019) with 49 strands. When in doubt, choose the heaviest weight wire that will fit your beads and the higher number of strands.

▶ Extra-fine wire (.010 to .012) is a much lighter weight, with a test strength of 5 to 7 pounds. It is designed for peyote stitch and bead weaving and is generally not recommended for stringing. *(See chapters 8 and 9.)*

Q **What are some of the plusses and minuses of using monofilament line for beading?**

A One of the advantages of monofilament is that it's clear, so it can be practically invisible when used for stringing or weaving. Its invisibility makes it perfect for floating designs, where you don't want to see the stringing material. Monofilament is available in a range of sizes and strengths, and you don't have to worry about matching the color to your beads, as you do when weaving with thread.

But monofilament is not a strong stringing material when compared to flexible beading wire or even a strong thread. Crimps squeezed too tightly during crimping can cut through monofilament. Monofilament also may become yellow and brittle with age, so it's not a great choice for beadwork that you want to last.

. . . .

Q If I want to string on thread, how do I finish the ends?

A The best way to finish a piece strung on thread is to add a bead tip (also called a knot cup) or clamshell at each end to make a sturdy connection with the clasp. Metal to metal is stronger than thread to metal. The bead tip is a little cup that the knot sits inside of, while a clamshell tends to be larger and closes over the knot to hide it. *(See* Examples of Findings *on page 77.)* Either style is easy to add. *(See* Adding a Clamshell *on the facing page.)*

A bead tip works the same way as a clamshell, except that it doesn't require a seed bead and doesn't close around the knot. Bead tips also tend to be smaller than clamshells, making them a better choice for finer-gauge pieces, such as delicate pearls. If your glued knot looks neat, it will tend to disappear inside the cup.

Overall, the weakest areas of this construction method are the little arm or loop of the bead tip or clamshell, and the

ADDING A CLAMSHELL

1. String an 11° seed bead and tie a surgeon's knot around the bead near the end of the thread.
2. Pass the thread through the inside of the clamshell.
3. Place a dot of glue on the knot and allow it to dry.
4. Snip off the short end of the thread.
5. Use chain nose pliers to close the clamshell, enclosing the seed bead and knot.
6. Use round nose pliers to carefully bend the arm or loop of the clamshell around one end of the clasp, so the clasp is secure but can still move freely. It's important that the join between the clasp and the necklace be able to move freely.
7. String the beads for the piece, followed by a second clamshell from the outside in, and add a seed bead.
8. Adjust the tension for the piece, snugging it up so there's not too much thread and the piece still drapes nicely.
9. Tie a couple of double overhand knots above the seed bead.
10. Glue, trim, and close the clamshell as for the first end, and then bend the loop of the clamshell around the second end of the clasp.

surgeon's knot

seed bead

clamshell

thread. This arm can only be bent a couple of times before it weakens and breaks. In base metal findings, the arm is stronger to resist bending, but also more brittle and prone to breaking. If you're stringing a necklace on thread, you may want to use silver plate clamshells instead of sterling silver for strength, and take care to bend the arms only once.

SEE ALSO: Basic Knots, page 15.

Q **What is the best way to secure the ends of the string when beading is completed? It seems that the knots come undone easily.**

A I encourage you to use good-quality flexible beading wire and crimps, which result in a flexible, permanent piece of jewelry. If you decide to string on a strong thread, you will place the knot at each end inside a bead tip or clamshell, as explained in Adding a Clamshell. *(See page 143.)*

Q **I always thought silk was the best material for stringing.**

A A lot of new beaders want to string on silk because they perceive silk as a fine material, but recent technological developments make flexible beading wire a much better choice. When you secure the wire with one small crimp on each end, you've eliminated the need for knots, extra rings, and relatively fragile bead cups or clamshells. Constructed correctly, a piece strung on flexible beading wire will last for years. Silk-strung pieces will gradually fray and need to be restrung every couple of years, depending on how frequently they're worn.

All About Crimps

Q **What is a crimp or crimp bead and how do I know which ones I need?**

A **Crimps** are seamless metal tubes or beads used to fasten the ends of flexible beading wire on a piece of strung jewelry.

A number of different types of crimps are available in different sizes. Some are better quality and easier to use than others. Here are some pointers:

Tube crimps (also called **cylinder crimps**) hold the flexible beading wire evenly with their straight sides. They're available in sterling silver, gold-filled, copper, and base metal with silver- and gold-plated finishes.

▶ **1 × 1mm micro-crimps** are tube crimps used for the smallest .010 flexible beading wire and for floating necklaces made on illusion cord or on a single strand of flexible beading wire (such as gold- or silver-plated or color-coated wire), to hold beads or groups of beads in place. Use micro-crimping pliers to flatten and fold them.

▶ **1 × 2mm crimps** are short tube crimps that can be used on most sizes of flexible beading wire, and also for illusion necklaces. Use them in pairs for extra strength.

▶ **2×2mm crimps** are the most versatile size for stringing jewelry. You can use them with most sizes of beading wire.

▶ **3×2mm crimps** are slightly longer and otherwise interchangeable with 2mm crimps. They work well with all sizes of beading wire, but will be more visible in the finished piece. For this reason, they work best with larger beads.

▶ **3×3mm crimps,** also called jumbo crimps, are used with multiple strands of beading wire as well as with thin leather and other types of cord. Use large crimping pliers to flatten and fold them.

Crimp beads are rounded crimps that look like a bead. They're usually 2mm to 3mm in diameter and are available in silver- and gold-plated, as well as gunmetal, antique copper, and other decorative finishes.

So what's the difference between crimp tubes and crimp beads? For most stringing, I do not recommend crimp beads unless you absolutely need one of the decorative colors. Because they're made of base metal, they're harder to fold smoothly and tend to crack more easily, so they're not a good choice for beginners. Tube crimps also contact the wire more evenly and are more secure than round crimp beads. For most stringing on flexible wire from fine .014 to heavy .024, I use 2×2mm tube crimps.

In general, I recommend avoiding any type of plated crimp tubes and beads. Even though they are less expensive than sterling silver and gold-filled crimps, the price difference is minimal, and base metal crimps too often crack and break. Because sterling silver and gold-filled crimps are softer, they do a better job of molding to the shape of the wire and holding it securely.

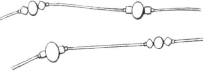

Tiny 1×1mm micro-crimps hold beads in place on a floating necklace.

SEE ALSO: Pliers and Cutters, pages 128–129.

CRIMP STYLES AND SIZES

Crimps are available in several different styles and sizes (length × width) as shown below (enlarged):

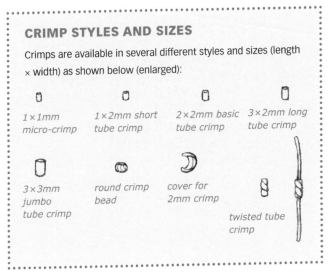

1×1mm micro-crimp

1×2mm short tube crimp

2×2mm basic tube crimp

3×2mm long tube crimp

3×3mm jumbo tube crimp

round crimp bead

cover for 2mm crimp

twisted tube crimp

Q How are crimps used?

A When a piece of jewelry is strung on flexible beading wire, the crimp tube joins the wire to the clasp, thus holding the entire piece together. So it's essential that the crimps are strong and attached correctly. The correct placement of the crimp is near the clasp, between a bumper or cushion bead and the strung necklace.

folded crimp

bumper or cushion bead

Q How do I use crimping pliers?

A Crimping pliers are used with tube crimps and crimp beads to create a firm, neatly folded crimp. A folded crimp is less visible and more secure than one that's simply been flattened with regular pliers. The pliers are available in three sizes, all of which work in the same way. *(See the box on* Crimping Pliers *on page 159.)*

Crimping pliers are usually packaged on a card with good basic instructions printed on the back. Keep this card for reference until you've applied enough crimps to be confident of the process. You'll also find crimping instructions on the next few pages, as well as in the Basics section of most beading magazines.

Take a good look at your crimping pliers. They have two ovals or
scoops in the jaws:

▶ The back scoop (closer to the
handle) has a point on top that will
make a dent, or crease, at the center
of your crimp.

▶ The front scoop is a smooth oval that's used for folding
the crimp in half onto itself along the crease.

To make a secure folded crimp, start by stringing one crimp
between the last and next to last bead from each end of the
piece. The last bead at each end is what I call the "bumper
bead." *(See the next page.)* It acts as a cushion to protect the wire
from the sharp cut edges of the crimp tube and gives the ends
of the piece a more finished look (more beads, less metal).

SEE ALSO: Pliers and Cutters, pages 128–129.

Q **So how does crimping work, exactly?**

A Attaching a crimp to the first end of a piece is easy.
Here's how:

1. String a crimp and a bead on wire. Pass the wire end
through the loop of the clasp and back through the first bead
and crimp tube, holding the two strands of wire apart so one
wire will lie on each side of the crimp. (Be sure that the wires
do not cross inside the crimp.)

2. Place the crimp in the back scoop of the crimping pliers, hold it gently without flattening.

3. Move the crimp with crimping pliers to adjust the size of the loop that passes through the clasp. You don't want this loop to be large and unsightly, but it needs to be large enough for the clasp to move freely.

4. Squeeze the crimping pliers firmly to flatten the crimp.

5. Look inside the crimp. Can you still see space inside it? If so, squeeze it again in the crimping pliers, or use chain nose pliers to flatten the crimp securely.

6. Turn the flattened crimp 90 degrees and place it into the front scoop of the crimping pliers so it's standing up.

7. Squeeze the crimping pliers gently to fold the tube in half. Be sure to watch the crimp as it folds, so you can reposition the pliers if needed.

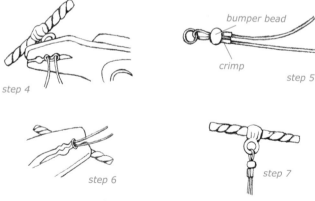

step 4

bumper bead

crimp

step 5

step 6

step 7

how to use crimping pliers

8. Make gentle squeezes around the tube to form a perfect cylinder.

9. Tug on the wire and clasp to make sure it's attached securely.

10. String some beads and pass the cut end of the wire through ½" to ¾" of additional beads. Snip off the excess so the end is hidden inside a bead (preferably with a snug fit).

11. String on the rest of the beads including the second crimp and bumper bead.

To crimp the second end of a piece, stringing instructions often say to "tighten the wire and crimp." But how tight should you make it? Before you crimp, determine how snug the wire should be. This is an important decision. On a finished necklace, the beads must have room to move so the strand is able to drape and hang fluidly around the neck. I call this extra room "ease" because that's what it's called in sewing. A stiff piece is clunky and unattractive. At the same time, you don't want the wire to be too loose, or you'll see wire between beads when the piece is worn.

To finish the second end of a strung necklace or bracelet:

1. Pass the wire through the loop of the clasp and back through the bumper bead, the crimp, and ½" to ¾" of other beads. You won't be able to pass through additional beads later as you did on the first end, so go through them now.

2. Make a guess at the correct amount of ease, and use transparent tape or a stopper clip to hold the end where you think you want it.

3. Drape the strand loosely around your hand twice. If it feels stiff or doesn't drape well, loosen the end stopper slightly.

4. Hold the strand by one end and see how much ease or extra room is between beads. Again, drape it around your hand. Has the extra wire disappeared? If not, tighten the strand by pulling on the wire end. If it's too tight or stiff, pull gently on the clasp end to loosen the crimp and wire.

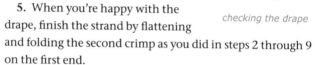

5. When you're happy with the drape, finish the strand by flattening

checking the drape

and folding the second crimp as you did in steps 2 through 9 on the first end.

6. Pull firmly on the wire end and trim it closely between beads so the end disappears. Never trim off the second wire end until the crimp has been securely fastened.

. . . .

Q **I'm having trouble getting my clasp loops the right size. Is there a way I can keep myself from making them too tight?**

A You can try using a new product called a wire guard. *(See page 83.)* It determines the perfect size for the loop of wire that passes through the clasp, and also protects the beading wire from excess wear against the clasp.

. . . .

Curvaceous

The larger the beads, the more room they need to be able to curve and drape. A good rule of thumb is to leave about a half-bead length of extra room or ease in the strand. In general, a necklace made completely of larger beads requires more ease than a necklace with a seed bead placed between each larger bead.

Q Will the crimp beads detract from my bead design?

A Shorter crimps, such as 1 × 2mm cylinders, can be less visible in a more delicate finished piece, but they do not hold the wire as securely as a longer tube crimp. To reduce the visibility of the crimps on a fine piece, try using two shorter crimps in place of one longer one. Place the crimps between beads where they will tend to disappear.

CRIMP BY TWOS

When several strands of flexible beading wire come together, it's preferable to crimp only two strands together in each crimp, rather than securing a larger number of strands in a single crimp.

clasp ring — bumper bead — crimps

Use two short 1 × 2mm crimps in place of one longer one.

Another option is to use a crimp cover. *(See* Crimp Styles and Sizes *on page 147.)* When closed, it looks like a small, round metal bead, neatly hiding a folded crimp and giving your work a clean professional finish. Crimp covers are available in sterling silver, gold-filled, silver-plated, and gold-plated. To attach one:

1. Hold the crimp cover gently in the front scoop of the crimping pliers.

2. Insert the folded crimp inside it.

3. Close the pliers carefully to shape the crimp into a smoothly rounded bead.

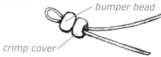

bumper bead

crimp cover

. . . .

Q When would I use a twisted crimp?

A Twisted tube crimps are one of the loveliest crimp styles and also one of the easiest to use. *(See* Crimp Styles and Sizes *on page 147.)* The twisted design, available in sterling silver and gold-filled, doesn't need to be folded, and looks beautiful when simply flattened with chain nose or flat nose pliers. The twisted ridges inside the tube help to grip the wire securely.

Twisted crimps are a perfect choice if you haven't bought your own crimping pliers yet, because they're smaller and more elegant than a flattened plain tube crimp. Match the crimp size to the wire you're using.

. . . .

Q My crimps sometimes come undone. What am I
doing wrong?

A First, make sure that the wires do not cross inside the
crimp. If the wires cross, the crimp will not grab the
wires securely, and it will tend to loosen and come apart.

If you're making a folded crimp
with the crimping pliers, after the
first crimp, look into each end of the
crimp tube. If you can still see some
space, crimp the tube again more
firmly, or flatten the crimp with chain
nose pliers. Tug on the wire after
crimping to check that it's secure.

> **CROSSED WIRES**
>
> When using any type
> of crimp, make sure the
> strands of wire do not
> cross inside the crimp.

Plated base-metal crimps can crack and break when flattened and folded. Using sterling silver or gold-filled crimps is
well worth the added security.

Also, it's essential that you are able to see what you're
doing. Make sure you have good light and magnification,
either with reading glasses (a little stronger than you actually need for normal vision works best); a magnifier worn
around the neck that rests on the chest (a style often used by
needleworkers); or a light with a built-in magnifier (the round
lighted magnifier works well). Use a small, portable light or
other style that can be directed precisely on your work area.

Practice making crimps correctly and securely, until you
don't have to worry about them coming apart again.

*SEE ALSO: Pliers and Cutters, pages 128–129; Magnification/Lighting,
page 130.*

Q I've seen round crimp covers that look like a bead. Can they be used instead of a crimp?

A No, a crimp cover never takes the place of a crimp. The cover is merely cosmetic, designed to wrap around and hide a folded 2mm crimp for a more finished look. After securing the crimp, attach the crimp cover. *(See page 154.)*

. . . .

Q I secured the crimps on a new necklace I'm making, but now realize that the necklace is too long. Is there any way I can take the crimps out and do it again?

A Yes, a crimp can be removed, if you're careful not to damage the wire. *(See* Nibbling Off a Crimp *on page 389.)* Whether you need to take off one crimp or both depends on the necklace design and the amount that you're shortening it. On a simple repeating design or a random or asymmetrical design, you may get away with removing just one crimp on one end. For a more complex symmetrical design, you may need to remove both crimp ends. After correcting the length, add a new crimp or crimps and finish the piece as usual.

. . . .

Q What if I'm stringing on leather cord?

A There are several different styles of crimp ends that work with round and flat leather cord, as well as with rattail, silk, and other fiber-wrapped cords. Depending on the style, the cord is inserted into the crimp, which is then either flattened or folded to anchor it. For extra security, add a dot of glue when inserting the cord, before crimping. Use the ring on the crimp end to join it to a clasp or other finding.

SEE ALSO: Leather Cord, page 199.

Stringing Tools

Q Do I need a special wire cutter?

A I recommend a flush cutter. The best one to use for flexible beading wire is made from harder metal so it can easily cut the multiple stainless steel fibers without damage to the cutting blades. Do not use regular wire cutters to cut flexible beading wire; it will ruin the blades.

If you're not ready to invest in a pair of good-quality cutters, reserve an old pair of scissors or snips for the job. Use a permanent marker to write "wire" on the plastic handle, so you remember which pair to use.

. . . .

Q What tools do I need for crimping?

A You can choose from one of several methods used to fasten crimps. Each creates a securely strung piece of jewelry with a slightly different result. Here's an overview:

▶ **Chain nose pliers.** Use this tool to flatten crimps, close crimp-ends for leather cord, and hold and manipulate rings and wire. Many expert beaders choose to flatten crimps with chain nose pliers first, before using the crimping pliers. This adds an extra step to the process, but it can provide additional security. Try it both ways to see which method works best for you.

▶ **Crimping pliers.** Invented in 1991, this special type of pliers allows the jewelry maker to flatten and fold crimps in half, so the result is smaller, smoother, and less obtrusive than a crimp that is simply flattened. The pliers are available in three sizes: micro (for 1mm crimps), standard (for 2mm crimps), and mighty (for 3mm crimps).

▶ **Magical crimper.** A relatively new design, this crimper flattens a crimp while rounding it into a small bead. It was created exclusively for use with 2mm sterling silver and gold-filled tube crimps and is available in two sizes, for use with .014"–.015" or .019" flexible beading wire. Make several squeezes to transform a 2mm crimp into a small round bead. Drawbacks include the tool's higher cost and the fact that each tool works with only one size range of wire.

SEE ALSO: Pliers and Cutters, pages 128–129.

CRIMPING PLIERS

Crimping pliers are available in three sizes: micro, standard, and mighty.

▶ Use the standard crimper for all regular stringing and crimping with 2mm crimps.

▶ Use the micro-crimper with tiny 1mm crimps, which will be virtually invisible in the finished piece.

▶ Use the mighty crimper with larger 2×3mm and 3×3mm crimps for crimping several strands of flexible beading wire or the ends of .5mm to 1mm cord, such as leather and rattail.

Stringing Shortcuts

Q **Is there a faster way to string beads than picking them up one at a time?**

A If you need to string a lot of loose, solid-color or randomly mixed seed beads that are not on strands, there's a wonderful tool called a bead spinner that can make the work go much more quickly. *(See page 134.)* With the bead spinner, you can string onto any thread or wire that will fit through the bead when doubled.

If your stringing material *doesn't* fit through the needle's eye, add a small loop of thin beading thread through the eye, and tie with an overhand knot. *(See page 16.)* Leave this loop in place and thread your stringing material through the loop.

If seed beads are on temporary strands, you can transfer them to flexible beading wire by guiding the wire into 1" to 2" of beads at a time, and sliding them off the thread.

. . . .

Q **I need to string a large quantity of beads for a multi-strand necklace. What's the quickest way to do it?**

A Because Czech seed beads are available in hanks on temporary strands, this feature can be used to your advantage when you need to string a lot of single-color beads. To transfer the beads to more permanent thread:

1. Tie the temporary thread in a knot around stronger thread or flexible beading wire.

2. Slide the beads carefully over the knot to the new strand.

temporary thread

new thread

Buying beads in strands also can save you a lot of time if you make French-beaded flowers on wire. You can slide the wire into the strand of beads 1" to 2" at a time or knot the thread onto the wire and carefully slide the beads to the wire, as described above.

SEE ALSO: How to use a bead spinner, page 134.

Bracelets and Necklaces

Q What are the standard lengths for bracelets and necklaces?

A If you're making pieces for gifts or to sell, you'll want to know the range of lengths that fit most people well.

Bracelets usually measure from 7" to 8" long; 7½" is a good length that fits many people. Remember that the larger the beads, the longer the bracelet will need to be to give the same fit, because larger beads take up more room inside the fastened bracelet. You can measure a bracelet flat, but the more useful measurement is found when it is fastened. You can test a bracelet's wearable length using a bracelet mandrel. Steel or plastic mandrels are sold as jewelry-making tools, but you can easily make your own quick version. *(See page 163.)*

Necklaces have a standard range of lengths *(see below),* but where a necklace falls depends on a woman's body structure, especially the neck and shoulders. Some women prefer short necklaces that would show up in a head shot. Others choose a long necklace, so they can enjoy playing with it during the day. A woman with a large chest may prefer a necklace that doesn't fall over the shelf of her bust line. Here are some length guides:

▶ Choker = 15" to 16"

▶ Princess = 18"

▶ Midchest or matinee = 24"

▶ Opera or rope = 30" to 36" and longer

Q How do I make a bracelet that ends up the right length? They all seem to fit a little differently.

A Making bracelets the right length can require a bit of trial and error. To decide on a good length, whether it's for your wrist or someone else's, it helps to measure another bracelet that fits well. This is the length you'll aim for.

Measure the closed clasp you plan to use, including any rings that will attach it to the bracelet you're making. Subtract this amount from the desired length of the bracelet. If the bracelet will be strung and fastened with crimps, allow ³⁄₁₆" to ¼" at each end for the crimp and loop. The number that's left is the length you'll want to string or weave for the bracelet, before the clasp is added.

· ·

Q How do I measure the length of a bracelet that has a toggle clasp?

A To accurately measure the length of a bracelet with any type of clasp, think of how the clasp overlaps or fastens when it's closed. For a toggle, the bar sits just inside the inner edges of the ring, so measure the bracelet from the inside edge of the post to the inside edge of the outer ring.

Measure from the post to the inside of the ring.

· ·

Q **What about bracelets made with big round beads, or really wide ones? They seem to fit more tightly.**

A If the bracelet you're making is extra-thick or wide, or strung with larger beads, simply measuring the length of an existing bracelet may not give you an accurate measurement. The new bracelet will need to be longer to fit around the wrist in the same way, because the thickness or bead size will affect the bracelet's inside circumference.

A bracelet mandrel helps with this measurement. A mandrel allows you to measure the bracelet's inside circumference, which is the space left over for your wrist. You can buy an inexpensive plastic version from a jewelry supplier.

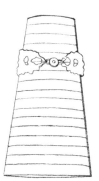

You also can make your own bracelet mandrel, using a large plastic drinking cup, as follows:

1. Cut out the bottom of the cup.

2. Slice an opening up the side of the cup.

Measure an existing bracelet on a mandrel and mark the length for a new bracelet.

3. Overlap the cut edges and tape them to make a bracelet-sized mandrel.

4. Place the favorite-fitting bracelet on the small end of the cup or mandrel and draw a line on the cup just under the bracelet to mark the size. You can mark many sizes on one cylinder.

5. Use the appropriate line on the cup to determine the ideal length for the new bracelet. Remember to allow enough

length for the clasp and any rings, as before. This method is much more accurate than measuring a bracelet when it's lying flat.

. . . .

Q It's difficult to imagine how my beads are going to look when strung into a necklace. What's the best way to play with an idea?

A A bead board, also called a design board *(see page 103),* is very useful for working out a new stringing design. For example, you might have five beautiful Venetian beads from your grandmother's necklace that you want to make into a new necklace. On the bead board, you can lay out the five beads to experiment with spacing, and then begin filling in between them with other beads of various sizes, shapes, and colors to make a pleasing arrangement. The groove trays are available in short and long lengths. If you plan to make any pieces longer than 26", purchase the longer board so you won't need to buy two different sizes.

When you have some ideas for stringing the piece, the next step is to use the end of your beading wire to pick up 1" to 2" of each design idea to see how they look. This will allow you to identify your preferences and make changes, and it also will lead to other ideas. Depending on how complex your piece will be, you may want to include several different designs in various parts of the necklace:

▶ Simple or intricate design repeats throughout the length of the necklace

▶ Larger or more important beads (focal beads) arranged at the center, with smaller beads and designs tapering toward each end

▶ Beads arranged in graduated sizes, with a smaller bead between each one

There are an unlimited number of design ideas just waiting to be unlocked by your imagination and your willingness to play. Once you decide on a design, you're ready to string the beads in order on flexible beading wire and fasten the ends with crimps. Remember that by making a piece, you're not ruining your grandmother's beads. You may wear it for a year and then decide to cut it apart and change the design to reflect your new ideas and expertise.

Q **I have trouble with the ends of the wire poking out and scratching my neck. Can you suggest a solution?**

A To prevent wire ends from poking out of the necklace, never cut the wire just after the crimp. It's important to continue to string the end through several beads (½" to ¾") after the crimp, preferably with a snug fit so the end stays buried. Snip the wire end closely between beads so the end remains hidden inside a bead.

Q Can I finish a necklace without using a clasp?

A You can create your own simple clasp by placing a large bead or button at one end and crimping or tying several knots between beads to anchor the end securely. On the other end, make a loop of seed beads that will fit over the button, and crimp or knot to secure it.

Or you can make a necklace with no clasp at all. A strand at least 24" long will fit over most heads. Here's how you do it:

1. String two crimps in the design at one end.

2. Pass the second end through the crimps in the opposite direction and continue through a few beads on each side of the crimps.

3. Adjust the ease and secure the crimps.

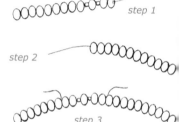

step 1

step 2

step 3

Q I just made a necklace I like on good-quality beading wire, but it feels stiff. What did I do wrong?

A Generic instructions to "snug up the beads" can lead to problems. It's just not specific enough. When you string beads on flexible beading wire, it's important to leave enough room for the beads to move. Otherwise the necklace won't curve gracefully around your neck, no matter how fluid or soft the wire may be.

To avoid stringing the piece all over again, you may want to try my method of removing a crimp, so you can add more ease. *(See* Nibbling Off a Crimp *on page 389.)* After removing the crimp, you'll need to string a new crimp and adjust the ease before securing it.

If you've already trimmed the second end, you may be able to shorten the necklace slightly so you'll have an end to work with. But if shortening it destroys the symmetry of the piece, you may need to start again with new wire. You can always save this piece of wire for a shorter necklace or a bracelet.

. . . .

Q I want to make eyeglass cords for my friends. How is that different from a necklace?

A An eyeglass cord or leash is constructed in the same way as a necklace, except that you use eyeglass findings in place of a clasp. String beads on flexible beading wire (at least .019 and 49 strands because eyeglass cords receive a lot of abuse), adjust the ease, and crimp the ends as usual.

eyeglass leash and findings

. . . .

Q I've seen necklaces where the beads seem to float in the air around your neck. Are these styles hard to make?

A Often called an illusion or floating necklace because the beads appear to float in thin air, this is not a difficult stringing job. Strung on clear illusion cord or fishing line, individual beads or groups of beads are held in place with a crimp at each end, to anchor them in the desired spacing.

You can use a very small crimp for this job, because the wire passes through the crimp only once (unlike at a clasp, where the wire needs to pass through twice). Try the tiny 1×1mm micro-crimps, which nearly disappear after crimping. You also will need a micro-crimper to flatten and fold the crimps.

An easy way to determine even spacing for your beads is to cut a plastic coffee stirrer or drinking straw to the length desired between beads or groups of beads. Slit one side of the tube so you can slide it off the wire after crimping. To use:

1. Slide the straw onto the cord after the last bead.
2. Add a crimp, the next bead(s), and another crimp.
3. Secure the crimps to anchor the bead(s) in place.
4. Slide the straw off the cord along the slit, and move it to determine the next placement.

Use a straw to evenly space beads.

Q Can I make a floating necklace or bracelet with something other than fishing line?

A For other interesting floating effects, you can use the same technique on flexible beading wire, which offers greater strength, especially for bracelets and for heavy or sharp beads. This technique can be especially beautiful using gold- or silver-plated wire, as well as on beading wire with colored coatings such as bronze, purple, red, white, or black. Use a multistrand clasp to create an interlocking, floating design, such as the bracelet shown here, making some strands longer than others.

Use a multistrand clasp to create a more intricate floating design.

Another variation of this technique is strung on silk or organza ribbon, silk cord, or waxed linen cord, with knots tied to hold each bead or group of beads in place. Choose the materials to reflect the style you'd like to achieve, whether breezy and sporty with seashells and linen, or crystals strung on shimmering silk.

SEE ALSO: Multiple Strands, page 185.

Q What makes a finished necklace strong?

A When jewelry comes to me for repair, I'm always curious to see where and how it has broken. It's almost always the thread that has frayed, the monofilament that has dried out and become brittle, or the bead tip that has been bent once too often. If the piece is correctly strung and crimped on beading wire, it seems to have a better chance of surviving much longer.

To assess the strength of a necklace or other piece of jewelry, I find it helpful to evaluate the piece in terms of its weakest link. That's the part that's most likely to fail first. I always examine a piece of jewelry critically to see if I can figure out where it might break first. I can use this information to strengthen the area so the piece will have a longer life span. Develop the habit of analyzing each piece you make for any of the following potential problems:

▶ Sharp edges and holes on your rustic stone beads that, over time, will saw through the too-thin beading wire. This is even more likely if the strand was crowded too tightly before crimping and the beads don't have room to move.

▶ A crimp with wires crossed inside, or a crimp that was never adequately flattened.

▶ Unsoldered jump ring or split ring that attaches the clasp was sprung open during construction and will never again close precisely, allowing thread or wire to work its way through.

> ### TROUBLESHOOTING
>
> On an eyeglass leash, the weakest link is usually the little rubber loop on the eyeglass finding. These rubber pieces tend to weaken and break long before the beaded strand has worn out. My solution is to add a split ring or spring ring to the rubber loop and attach the flexible beading wire to this ring. That way, when the rubber finding breaks, you can easily replace it without restringing the entire piece.

When doing this evaluation, it also makes sense to determine how much the piece will be worn. If it's a formal necklace such as one for a bride, it is unlikely to receive frequent wear. But if your project is one of those perfect bracelets that you reach for every time you wear black, then it needs to stand up not only to banging around on a mouse pad all day, but to being worn day after day, week after week. I often wear my favorite pieces every day, and I expect them to last for years. When assessing the strength of a piece of jewelry, keep its work life in mind.

Q I make bracelets that I really like, but when worn, they always seem to turn upside down so the clasp sits on top of my wrist. I've tried making them tighter, but it doesn't seem to help. What can I do about this?

A Yes, our ideal for a bracelet is for the center or focal area to sit nicely on top of the wrist. But it's an undeniable law of gravity that if a bracelet is heavier in the focal area than it is in the clasp area, then it's going to flip upside down, and all you'll see is the clasp. If you're tired of turning your bracelets around all day long, the solution is to design a bracelet that's weighted correctly so gravity will help it hang with the clasp at the bottom.

To make the laws of physics work for you instead of against you, you need to plan to make the focal area of the bracelet lighter than the clasp area. Experiment by arranging lighter beads in the focal area such as wood, seed pods, bone, cork, amber, polymer clay, metal mesh, or filigree Bali beads. Place heavier beads on either side of the clasp, such as stone, solid metal, or glass tube beads with wire wrappings.

Using these principles, you'll be able to make bracelets that look as beautiful on your wrist as they do sitting on the table. A couple of other quick solutions will work in a pinch:

▶ String a bracelet on stretch cord, making it snug enough to grip the wrist so it won't flip over easily.

▶ Design a bracelet that has no top or "right" side, so it looks great no matter which way it turns, such as one strung on memory wire.

▶ Use a gorgeous clasp that's meant to be seen, so it will look great as the focal point of the bracelet.

CHAPTER 6

Other
Stringing
Techniques

Memory Wire

Q When is it a good idea to use memory wire?

A Steel memory wire is another stringing material that can be used to make quick, fun bracelets and other jewelry. Memory wire is made from hardened steel that retains its shape, as long as it's handled gently. It's available in four sizes that are used for different purposes (the measurement equals the diameter of the memory wire loop):

▶ 1¾" for a snug bracelet

▶ 2¼" for a bangle bracelet

▶ 3¾" for a necklace

▶ ¾" for a ring

Available finishes include regular dark steel, stainless, and bright shiny steel, as well as bright gold- and silver-plated in fewer sizes. Memory wire is inexpensive and usually sold by the loop or in packages of 12 loops.

. . . .

Q When stringing bracelets on memory wire, how do I figure out the length or number of loops I need?

A For a bracelet, one factor in deciding the number of loops of memory wire is whether or not the finished bracelet will slide on over your hand. I've made memory wire bracelets with as many as 26 loops or wraps using 11° Delicas on 2¼" wire, but it would take forever to put on this bracelet if it didn't fit over my hand and had to be donned one wrap

at a time! Test the fit with plain wire before you begin to add beads.

Other factors include the bead size you're using, and how you want the finished bracelet to look. If you're stringing 11° Delicas or seed beads, eight wraps may be a good choice, and the finished bracelet doesn't take so long to put on. For chunkier beads, such as Czech glass, I find that three to five wraps work well. You can also wrap the strung beads with regular wire to embellish the design. As always, test your design by making one bracelet and see what number of wraps you prefer.

If you like the look of a 26-wrap bracelet, but want it to be easier to wear, you can make sets of coordinating shorter bracelets with eight to ten wraps each and wear them together. It's fun to shade the colors, stringing a couple of wraps before progressing to the next bead color.

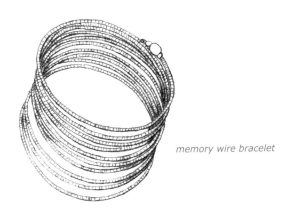

memory wire bracelet

Q **Can I make a necklace from memory wire?**

A Necklace lengths for memory wire are a little different. Because you don't want to choke the wearer, memory wire necklaces usually wrap the neck only once, with a short overlap. To create a necklace, you'll need one-and-a-half to two wraps of wire (since our necks are not 3¾" in diameter). Memory wire tends to relax when you string the beads. How much it relaxes depends on the size and weight of beads used. For example, the 2¼" wire relaxes to 2⅜" when strung with 11° seed beads and to 2½" when strung with 6mm beads.

Again, testing is a good idea. Be sure to make notes of what works, so you don't have to reinvent the necklace the next time you make one. A memory wire necklace also looks great with a pendant strung at the center.

Q **How do I cut memory wire?**

A Please, please, do not use your good wire cutters to cut memory wire. Many a nice pair of cutters has been instantly ruined while trying to cut memory wire. Because the wire is hardened, most of the cutters made for memory wire snap or break the wire, rather than cut it. Purchase a special pair of memory wire cutters, or use piano wire cutters.

If you're not ready to purchase this extra tool for working with memory wire, you can politely ask that it be cut into bracelet or necklace lengths at the bead store where you purchase the wire. Most stores will try to accommodate this request, or they will let you use their memory wire cutters.

SEE ALSO: Pliers and Cutters, pages 128–129.

Q Is it tricky to finish the ends of a piece made on memory wire?

A There are several ways to finish cut ends of memory wire so the beads don't fall off. The quickest option is to turn a small round loop or triangle loop in the wire end using round nose pliers. When you first try this, you'll realize that this wire is very hard! Here's the best way to go about it:

1. Grip the very end of the wire with the round nose pliers, so that no wire sticks out, and hold it tightly.

2. Use the opposite thumb to press the wire firmly against the jaw of the pliers and turn the pliers away from you to form a curve, following the natural curve of the wire.

3. Reposition the pliers to grab the next section of wire and repeat until you have created a full loop. (If you have difficulty turning a round loop, use chain nose pliers to make a small triangle loop.)

4. Disguise the end loops in memory wire by stringing a larger bead or decorative set of beads just next to each loop. It's just an optional way to trick the eye, so it doesn't really notice the small loop.

Another finishing option is to glue one of the beads from your design on the end of the wire, or use a half-drilled bead end made just for this purpose. Either way, I find that the glued beads will not stay in place unless you use very strong glue, such as two-part epoxy, which is available at hardware stores.

glued bead at the end of a memory wire bracelet

Stretch Cord

Q **Why would I make a bracelet with stretch cord? It seems a bit amateurish.**

A Some people turn up their noses at bracelets made on stretch cord, feeling that it's not "real" jewelry. But this style of bracelet is quick and fun to make and wear. If the beads are beautiful, it can look great. It's ideal for people who are allergic to metal, take their jewelry off a lot, or have trouble fastening clasps. I confess that I find metal clasps to be chilly on my bare arms during Boston winters, so there's another argument in their favor.

. . . .

Q **What is stretch cord, anyway?**

A There are a number of brands of stretchy, clear elastic jewelry cord available in beading stores. Most are made from a high-tech polymer that's very strong and doesn't crack, yellow, or harden over time. Because the ends do not fray, you can use the cut end to pick up beads without the need for a needle. It's also usually latex-free (check the package), which is ideal for people with allergies, and it's easy to knot. Here are a few pointers:

▶ Stretch cord comes in several diameters for different sizes and weights of beads; .5mm, .7mm, and 1mm are the most popular. For the 1mm size and larger, always knot the ends together with an overhand knot, as square knots will work their way open.

▶ Use the larger sizes of cord for large or heavy beads, or those with large holes. Do not use heavy beads with the thinner weights (unless you use the cord doubled), as the piece will droop, causing the cord to show between beads. For the smaller .5mm and .7mm cord, you can tie two overhand knots, a square knot, or a surgeon's knot, then turn the piece over and tie a second knot.

▶ Make the piece more secure by stretching the knots thoroughly to tighten them and add a dot of glue or clear nail polish. If you tie tight, secure knots, the glue is optional.

▶ Some brands of strong elastic stringing materials have even more stretch and recovery, a fibrous construction, and a milky appearance. For extra strength on larger beads or beads with larger holes, pass through the bracelet twice before knotting as above.

SEE ALSO: Basic Knots, page 15.

An Armful of Beads

I have a particular love of stretch cord, because it is how I first became interested in making beaded jewelry. As a low-risk way to try playing with beads and colors, I decided to make one stretch bracelet every day. I'd spend about 10 minutes arranging colors for each one, string 1" or 2" to test the idea, and come up with a fun design. I spent no more than 15 minutes making each bracelet. In about a month, I had 40 interesting stretch bracelets that I wore all together as a 4" wide, funky cuff of bead beauty and chaos. I made some bracelets slightly larger, so they would fit further up my arm.

I loved wearing this rich armful of colorful bracelets, and many people asked me about them. I still drag them out occasionally to inspire beginners with an easy, painless way to get started playing with beads and jewelry making.

Q What about crimps? Can't I crimp on stretch cord?

A I don't recommend using crimps with any of the stretch cords. Crimping can cut through the cord or cause it to fray. For the same reason, when choosing beads to use with any of the stretch cords, check to be sure there are no sharp edges. A sharp bead can cut through the stretch cord and cause the piece to break.

Q **My stretch bracelets keep breaking. What am I doing wrong?**

A When you make a stretch bracelet using one of the good-quality stretch cords available, the weakest area is your knot! That's why it's important to use the right type of knots and tighten them securely. Don't cut the ends too short.

Another reason a bracelet might break is that you're using beads or crystals with sharp edges. Avoid them; they may cut through the cord.

Finally, handle your bracelets gently. The stretch cord itself is strong and should not break unless it's stretched to many times its normal length.

....

Q **When using a stretch stringing material, what is the best way to hide the ends after knotting?**

A If any bead in the design has a larger hole, you can string it last if you'd like to hide the knot inside the hole. Here's how:

1. Apply glue or nail polish to the knot on the beaded strand.

2. Insert one end of the cord through the large-hole bead and pull on this end gently until the knot rests inside the bead hole.

3. Allow the glue to dry for a half hour or more.

4. Trim the cord ends at least ⅛" from the knot. Be careful: If you cut the ends too short, the knot may come undone.

Repeated stretching from putting on and wearing the bracelet may eventually pull the knot out of its glued hiding place. Don't worry if you're not able to hide the knot inside a bead. If you're using clear cord, knots tend to disappear when placed next to a larger bead in the design. This is because the eye is distracted by the larger bead.

· ·

Q **What kinds of beads do I need in order to make some other designs?**

A There are an infinite number of fun patterns and arrangements of beads that you can make using stretch cord. Flowers, dangles, and straight stringing can all be combined using a variety of shapes, sizes, and colors. What you

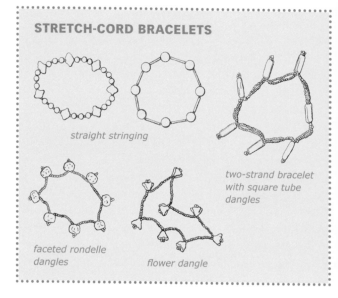

STRETCH-CORD BRACELETS

straight stringing

two-strand bracelet with square tube dangles

faceted rondelle dangles

flower dangle

make will depend on the beads you have on hand and what's available in local stores.

The simplest bracelets are my favorites. Here are just a few suggestions:

▶ Use 12 bright red semiprecious stone chips separated by ½" of bright green opaque Delicas. The result looks like a string of chili peppers.

▶ Use 4mm round garnets and seven 10mm black Czech Saturn-shaped beads, separated by bright orange Delicas.

▶ Try eight African dotted bone beads, with a gray 8° seed bead on each side, and ½" of bright red Delicas between each group.

If you feel the Delicas on these strands look too narrow, substitute a larger Delica or seed bead or a short bugle bead. Each strand doesn't seem narrow when several are worn together, so it depends on how you plan to use them.

. . . .

Q **What if I want my stretch bracelets to look more like a set?**

A Certainly, your colors don't have to be as diverse as mine! You can make a set of 5 to 10 bracelets that all have the same three or four colors, so they look great together. A set like this is also a wonderful, quick gift that you can make for a friend — especially if you know the colors she loves and wears often. It's a great way to explore interesting color combinations.

. . . .

Q What is a flower dangle and how do I make one?

A Flower dangles are a collection of beads that have a center and look like flowers when they hang off a strand. You'll need about six to eight larger beads to make dangles for a stretch-cord bracelet, and there are a couple of ways to create the dangles. Experiment and take notes about spacing between dangles, so the bracelet is both symmetric and fits you.

One option is to create dangles separately and string them on the cord. I placed some bright orange drops with vertical holes onto headpins with a seed bead at the bottom, and turned a loop at the top of each. I then strung eight of these dangle beads separated by ¾" of 8° seed beads in two colors: two light opal green, alternating with one transparent purple. Creating dangles in this way is not only for stretch cord; beaded dangles work equally as well on flexible wire with crimped ends and a clasp.

Another method to make a stretch bracelet with dangles uses the cord throughout. Here's how:

1. Start by stringing ¾" to 1" of beads for the first section between dangles. These can be 8°, 10°, or 11° seed beads, plain or in a pattern.

2. String a larger 6mm to 10mm dangle bead and three to five tiny 11° Delicas or 15° seed beads for the flower center.

3. Pass the stretch cord back through the larger dangle bead. If it's a tight fit, stretch the cord to make it narrower. Pull the cord tight so the dangle is seated firmly.

4. Repeat steps 1 through 3 until you reach the desired length.

5. Snip the cord a couple of inches away from the beads, and knot the ends.

6. Finish with glue for added strength, if desired.

Your local bead store will reveal many other interesting options for dangle beads. These may include:

▶ Czech glass or semiprecious stone flowers

▶ Pyramid shapes

▶ Faceted drops

▶ Squares

▶ Fat faceted rondelles

▶ Table-cuts

▶ Leaves

▶ Faceted donuts

▶ Square tube beads

If a strand doesn't look right or isn't a good size, snip it apart and start again. Remember that each strand takes only about 15 minutes to make, so be willing to play and experiment.

Multiple Strands

What is meant by multistrand bead stringing? Is it hard to do?

Multistrand work is a slightly more advanced version of the basic stringing detailed in chapter 5 and offers a way to make your designs more intricate. Most of the same information applies to both necklaces and multistrand bracelets. There are several ways these pieces can be constructed, and there are also several different styles:

▶ All strands the same length

▶ All strands twisted together

▶ All strands in different, graduated lengths

twisted

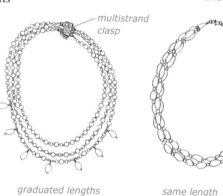

multistrand
clasp

graduated lengths   *same length*

. . . .

Q **Can a stretch bracelet be multistrand?**

A One fun way to make a multistrand stretch bracelet is to make several dangle strands that are alike or use the same beads, and join them using a multihole spacer, such as one of the beautiful Bali silver ones. This is a great use for a single, leftover spacer. Here's how:

1. Cut six strands of stretch cord in equal lengths large enough to fit your wrist, plus 8" to 10".

2. String beads on each strand, making dangles. Tape the ends until you're ready to join them.

3. Knot two strands through each of the holes of a three-hole spacer.

4. Add glue or clear nail polish to the knots, and pull all the knots inside the spacer.

5. Allow the knots to dry at least a half hour.

6. Trim the stretch cord ends about ⅛" from each knot.

Another fun multistrand stretch design that I call the "bubble bracelet" looks like a chunky single strand, but includes little three-strand bubbles along its length. Color combinations are only limited by your imagination!

bubble bracelet

Use large-hole beads such as 4mm Miyuki squares and 6° seed beads, with Miyuki 3.4mm drops for the bubbles. A color mix is fun to use for the drops. Try one of the prepared mixes or mix several colors to make your own. Here's how you make it:

1. Cut three strands of .5mm stretch cord the length of the desired bracelet plus 4" to 5".

2. String five beads onto all three strands, held together, in a pattern: 6° seed, square, seed, square, seed.

3. Separate the three strands and string seven drops onto each one individually.

4. Bring the strands back together and repeat the five-bead sequence, as in step 2.

5. Alternate this pattern (steps 3 and 4) until you reach the desired length and end with the drop beads.

6. Tie all three strands together tightly using an overhand knot, followed by another overhand knot on top of it, and tighten securely.

7. Add a dot of glue and pull the knots inside a 6° seed bead.

8. Allow the glue to dry for at least a half hour.

9. Trim the stretch cord ends about ⅛" from the knot.

. . . .

Q How do I make a necklace with more than one strand?

A The easiest way to make a multistrand piece is to use flexible beading wire and a multistrand clasp. For example, if you want a three-strand necklace: buy a three-strand clasp, string three separate strands, then crimp one strand into each hole of the clasp. Strands can be all the same length, and worn either straight or twisted. Strands also can be graduated in length, with each lower strand slightly longer than the one above it.

To create a twisted look, you can gently twist a multistrand piece before fastening the clasp. To make a permanently twisted piece, use a multistrand clasp, then interlace and twist the strands before crimping. *(See the floating bracelet design on page 169.)*

option 1

Other techniques for joining two or three strands to a single-strand clasp work best with strands of smaller beads near the ends. (Adding crimp covers can give the second and third options a more polished look.) Try these:

option 2

1. Crimp each strand separately into the ring of a single-strand clasp.

2. Bring two fine strands into one crimp and crimp them together.

3. Crimp each strand into a jump ring, and then join those rings into the ring of the clasp.

option 3

Q **How do I make a necklace with strands that are different lengths?**

A To make a necklace with graduated strands, string each strand slightly longer than the one above it, so the necklace lies smoothly around the neck. The length of each new strand depends on the look you want and the size of your beads, but making each strand 1½" to 2" longer is a good place to start. Decide on the length of the shortest (top) strand first, so you don't end up with a necklace that's going to choke you.

Q What's another way to join two strands smoothly to a single strand clasp?

A To transition to a single-strand clasp, you can first crimp the two strands together and then join the remaining strand to the clasp. To disguise the first crimp, one solution is to use a crimp cover, so it looks like a round metal bead in the design. Another option is to use a decorative accent bead with a larger hole to cover the join, so the folded crimp can slide inside it. Here's how that works:

1. String a few smaller seed beads (11° or 8°) on each end before adding a bead over both strands, the crimp and the decorative bead, so the two strands will lie smoothly side by side.

2. Test the hole of the decorative bead so you know that the folded crimp will fit inside. (If the plain crimp fits, the folded one, which is smaller, should also fit. If the crimp nearly fits and your decorative bead is metal, such as a Bali silver bead, you can use a reamer or broach to open up the hole until the crimp fits inside.)

Use a decorative bead to cover the crimp and join.

3. Finish the rest of the necklace as usual for a single-strand necklace.

Q How do I use a cone?

A A final method for making a multistrand piece involves that mysterious finding called a cone. *(See* Examples of Findings *on page 77.)* The cone is a fancy cover for a group of strands, and serves as a bridge to a single-strand clasp. If you want a multistrand necklace with strands that all bunch together, this is the method to use. A cone is a graduated cylinder that's open at both ends, designed to bring three to 12 strands together and hide the crimps or knots used to finish the strands. Cones are available in a wide variety of widths and lengths to accommodate differ-ent numbers of strands and various sizes of beads.

> **DISAPPEARING ACT**
> ········
> If you want the crimp to disappear, use a large-hole bead as the cushion bead. The folded crimp will slip inside it.

Here's one way to join a multi-strand necklace using a cone:

1. Cut a 3" piece of 20- or 18-gauge wire and make a simple or wrapped loop at one end. Test the loop to make sure it fits and is hidden inside the cone.

2. Crimp or knot all the strands into the wire loop, adding smaller beads at the ends, if needed, so the strands taper to nestle inside the cone.

3. Insert the straight end of the wire into the wide end of the cone and snug all the strand joins inside the cone.

step 1

step 2

4. Make a second loop in the wire at the top of the cone, and join it to the ring of the clasp. For a decorative touch, string a bead after the cone and before the loop.

step 3

An alternative method uses flexible beading wire in place of the regular wire.

1. Cut a 4" piece of flexible beading wire. String a crimp tube and make a small loop at one end. Crimp and fold the tube securely.

2. Follow steps 2 and 3, above.

3. String a bead, a second crimp tube, and a cushion bead, pass through the ring of the clasp, and back through the bead, the crimp tube, and the cone. Crimp and fold the tube securely.

The beaded strands don't have to fit completely inside the cone. But if they don't nestle into the cone enough to hide the loop and crimps or knots, add a couple of smaller beads at each end of the strands, or switch to larger cones.

Tricky Stringing Solutions

Q **I want to make a three-strand necklace using larger beads, and my clasp has holes that are too close together. How do I make the beads fit the clasp?**

A You're right that if you try to bring larger beads into a smaller multistrand clasp, the beads will bunch up and won't lie smoothly. Two solutions to this problem:

▶ Change to smaller beads as you near the clasp, so they fit neatly side-by-side when crimped into the clasp.

▶ Purchase a clasp with more holes and leave some holes empty to create more room for the larger beads. For your three-strand necklace, you might purchase a five-strand clasp, and crimp strands into the first, third, and fifth holes. The empty second and fourth holes will hardly be noticeable in the finished necklace.

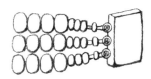

Solution 1: Use smaller beads near clasp.

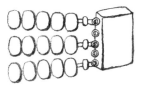

Solution 2: Create more room with a five-strand clasp.

Q I have a beautiful large Chinese pendant with a bar across the top, but there's no hole to string through. How can I use it as a focal piece for a necklace?

A One solution is to string the left and right sides of the necklace separately, looping each side through the bar on the pendant as shown below. Consider these tips before you start:

▶ Use the largest size of flexible beading wire that fits through all your beads twice.

▶ For a fine finish, use French coil to cover each piece of wire where it wraps around the bar. *(For more on using French coil, see page 211.)*

Option 1: Hang the pendant from two beaded strands.

▶ Alternatively, use color-coated beading wire (such as bronze, gold, silver, or black) that coordinates with the pendant and the finished necklace.

▶ Join both strands at each end to a clasp as usual.

Here's how to make it work:

1. Cut two pieces of beading wire to the length desired for the necklace plus 3".

2. On one piece, string a length of French coil long enough to wrap around and cover the bar. Slide it to the center and wrap the wire around the left side of the pendant bar.

3. String some smaller beads, then string beads in pattern on both strands for that side of the necklace.

4. Add a crimp, a bumper bead, and then the clasp to the end, and bring both strands back through the bumper bead, crimp, and at least ½" of beads on the strand.

5. Secure strand temporarily with transparent tape or a stopper clip.

6. Repeat steps 2 through 5 for the right side of the necklace.

7. Check and adjust the necklace length, the balance, and the amount of ease on each beaded strand.

8. Finish by fastening the crimps.

An alternate option is to create a two-strand necklace by passing both strands through a larger bead at each side of the pendant and then stringing each strand of wire separately to the back, as shown at right.

Option 2: String separately for a two-strand necklace.

· ·

Q I have a three-strand necklace that needs to be restrung. It was strung on thread, and a strand broke. The strands come together at each end into a larger silver bead with a big hole, but it's not wide like a cone. How can I restring the piece using beading wire instead of thread, so the ends are hidden inside that bead?

A Solving this kind of problem with a necklace you already own can be tricky. Some people might try to fix only the broken strand, but you're right to restring the entire piece on beading wire. When thread starts to break in one area it's an indication that the other strands may soon follow.

When you don't have enough room to crimp multiple strands of beads into a stiff wire loop in the standard way you would with a cone, try this. Use a small loop of beading wire with a single crimp to join the strands instead, and hide the loop and crimp inside the large-holed bead, as follows:

1. Cut a 5" piece of flexible beading wire.

2. String a crimp bead, curve the wire in half, and use transparent tape or a stopper clip to hold both ends. (This is the beading wire loop.)

3. Cut a piece of beading wire for each strand of the necklace, allowing about 1½" extra at each end.

4. Crimp one end of each strand securely into the prepared loop.

5. Remove the tape/clip and insert both ends of the wire loop through the wider end of the large-holed bead.

6. String one end of the wire through the clasp ring, and complete the loop by inserting the second wire end through the crimp bead.

7. Pull both ends to adjust the size of the loop, making sure that most of the loop, the crimp, and the ends of the three strands are hidden inside the large-holed bead.

8. Carefully pull the crimp out of the top of the large-holed bead and tighten the loop again. Flatten and fold the crimp, and then use pliers to rotate the loop so the crimp is hidden inside.

9. String the beads on the three strands, one at
a time; secure each end temporarily with tape or a
clip until all are ready.

10. Prepare a second short piece of beading wire the same way as the first one (steps
1 and 2), adjust the ease on each strand,
and crimp the second end of each
strand into it.

11. Repeat steps 6 through 8 for
the second loop.

*A large-holed bead can hide
the join for three strands,
using a beading wire loop.*

If this single-crimp method
seems too tricky, you can use the second method shown on
page 192 for working with regular cones. It results in an extra
crimp tube above the large-holed bead. If desired, you can hide
it inside a larger-hole cushion bead strung after the crimp.

. . . .

Q **If I want to make a necklace with no clasp, and my
beads are too small for the wire to pass through
twice, how do I finish the necklace so it looks nice and is
secure?**

A For strength, I like to use two cylinder crimps on a
strand that will not include a clasp. *(See page 166).* One
solution that works well is to add a balanced group of beads
with larger holes around the crimps, so no wire ends protrude
to scratch your neck. To add symmetry and allow the crimps
to blend into the design, add a group of large-hole beads on
either side of and between the crimps.

Remember that beads with larger holes do not necessarily have a larger outside diameter than beads with smaller holes. For large-hole beads that have room for two strands of most flexible beading wire, try using 8° or 6° glass seed beads, or 3mm sterling silver or gold-filled large-hole hollow metal beads. For balance, you may choose to integrate the large-hole beads into the design of the necklace, as well.

A necklace 24" long or more will usually fit over the head, but swingy rope-style necklaces can be as long as 36". Use heavy .024 wire whenever possible on longer necklaces. They need strength to withstand the extra tugging from toddlers and snagging on furniture that they tend to attract.

To plan the necklace, measure or estimate the length of the large-hole bead section and subtract this amount from the length you string for the main body of the necklace. You'll also want to be sure that the focal bead or center front remains centered. String the two sides of the necklace the same length, and then add the large-hole beads and crimps at one end. Complete as for the no-clasp necklace on page 166.

Q Can I make a necklace that uses both wire and thread?

A Sometimes, a piece of jewelry may combine both wire and thread techniques in its construction. You may find designs that are written using thread only, where you can make the piece more durable by stringing the base on flexible beading wire. Such examples include:

▶ Branched coral and looped techniques

▶ Some netted designs

Often the first row of beads can be strung on flexible beading wire and crimped to create a strong base, and then the thread-woven beadwork is stitched into this base. Besides providing strength to a complex piece, the wire base row can also add support for a larger focal bead, if desired.

Here are two other examples of combination beading techniques:

▶ A crocheted rope bracelet or necklace *(see page 326)* can have beading wire strung through the center of the rope so beadcaps and a clasp can be added.

▶ Some beaded ring designs have a thread-woven top (often a variation of right-angle weave) with a stretch band that enables the ring to fit different sizes.

Leather Cord

Q I'd like to make a necklace using beads on leather. What's the easiest way to accomplish this?

A Necklaces strung on leather often have a rugged, casual look. It's one type of necklace that some men are willing to wear. For stringing on leather, you'll need beads with large holes, such as large-hole lampwork beads, ceramic beads, faceted roller beads, or pony beads (very large seed beads). Test your bead holes on the cord you plan to use.

Round leather cord is available in .5mm, 1mm, and 2mm diameters, while flat leather or suede thong is ⅛" to ³⁄₁₆" wide. Both are available in a variety of colors. Synthetic leather round cord looks like leather, but it is stronger and more durable, especially in the narrow .5 and 1mm sizes.

Q How do I finish the ends of leather?

A To finish the ends and attach a clasp, you can use one of several types of findings. A round **coil crimp end** is made from wire shaped in a spiral. A flat, metal **fold-over crimp end** works best with flat leather thong. Each style has a loop on one end for attaching the clasp.

To apply crimp ends to leather cord:

1. Place glue on the leather end.

2. Insert the leather end inside either a coil or fold-over crimp end.

3a. Use chain nose pliers to flatten the last wrap on the end of the coil, enough to grab the cord firmly without cutting it.

attaching coil crimp ends to leather cording

3b. Use the pliers to fold each side of the fold-over style over the leather so they overlap and hold the leather securely.

attaching fold-over crimp ends to leather cording

For a casual necklace, tie the ends of the cord in sliding knots *(see page 18)*, so the necklace can fit over the head and then be tightened. To make the knots, see the illustration below. Like thread, leather cord doesn't last forever. It will need to be replaced when it starts to dry out and crack.

adjustable knots for leather cord

Silk Cord and Knotted Strands

Q I always see pearls strung with knots between each one. What are the advantages and disadvantages of this style of stringing?

A The practice of stringing pearls on silk began centuries before there was a fluid, high-tech material available for stringing, such as the flexible beading wire we use today.

A knot was tied between each pearl because, at that time, pearls were more valuable than diamonds. Plied silk didn't last forever, and if the strand broke, the knotting prevented all but one pearl from being lost.

Nowadays, many people still choose to knot pearls onto silk cord because it's a traditional style that evokes quality and elegance. Brides often choose it, and anyone who owns a beautifully matched set of pearls, even though they no longer cost as much as diamonds, may prefer to wear them in the traditional style.

The disadvantage of knotting pearls on silk is that the pearls will need to be restrung every few years, with some experts saying as frequently as every two years. Silk frays, stretches, and wears out, so it's not such a permanent stringing method.

I encourage anyone who's not terribly attached to the knotted style to consider switching to flexible beading wire the next time those pearls need to be restrung. Adding a carefully chosen small seed bead between each pearl can replicate the spacing, length, and even the luster of the silk knots, resulting in a more durable, reliable, and still very elegant necklace.

. . . .

Q I want to string some beads on silk and tie knots between each bead. How do I know what size cord to use for knotting it?

A When knotting between beads, use the largest cord that fits comfortably into the holes of your beads, so you don't run the risk of a too-skinny knot slipping inside one of the bead holes. (It happens!) The easiest way to determine which size cord to use is to test it in the bead.

Most bead stores sell silk bead cord in closed packages or spools, so you can't easily try it out. So it's a good idea to maintain your own sample set of the sizes you use most. Whenever you finish a project using silk cord, save about a foot of the cord and tape it into your beading notebook. Jot the thread size next to it. Try to accumulate samples of the basic sizes, so you'll have them available to test with your beads the next time you want to do knotted bead stringing.

The easiest silk cord to find is a brand from Germany. (*See* Resources.) Packaged on cards with an attached needle, it's available in 20 colors in sizes from 0 (thin) to 16 (thick). Each 2-meter package is enough to make about two necklaces.

Another high-quality silk is sold on spools in 42 colors with a different sizing system from A to FFF. If you're using silk cord on a spool, you'll string it on a twisted wire needle and use it doubled throughout the piece. Test the doubled cord in your bead holes to determine the correct size.

Before you decide to knot a strand of beads, examine the holes closely. If the bead holes are larger on one side of the bead than the other, or if the holes are sharp, jagged, or uneven, these beads are not good candidates for knotting. Why? If you use the largest cord that fits into the smaller hole, the knot on the larger side will slip inside the hole and disappear. This looks very unattractive in a knotted piece, and should be avoided. If the holes are sharp, they will fray and chew through the silk, ending in a broken strand.

In general, pearls have smaller holes and tend to work well with carded silk cord in sizes 2 to 4, if using a single strand. For Czech glass, you can usually use sizes 6 to 8 silk cord. For chunkier semiprecious beads with larger holes, use the largest thread that fits comfortably into the holes. This may require that you use two or more strands of cord to achieve a good fit.

. . . .

Q **I know the knots will make my necklace longer. How do I know how long the finished piece will end up?**

A A general rule of thumb for pearls is that the knots and clasp will add about 2" in length to your necklace. If you start with a 16" strand of pearls and knot between each bead, the finished piece will measure about 18" with the clasp.

You can also estimate the finished length this way:

1. Tie a test knot in your stringing material, string a bead, and measure the combined length.

2. Multiply this length by the number of beads on your strand or the number of beads you plan to use.

3. Measure and add the length of the clasp.

4. Adjust your plan so the necklace or bracelet comes out just the right length.

. . . .

Q **What's the best way to knot pearls?**

A There are many different methods for knotting pearls, and each beading expert seems to have her favorite tricks and secrets. As with all these techniques, it is a matter of habit and personal preference, not absolutes. I prefer a traditional knotting method using a double strand of silk and overhand knots, which can be tightened with tweezers, an awl, or a large tapestry needle, or by using fingers alone. Here are some pointers:

▶ The benefit of tightening the knots using the fingers alone is that tweezers may slip and the knot may tighten before it's close enough to the bead. Also, if used aggressively, tweezers can begin to fray the silk before the necklace is even worn. *(See page 206.)*

▶ The trick to making tight, even knots without gaps is to string the beads on a double-strand of cord, so the cords can be pulled apart for the final tightening of each knot.

▶ To make a knotted necklace or bracelet, you'll also need a clasp and two bead tips or clam shells: one to join each end of the knotted strand to the clasp.

▶ If you're working with carded silk cord, you can cut off the attached needle, string on a twisted wire needle, and use the cord doubled. Always test the doubled cord for fit in the bead holes to be sure you're using the correct size.

▶ If you want to knot a piece that's more than 20" long, use two cards of silk and don't cut off the needles. Pass first one needle and then the other through all the beads.

▶ Before handling silk or beginning to knot, always wash your hands. It's easy to transfer dirt and moisture from your hands to the silk, which will take on a grubby look that you will not be able to wash out or remove.

▶ So the piece doesn't stretch later, prestretch the silk cord before knotting it. Remove the entire cord from the card, dampen it with water, and hang it to dry overnight with a weight tied on the ends.

▶ Whether you tie a single or double overhand knot at each end depends on the size of silk cord you're using. You want the knot to sit inside the bead tip without spilling out or falling through the lower opening. For thinner cord, use a double overhand knot; for thicker cord, use a single.

Q How do I make the knots?

A After the cord has been dampened in water, prestretched and dried, knot the strand as follows:

1. Knot the end of the cord and string a bead tip, passing through the cup so the knot sits neatly inside the cup. String all the beads and slide the first bead to the end of the cord.

2. Wrap the cord above the bead around your hand and drop the bead through the loop, forming an overhand knot.

3. Lay the work on the table. Use either your finger and thumb or a tweezers to reach through the loop and grab the cord where it exits the bead. Pull the cord to tighten the knot, so the knot forms below the tweezers or fingers.

4. Remove your fingers or tweezers from the knot, snug the knot close to the bead, and tighten it by separating the two strands and pulling them firmly apart.

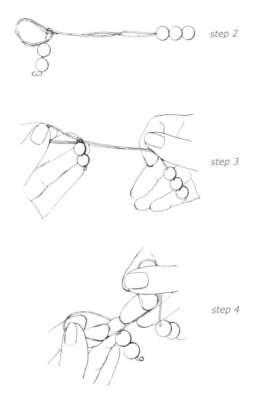

step 2

step 3

step 4

Your knots will become smoother and more even as you make more of them. Be sure to practice tying a few knots before you begin knotting a real piece.

SEE ALSO: Basic Knots, page 15.

A Master's Secret

Here's a tip from master beader Terry Kwan of Boston. When using silk cord doubled, Terry prepares the cord for stringing before prestretching it, as follows:

1. Measure and cut the cord, using twice the finished necklace length and then doubled (or four times the necklace length).

2. String on a twisted wire needle, bring the two ends together, and tie a single or double overhand knot at the end, depending on the size of the cord.

3. Dampen the silk and hang both the needle and knot end loops around a doorknob. Place a stapler (or any heavy object) in the lower loops to weight the silk, and allow it to dry overnight.

4. Now you're ready to begin knotting.

Q **What about nylon cord for knotting? I've seen it packaged on cards, too.**

A Plied bead cord for knotting is available in both silk and nylon. Silk is the traditional choice, while nylon is stronger, frays less, and is less fluid. The cords labeled "high-performance nylon" are said not to stretch.

Personally, if I'm not going for the sheen and fluidity of silk, I would rather string on flexible beading wire. But if you want a piece to be both knotted and more durable, nylon beading cord is worth a try. Use it as you would silk cord.

Q How do I decide between tying single knots and tying double knots?

A Double knots are used only if a single knot isn't large enough to hold the bead in place. The result will never be as smooth or as even as with single knots, so use a double knot only in a dire emergency (for example, when the knot is disappearing inside the bead hole).

. . . .

Q When I'm planning to knot a necklace, why would I buy more expensive carded silk cord rather than using less expensive silk cord on a spool?

A Carded silk cord is convenient to use because each card holds just enough for one or two necklaces, and the cards are relatively inexpensive at $1.25 to $1.50 each. Silk cord on a spool is much less expensive per yard, but the initial outlay is greater. A ½-ounce spool of size E holds 200 yards and costs around $12.50 per spool.

Whether carded or spooled, both types of silk are available in a range of beautiful colors. The best choice for you depends on the quantity of knotting you do, and the variety of colored silk cords you want to have on hand.

. . . .

Q How much cord do I need to knot a necklace?

A When using silk cord to knot between each bead of a necklace, you should allow double the length of the finished necklace, and then measure twice that if you plan to use the cord doubled.

. . . .

Q I knotted a pearl necklace and it looked really nice when it was finished. But now that it's been worn several times, there are spaces between the pearls. Why did this happen?

A There are two reasons that spaces could open up between your knotted pearls:

▶ The knots may not have been formed tightly enough. Be sure you snug each knot close to the bead and tighten it firmly.

▶ Silk cord can stretch after knotting, especially if you did not prestretch it. *(See page 206.)* It's normal for a newly knotted strand to look a little tight at first. The weight of the beads when wearing the strand will help it to relax and hang smoothly, with no gaps.

. . . .

Q I'm almost through knotting a pearl necklace (two more pearls to go), and the needle broke off. How can I finish stringing the pearls?

A This should not happen, because the correct way is to string all the beads on the cord first, before you begin knotting. The twisted wire needles strung on silk cord are not terribly strong. When stringing, especially if the beads fit tightly on the thread, always pull on the cord as you bring it through a bead, rather than on the needle. Repeatedly pulling on the needle can cause it to weaken and break.

Now that yours is broken, though, it would be a shame to start over. One trick you can try is to dip the end of the thread in glue or clear nail polish, and allow it to dry. You may need to dip it twice and roll it between your fingers, so it's stiff enough to serve as the needle. Use the end of the thread to string the remaining pearls.

Q **What is French coil, and how is it used?**

A French coil or French wire is finely coiled wire, like a tiny spring, used over the stringing material where it goes through the ring or clasp. This wire can add polish to the piece and is said to protect the stringing material from wear against the metal clasp, but its main function is decorative.

Although usually used with thread, French coil can also add an elegant detail to a design strung on beading wire. French coil is available in four sizes from fine to extra-heavy. Often used in finishing better-quality strung jewelry, such as pearls, French coil is very fragile, so handle it carefully to avoid crushing or distorting it.

HOW TO USE FRENCH COIL

Here's how to use French coil on flexible beading wire with a twisted tube crimp.

1. Cut about ⅜" lengths with scissors and carefully slide a piece of French coil over the stringing material. (Take care, as the coil is easy to distort.)

2. Pass the stringing material through the ring of the clasp and back through the last three beads (and the crimp, if used), forming a neat loop of French coil around the clasp.

3. Pull on the end of the stringing material to snug up the coil without crushing it.

4. Knot or crimp the stringing material as usual. If using thread, pass through one bead, snug up the loop and knot after each bead for a total of three beads. Add a dot of glue to the final knot. Allow to dry before trimming closely.

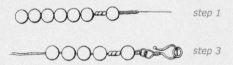

step 1

step 3

CHAPTER 7

Working with Wire

Defining Wirework

Q I see classes offered on wirework, but I don't understand why I need to know about that. How is wire used in beading?

A The ability to manipulate wire is a skill that's essential to well-rounded beadwork. You can use wire in a basic way to join pieces together or in a more advanced way to create an entire necklace of wire links. "Chain mail" techniques, once used to make medieval armor, are now popular again. It's a beautiful way to work with wire, creating wearable wire-mesh jewelry pieces from the simple to the ornate. In chain mail, hundreds of jump rings are joined together to create a heavy, slinky mesh fabric that can be formed into a bracelet, necklace, earrings, or other objects.

Wirework may be disguised by other names that you recognize. For example, a jump ring is simply a round or oval loop made of wire. A headpin is a piece of wire with one end either flattened or embellished with a decorative stopper so beads don't fall off. An earring hook, a hoop, a length of chain, or a simple S-clasp can easily be made from wire. You can purchase wire and tools and learn to create these pieces yourself. Or you may just become comfortable using and manipulating the wire-based findings that you purchase.

You may recognize these wire components of beadwork as findings we discussed in chapter 3. Findings include all of the parts used in beaded jewelry that are made of metal.

Types of Wire

Q My local bead store sells so many different kinds of wire, and I see even more options in catalogs. How do I know which type to buy?

A The choices for wire can seem overwhelming, but you don't need all of them! First, let's look at the options, and then I'll recommend a good basic wire for much of the wirework you'll be learning at the beginning.

▶ **Wire shapes.** These include: round, half-round, square, triangular, and twisted. (*See* Profile of Wire/Shapes *on page 216.*) Round wire is by far the most commonly used shape.

▶ **Wire gauges (or diameters).** These range from heavy 10- and 12-gauge to extra-fine 34-gauge. (*See* Profile of Wire/Guide to Gauge *on page 216 for examples of common sizes.*)

▶ **Wire materials.** Includes: base metals (such as brass and copper; called "base" because they oxidize or corrode relatively easily); precious metals (such as gold, sterling silver, fine silver, and niobium); and combination metals (silver-plated, gold-plated, and gold-filled).

▶ **Wire measures.** You can purchase wire by weight (ounce or pound), by length (foot, yard, or meter), or by the spool or reel. As with needles and seed beads, the larger the wire gauge number, the thinner the wire.

....

PROFILE OF WIRE

SHAPES

☐ square

◐ twisted

⌒ half-round

△ triangular

○ round

GUIDE TO GAUGE

Gauge	12	14	16	18	20
Diameter (in mm)	2	1.5	1.25	1	.75

Gauge	22	24	26	28
Diameter (in mm)	.64	.5	.4	.3

Q What do the gauge sizes mean?

A Even though wire in the United States is sized by gauge, in other parts of the world wire is measured by the diameter in millimeters. The Guide to Gauge chart *(see above)* shows the approximate diameter of our various gauge sizes.

Q When would I want a hard wire versus a softer one?

A The hardness or softness of wire is referred to as "temper." The three most common tempers are:

▶ **Dead-soft.** Easy to work with and to bend with your fingers and tools.

▶ **Half-hard.** A little stiffer, so it's better for holding a crisp angle. Half-hard wire is more difficult to work with in the heavier gauges from 10 to 16, so gauges 10 to 14 are usually only available in dead-soft. Both dead-soft and half-hard are appropriate for most wirework.

▶ **Hard.** So stiff that it's generally not recommended for use in wirework, beading, or jewelry making.

Bending and working with wire will harden it (called work-hardened), as does hammering or planishing (flattening the wire's shape with a hammer). Hardening can make the wire hold its shape, but it's also more brittle and prone to break. To soften wire that's been hardened, you can heat it, which is called annealing.

For most basic, beginning wirework, you'll want to start with round, 18- or 20-gauge dead-soft or half-hard wire. The metal used depends on the color you want and the quality of the finished piece. Precious metal wires such as sterling silver, fine silver, and gold-filled are relatively expensive. Most wirework and jewelry makers practice and work out their designs in less expensive copper or silver-plated copper wire, and then they may turn to precious metal wire for the final product.

Can you explain more about the different metals for wire?

Let's look at them one at a time.

Sterling silver. Like other sterling findings, sterling silver wire is 92.5 percent pure silver, alloyed or mixed with 7.5 percent other metals, such as copper. The term "sterling silver" is very old, and was in use in England by the thirteenth century.

Sterling tarnishes, so it's best to store it in a ziplock bag when not in use. It's not only the pure silver itself that tarnishes, but the copper used in the alloy that reacts with oxygen and then darkens. You can also buy special papers, fabrics, and bags that have been treated to retard tarnishing. Some people store sterling pieces in double ziplock bags to further reduce exposure to oxygen.

Fine silver. Wire made from 99.9 percent pure silver tarnishes more slowly than sterling silver. It is softer than sterling silver and slightly more flexible. For this reason, fine silver is a great choice for crocheting and knitting projects. It can also be heated without changing color; therefore, fine silver is the wire of choice for inclusion in lampworked beads or for precious metal clay.

Gold-filled. Gold-filled wire is durable, does not tarnish, has most of the same properties as gold wire, and has a long life span, so it's a great alternative to real gold. This wire is more expensive than gold-plated wire, because it is made with a thicker layer of gold. It's also less expensive than real gold wire, which is gold all the way through.

Gold. Available in alloys from 10- to 24-karat (41.67 percent gold to 100 percent gold), gold wire comes in a variety of different colors, including yellow, green, pink, red, and white gold. Gold wire is expensive and is usually available from fine jewelry suppliers.

Copper. Beautiful and inexpensive, copper wire is an excellent choice for practicing wirework techniques. A rich, red-brown color, copper can be polished to a bright shine or allowed to oxidize, which darkens the color to an interesting green patina or deeper brown. Dipping the piece in a liver of sulfur solution or one of the other oxidizing products will speed the process. *(For tips to prevent tarnishing, see page 220.)*

Copper wire also is available with poly/nylon enamel coatings. Such coated wire is sometimes called art wire or artisan wire and is made in at least 30 brilliant colors. Use tools carefully to avoid marring the coating, and protect finished pieces so they won't become scratched.

Silver-plated and brass-plated copper wires also are excellent inexpensive choices for learning and practicing a new design, as well as creating finished pieces. Gold-plated copper wire is also available, but it's more expensive.

Q How is precious metal wire sold?

A Some local bead stores may sell sterling and gold-filled wire by the foot. If you need a larger quantity, you also can purchase it by the ounce. If you're buying wire online or from a wholesale source, you may run into a different measuring system called "troy weight." This is an ancient system of measuring precious metals that dates from before the eleventh century. A troy ounce is about 10 percent larger than a standard ounce; it equals 31.1 grams, while a standard ounce weighs 28.35 grams.

· ·

Q I love the look and color of copper wire, but I don't want it to tarnish or turn my skin green. How can I prevent this?

A Some people prefer the tarnished or "aged" look of copper, but if you're not one of them, you could spray the copper with polyurethane or another sealer to keep it from tarnishing. Personally, I don't recommend this practice, because when the sealer begins to wear off, the copper piece may tarnish unevenly and look blotchy.

You can't really prevent copper from tarnishing, although storing your jewelry in a ziplock bag will slow it down. But this won't be a problem if you keep your copper jewelry clean and bright. Here are some suggestions:

▶ Clean the piece in a tumbler, if you have access to one.

▶ Use an old toothbrush to scrub the piece with a paste of baking soda and water. Rinse well, pat dry, and allow the jewelry to air-dry thoroughly.

▶ Clean with a mixture of lemon juice or white vinegar and salt, rinse, and neutralize the acid by rubbing the piece with baking soda. Rinse again thoroughly and allow to air-dry.

....

Q I've seen designs made with twisted wire that look really interesting, but my local bead store doesn't stock twisted wire. What should I do?

A You can make your own twisted wire by using plain round wire in a thinner gauge. Remember that the finished twisted wire will be twice the diameter of the plain wire, so two strands of 24 gauge will result in 18 gauge twisted wire. (*See* Profile of Wire/Guide to Gauge *on page 216.*)

Option 1

1. Bend the round wire in half lengthwise and secure the ends by clamping them in a vise, if available.

2. Insert a hook into the loop of the wire, preferably a hook made of wire and held in a strong pin vise. Or you can insert the hook into a hand drill, and place the wire loop onto the hook.

3. Pull the wire taut, and gently twist it until the entire length of wire is evenly twisted.

Option 2

1. Screw a cup hook into a door frame (in your work room, laundry room, or another inconspicuous place).
2. Place the loop of the wire on the cup hook.
3. Secure the ends in a pin vise and twist the wire while pulling the pin vise firmly away.

Whichever method you choose, be careful not to twist too much, especially with thinner gauges, or the wire will snap.

Wire Findings

Q Tell me about the wire rings I'll need.

A Several types of rings are used in jewelry making. These are the most commonly used wire rings:

▶ **Jump ring.** A loop made of wire that's used to join jewelry parts together. In fine jewelry, jump rings are often soldered closed so they are more secure and can't be pulled open. Since beaders seldom bother with soldering, this type of ring is not the best choice when joining to thread, which may work its way through the opening.

▶ **Soldered jump ring.** A jump ring that's been soldered shut, which is perfect to use whenever the ring doesn't need to open, such as for a necklace closure where it will be strung and crimped.

▶ **Split ring.** A ring made of wire wrapped around twice, like a tiny key ring. This type of ring is more secure than an open jump ring, especially when used with thread. Split rings are available in both round and oval shapes. Because split rings can be difficult to open and because the wire is thin and easy to distort, there are split-ring pliers and tweezers available that make it easier to open and hang onto split rings. (*See* Pliers and Cutters *on pages 128–129*).

jump ring *soldered jump ring* *split ring*

SEE ALSO: Basic Wirework Techniques, page 231.

Q **What is a headpin?**

A A headpin is a length of wire with a flattened head on one end to keep beads from falling off. Headpins may be simple (with a flat round head) or decorative (with a ball, scroll, flower, or other decorative head).

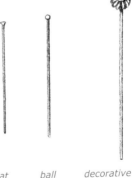

flat head *ball head* *decorative head*

Q **What is the pin that has a loop on one end?**

A This type of pin is called an eyepin. The end loop keeps beads from falling off and offers a place to hang another bead, link, or segment below the pin. While you can purchase eyepins, they're also easy to make by cutting lengths of wire and using round nose pliers to make a loop at one end.

Wire Tools

Q **What kinds of pliers do I need?**

A You'll need a basic set of jeweler's pliers for working with wire and other metal findings. Jeweler's pliers feature smooth jaws, rather than the serrated jaws of many other pliers. When working with wire, serrations can damage the wire, leaving noticeable marks and dents behind, making it impossible to create smoothly finished wirework.

Inexpensive jeweler's pliers are fine for a beginner, but as your work becomes more refined, you'll probably want to invest in high-quality German tools. They're more expensive, but if you reserve them only for jewelry work, they will last for many years.

SEE ALSO: Basic Tools, page 124.

Q **Are there any special wire cutters I need to buy?**

A There are different styles of wire cutters that can be used for wirework, but my favorite style is called a flush cutter, as discussed in chapter 4. If you purchase the one made for cutting flexible beading wire, you can also use it for dead-soft and half-hard wire. A good pair of flush cutters makes a straight, smooth cut on the back side of the pliers, which saves you time in filing and smoothing cut ends of wire.

SEE ALSO: Basic Tools, page 124.

JEWELER'S FILES

Jeweler's files can be useful for filing and smoothing the rough ends of cut wire. They're available in various shapes, such as those shown below. Emery boards from the drugstore also can be used for smoothing cut ends of wire and sharp edges.

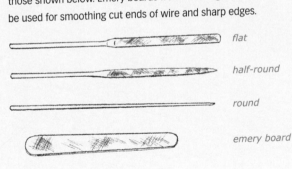

flat

half-round

round

emery board

Q What other tools do I need when doing wirework?

A Here are a few items you may find useful, depending on the kinds of wirework you are doing.

A small hammer is used to flatten and harden wire while adding strength, shape, and design features to many findings such as clasps and ear wires. Shaping the wire with a hammer is also called planishing. There's a wonderful small hammer available that has interchangeable faces and works well for planishing. One side has a brass face that you can use for flattening and shaping wire. On the other side is a nylon face that will work-harden wire without flattening it (that is, harden it by hammering). The hammer's best feature is that the replacement inserts are inexpensive and easy to install when a face becomes dented or scarred.

A ball-peen hammer has a flat head on one side and a rounded peening head on the other, both of which are metal. The round side can be used to set rivets or make decorative texture marks in metal.

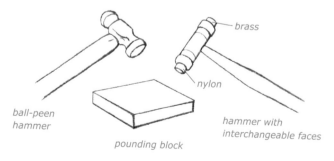

brass

nylon

ball-peen
hammer

pounding block

hammer with
interchangeable faces

A **steel pounding block,** used with either hammer and sometimes also called a bench block or anvil, provides a foundation for hardening and shaping wire. You can use a small block of steel or the flat side of a large, old hammer head (watch for these and other useful tools in yard sales).

A **Dremel tool** is a small variable-speed tool that works like a miniature electric drill. While not an essential piece of equipment, a Dremel can be helpful for drilling holes in coins, shells, and other objects to create beads, as well as in cutting and polishing wire and metals. Sets with varying numbers of attachments and accessories are available at home centers and hardware stores. (*See* Resources.)

A **polishing cloth** is a piece of fabric that's been chemically treated so it removes dirt, fingerprints, and tarnish from precious metals and wire.

Tool Tips

Q **Why do I need to hammer on the wire?**

A Hammering or planishing is used for several reasons. Gentle hammering and bending of wire:

▶ Flattens wire and creates graceful shaping

▶ Makes the wire more brittle

▶ Hardens the wire, so it holds the shape and becomes stronger

If you want to harden wire evenly without flattening it, use the nylon face of the hammer. To soften hardened or half-hard wire, you can anneal or soften it by heating the wire over a flame. However, once wire has been hardened by hammering, or work-hardened, it becomes easier to break, so work with it carefully.

. . . .

Q **I'm just getting started with wirework. Do I need to invest in the expensive German tools right away?**

A The quick answer is "no." Good-quality, basic hand tools are available in a wide range of prices. If you're just starting out, you'd probably rather spend your money on beads and other materials, than on tools!

It's fine to start with the relatively inexpensive hand tools made in Pakistan, but don't just buy the first cheap pair you see. Try grasping the pliers and opening and closing the jaws to see how they fit your hand and how well they operate. You don't want to end up with shoddy tools that really don't work well and don't last.

On the other hand, if you're a person who loves fine tools or plans to do a lot of beading and wirework, it makes sense to invest in higher-

Tool Stash

If you do purchase top-quality jewelry-making tools, I suggest you store them separately from the other household tools. You don't want to find someone using them to tinker in the garage, or worse, find a pair after they've been left in the driveway for a couple of weeks (my son at nine years old comes to mind).

quality German hand tools. You just can't beat the quality and durability of their steel and construction.

The two hand tools in which German quality matters most are the round nose and chain nose pliers. On the round nose pliers, it's wonderful to have tips that are truly round, strong enough to keep their shape, and taper to a very narrow tip. On the chain nose pliers, the tips taper to a smaller end so they fit into tiny spots more easily. If you also have a less expensive pair, it won't go to waste. It can be your second pair, because it's often handy to have a set of chain or flat nose pliers for each hand.

Q I'm having trouble working with wire without leaving dents and scratches from my hand tools. Do you have any suggestions?

A As you work more with hand tools and get the feel of the wire, you'll learn to hold and shape the wire gently without using a tight grip or a lot of force. Once you learn to use your tools correctly, you'll start to leave fewer marks.

Even with practice, though, it can be difficult to work with soft or fragile metals, such as color-coated wire, without leaving dings in the finish. There are several options that can help:

▶ Cover or coat the jaws of your pliers to cushion the wire from damage. The quickest solution is to place a piece of thin fabric between the wire and your pliers.

▶ Wrap the jaws of your pliers with pieces of masking tape or self-adhesive moleskin. To later remove any tape

or adhesive residue from your pliers, rub
them with a little cooking oil or use a gum-
removing product or nail polish remover.

▶ Dip the jaws of the pliers in a liquid-
rubber product. Designed to cushion the
handles of tools, they also work well to
cushion the hard edges of the pliers' jaws.
You'll find these products at hardware and
beading stores. After dipping the tool, allow
the coating to dry thoroughly before use.

*wrapping pliers
jaws with
masking tape*

The best part is that you can easily peel the rubber coating
off when it's no longer needed.

. . . .

Q **I want my wirework to have a smoother look. How
do I make neater ends and flat joins?**

A You're right that if you just nip off the end of the wire
with any old cutters, you will end up with a gnarled
bite, also called an angled cut. To make a
clean, square end, or flush cut, consider
the following:

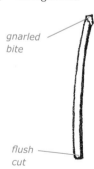

*gnarled
bite*

▶ Use the flat (back) side of a sharp pair
of flush cutters.

▶ Hold the cutting surface at a 90-
degree angle to the wire.

▶ When you cut, the back side of the
cut will be flat and square, the front
angled.

*flush
cut*

▶ Flip the cutters over and cut again if you need to make both ends flat.

▶ When snipping ends or cutting off short pieces, place a finger on the wire end to keep bits of wire from flying.

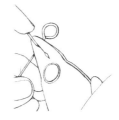

Use a finger to keep cut bits of wire from flying.

Basic Wirework Techniques

Q **What's the best way to close a jump ring so the ends meet without any gaps?**

A Never open the jump ring by making the circle wider, as it will be impossible to return the ring to a smooth circle. To open and close a jump ring, always use two pliers (one in each hand) and a twisting motion, as shown on page 232. Chain nose and round nose pliers work well for me. You might prefer chain nose and bent chain nose pliers, or two sets of bent chain nose pliers. Practice with the tools you have available to see what works best for you. Here's how:

  1. Grasp the jump ring on either side of the opening with a pliers in each hand.

  2. Rotate one set of pliers toward you, while rotating the other set of pliers away from you.

3. Reverse this motion to close the jump ring.

For a smooth tight join, push the ends slightly together while closing them, a little beyond where they meet, and then pull back just a bit to bring the ends together perfectly. You can feel the ends pressing against each other when you've done it right. Now they'll stay that way.

Twist to open and close a jump ring.

Q It can be tricky to find jump rings in just the right sizes for some projects, such as chain mail designs. Is it possible for me to make my own jump rings?

A Yes, it's possible to make your own jump rings, but it takes care and precision to make high-quality jump rings. I know that purchasing hundreds of jump rings for a chain mail project can seem expensive, but don't undertake the project of making your own jump rings lightly, just to save money! Perfect jump rings make smoother, stronger chain mail. Some designs have very specific size requirements so the pattern will fit together correctly. If the rings are not the exact size and gauge, some patterns will not work. With that said, if you still want to try making small amounts of your own rings, here are some pointers you'll need to consider.

Materials

▶ Use wire of the correct gauge for the rings you want. Most jump rings are made with 18- to 22-gauge wire, although rings for certain designs may be made with wire as heavy as 10-gauge.

▶ Avoid mixing rings you make with purchased rings of the "same" size and gauge. They will never be exactly the same.

▶ Thinner gauge wire (with a higher number) is easier to bend, while thicker wire (with a lower number) makes a stronger, more stable jump ring. The thicker the wire, however, the trickier it is to make accurate jump rings.

▶ You'll need mandrels (steel rods) or wooden dowels of the right size so the jump rings will have the interior diameter required. When using the wooden dowel technique that follows, it also helps to have a drill such as a small-size, variable-speed rotary tool or Dremel.

▶ For cutting rings, you'll need a jeweler's saw with 2/0 blade or electric cutting tool to make straight even cuts.

▶ A tumbler is a wonderful tool for hardening, cleaning, and polishing the jump rings before use.

▶ Always wear eye protection when working with metal.

Technique

1. Start with a wooden dowel that's the same size as the inside diameter of the jump rings you want to make.

2. Drill a hole through one end of the dowel, and insert the end of the wire into the hole. This will anchor the wire to the dowel and keep the wire coil from spinning.

3. Wrap the wire neatly around the dowel, with each coil placed firmly against the one before.

4. Cut the wire where it goes through the hole to free the coil and slide it to the other end of the dowel.

step 3: wrap the wire   *step 4: cut the wire*

5. Hold the coil securely with your nondominant hand and use the saw or cutting tool to cut a shallow, vertical slot at the end of the dowel.

6. Hold the blade at the top of the slot as a guide and gradually feed the coil toward the blade as you saw or cut through

the top of the coil. Take care to cut only one side of the rings, not all the way through. If the coil becomes hot during cutting, use a piece of fabric or rubber to protect your fingers.

7. Take a look at the cut rings once they slide off the dowel. If the ends of the jump rings aren't flat, file each end smooth and flat with a jeweler's file. Don't file back and forth; pass the file in one direction only.

8. Use the jump rings as you would any manufactured rings, being sure to open and close them properly. *(For more about jump rings, see page 222.)*

Notes

▶ Wooden dowels have the disadvantage of being fairly soft. So the coils may be difficult to remove before they've been cut apart, or may become slightly smaller than planned. An alternative is to use a metal mandrel, such as a knitting needle of the right diameter, and then slide the coil off the needle before carefully sawing the rings apart.

▶ If you need only a few rings and don't have a jeweler's saw or electric cutting tool, you can snip the rings apart using a flush cutter, flipping the cutters over to make a smooth cut on each end, as described earlier in this chapter. *(See page 230.)*

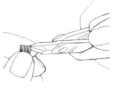

snipping jump rings with a flush cutter

▶ If you need to make a large quantity of jump rings, you might consider investing in a jump ring maker with several sizes of steel mandrels and a tumbler. With these tools, you are more likely to end up with smooth, perfect jump rings. You can find more about making jump rings on the Internet.

. . . .

Q **When I make my own jump rings from a coil, they don't close evenly. How can I make a jump ring with a smooth seam or join?**

A To make a clean jump ring that closes smoothly, you first need to cut each end of the ring with flush cutters. After making the first cut, flip the pliers over to cut the second end. Now examine the ends. If they aren't smooth and flat, file them with a jeweler's file as described earlier. *(See page 235.)* When you close the jump ring, the two flat, square ends should match neatly.

. . . .

Q **I have a pile of jump rings to open for a chain mail project I'm making. Is there any way to make this job go faster?**

A For opening and closing jump rings, I can suggest a tool that you can quickly make yourself, and another inexpensive tool that you can purchase.

Make a tool

1. Use a 6" to 8" length of wooden dowel that's ⅜" to ½" diameter.

2. Drill a small hole in each end, and insert a slot-head screw. Choose a screw with a deep slot wide enough to hold

your jump rings. (To make the tool more versatile, insert a different-size slot-head screw into the opposite end; use one end for larger wire and the other for smaller wire.)

step 4

3. Hold the dowel tool in your non-dominant hand and use it to stabilize one side of the jump ring by positioning one side of the ring inside the screw slot.

4. Hold a set of pliers in your dominant hand, grasp the jump ring near its opening, and rotate the ring open or closed.

Buy a tool

Another option is to purchase a metal jump ring opener that you wear like a ring on the index finger, with different sizes of slots to stabilize one side of the jump ring. It works in the same way as the dowel. Either tool allows you to open and close jump rings more quickly with only one set of pliers, once you become accustomed to using it. It's just easier to get the tool into position than it is to manipulate a second set of pliers.

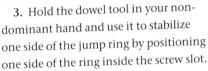

Q I'm learning to make easy earrings by placing beads on a headpin, making a loop above the beads, and then hanging the loop from ear wires. But my headpins don't hang straight. How can I fix this?

SELF CARE

Learn to use your tools correctly so you're not gradually injuring your wrists or hands. Never make a loop in one continuous motion; rather, move the pliers in several small, repeated segments as you rotate the loop away from you.

A If you make a loop that's shaped like a teardrop or "P," as shown below, the earring will not be centered or hang straight. Your goal is to make a round, closed loop centered over the headpin or wire.

Here's how you make a round, centered loop:

1. Use round nose pliers to grasp the very end of the wire so it doesn't protrude beyond the pliers. Test this by running your finger along the jaws of the pliers to be sure you can't feel the end of the wire sticking out.

2. Press the wire firmly against the jaw of the pliers with your nondominant thumb and rotate the pliers away from you about a quarter-turn.

3. Reposition the pliers and rotate again, pressing firmly.

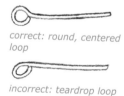

correct: round, centered loop

incorrect: teardrop loop

incorrect: P-shaped loop

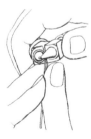

center the loop

238

4. Continue in this manner, working in short quarter-turns until you have formed a complete loop, with the cut end touching the wire. At this point, you have a P-shaped loop.

5. Grasp the wire at the base of the loop with the pliers as shown and bend it toward you until the loop sits squarely on top of the wire. Now your earrings will hang straight. This is the correct simple loop to use in all of your jewelry.

. . . .

Q **What if I have too much length at the top of the headpin? Is there a way to make a good loop other than just guessing the length and cutting it?**

A If you have extra length in the headpin, you can use a trick I learned from wirework guru Linda Linebaugh, who taught me many wire techniques. Rather than cut the headpin and hope you'll have enough length to make a well-formed loop, try this:

1. Start at the end of the wire and make a loop, as described in the question just before this one.

2. Continue rolling the wire around the pliers until you reach the top bead.

3. Use flush cutters to cut off the excess wraps of wire just at the end of the last full wrap. (You can use the extra wraps as jump rings, if you like.)

4. Center the loop, as usual.

wrap the excess length of a headpin

. . . .

Q When I'm making earrings, how can I make the loops the same size so they look like a matched pair?

A The easiest way to ensure that your loops will be the same size is to shape both loops at the same spot on your round nose pliers. Use a fine-point permanent marker to mark the tips of your pliers at the diameter you want for the loops. Bend the wire around the pliers at this point every time, and you'll get loops that are always the same size. You can make several tiny marks for loops of different sizes. It's easy to remove the marks with acetone, nail polish remover, or an emery board if you need to reposition them.

When you're first learning to make perfect loops, it's easiest to begin near the center of the round tips of your pliers. After you've had more practice, try making tiny loops near the very ends of your pliers. These small loops look beautifully polished on delicate earrings and other fine jewelry.

> ### MATCHED SET
> Whether you're making a basic earring with beads on a headpin or a more elaborate design, it usually looks best to match the size of the hanging loop to the one on the earring finding. The two loops then create balance in the design.

Q I like the look of wrapped loops. What's an easy way to make them?

A To make a wrapped loop, think of it in two stages. The first stage consists of steps 1 through 3 below. After step 2, you can insert a chain link, ear wire or other finding, or

240

another ring inside the loop before you close it. For the second stage, continue with the remaining steps to finish the loop.

1. Use chain nose pliers to bend a crisp 90-degree angle about 2" from the end of the wire.

2. Use round nose pliers to hold the wire just above the bend (a). Use the thumb and index finger of your nondominant hand to bend the wire around the top round jaw of the pliers until it meets the lower wire (b).

3. Remove the pliers from the loop and insert the lower round jaw of the pliers into the loop. Continue bending the end until it is perpendicular to the vertical wire.

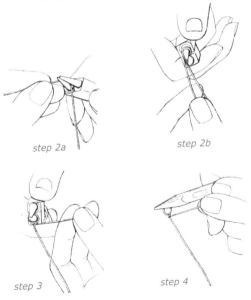

step 2a

step 2b

step 3

step 4

4. Switch to chain nose pliers and grasp the piece flat across the loop. Use your fingers or a second set of pliers to wrap the wire end tightly around the lower wire just below the loop, making two or more wraps. The wraps should touch each other snugly.

5. Use the flush cutters to trim the wire end close to the last wrap, then check the trimmed wire end. If you can feel the cut end or it sticks out, which may scratch the wearer, use chain nose pliers or the front scoop of your crimping pliers to squeeze and tuck the wire end neatly against the last wrap. Smooth the end with a fine file or emery board, if needed.

....

Q **Why would I want to make a wrapped loop instead of a regular loop?**

A From a design standpoint, wrapped loops are popular in jewelry because they can add a playful, organic style to a piece. But there are also structural reasons to use a wrapped loop. If you prefer to work with thinner wire such as 24-gauge because it's easier to bend and kinder to your hands, you'll need to use a wrapped loop for added strength. A simple loop won't stay closed in wire that's thinner than 22-gauge (actually 20-gauge is preferable). Sometimes, it's necessary to use thinner wire, because the bead has a small hole, such as a pearl, and larger wire won't fit. So always use wrapped loops when working with thinner wire.

Making Jewelry Components

Q **What other jewelry parts can I make with wire?**

A Besides jump rings and loops, you can use lengths of wire to make components or parts for jewelry, such as a dangle for an earring, a pendant for a necklace, one end of a clasp, or a link that can be joined with other links to make a bracelet or a necklace. A wire component is usually joined to another jewelry component with either a simple loop or a wrapped loop.

....

Q **What is it called when a wire piece has a loop on each end?**

A Some people call this wire formation a barbell, because it resembles a hand weight. I call it a "link," because it can be used to join, or link, two other jewelry components. A link may have a bead strung at the center, or two plain links can be placed together as part of a chain to add texture and interest.

a link with a bead

two links used together as an accent

Links can be made from any type of metal wire used in regular wirework. The choice of wire really depends more on the design and the finished look you want to achieve. For example, if you love the way copper and green look together, use copper wire with a green bead at the center. If you love how silver and black play off one another, join sterling silver links together to form a chain, and attach a gorgeous black pendant at the center.

Depending on the other pieces it will connect, the link may have one loop facing vertically and the other end facing horizontally (rotated 90 degrees), or both loops may face in the same direction, as shown on page 243. Again, the direction of the loops has more to do with the design and function than with a set principle on how links are made.

. . . .

Q When I put a wire through a bead and try to bend it, the bead sometimes breaks. This especially happens with crystals, which are expensive. How can I avoid this problem?

A To avoid breaking beads, be careful to bend the wire without placing stress on the bead hole. Make the bend just above the hole, rather than using the bead hole to push against. For a wrapped loop, you can hold the wire above the hole with the tips of fine chain nose pliers and bend the wire above the pliers. This creates a small space for the wrap. If you want a simple loop, you don't need this much space.

. . . .

Q I've seen wire pieces that look like the number eight. How do I make these?

A A simple figure-eight wire shape is sometimes used as a link in a chain, or in place of a jump ring as a closure

MAKE A WIRE LINK BRACELET

Using either simple loops or wrapped loops, you can create a quick, fun bracelet made from wire links. Each link can hold a bead: a piece of chunky furnace glass, lampwork, or a Czech glass bead. You'll need six to eight of these beads, depending on the size of the bead and the desired length of the bracelet.

1. Cut three to four 6"-long pieces of 18- or 20-gauge half-hard wire. (You'll be making two links from each 6" wire.)

2. Make a fairly large loop, maybe 4 to 5mm, on one end and slide on a bead. Use a loop size that looks balanced with the beads you've chosen.

3. Make a loop of the same size in the wire end on the other side of the bead.

4. Cut the wire and turn the second loop perpendicular to the first.

step 3

5. Form a loop on the cut end of the wire and put it through a loop of the first link before completing it.

6. Finish as for the first link, adding a bead and a second loop.

step 5

7. Repeat making and joining links until the bracelet has about seven links, or is the length desired.

8. Use a jump ring to join half of a snap clasp or a toggle to each end.

to fasten a hook or lobster claw. To make a figure-eight:

1. Cut a 1½" piece of 20-gauge round wire.
2. Make a simple loop at one end of the wire.
3. Turn the piece and repeat at the other end, bending the wire in the opposite direction, as shown.
4. Hammer the piece lightly to harden it.

simple figure-eight link

Q How do I make an S-clasp?

A An S-clasp is similar to a figure-eight, just a little fancier. For an attractive S-clasp about ⅞" long or smaller, use 20-gauge round wire. For a larger S-clasp, use about 4" of 18-gauge wire and make larger loops. Here's how you make a small one:

> **MAKESHIFT TOOLS**
>
> If the largest section of your round nose pliers doesn't make a large enough loop for the S-clasp you want to make, try using the shaft of a round, disposable ball-point pen, mascara tube, or knitting needle.

1. Cut a 2½" piece of wire.
2. Make a tiny loop at each end, facing in opposite directions.

step 2

3. Use the large diameter of a round nose pliers to bend the wire above the tiny loop in the opposite direction to make a larger loop. Keep bending until the small loop and the wire nearly touch.

4. Turn the piece and repeat at the other end.

step 3

5. Use a hammer and steel block to lightly hammer and flatten the curves gracefully.

step 4

SELECTIVE FLATTENING

When planishing wire, hang any area that you don't want to flatten off the edge of the block. That way you can't strike and ding it by accident.

S-clasps can be used in a number of ways. Try one of the following:

▶ Add a bead at the center before making the second end loop.

▶ Join as links to make a bracelet.

▶ Use a jump ring to attach each end of a necklace to the S-clasp. (To use it as a clasp, the sides should be nearly closed, so the ring just squeezes through.)

Q I've often seen spirals on wire pieces. Are they hard to make?

A A wirework spiral can be used as a decorative finish at the end of a wire. It's versatile and easy to make.

▶ Make your own headpin with a small spiral to serve as the head.

▶ Wind a leftover end of wire into a neat spiral rather than making a simple loop or cutting it off.

▶ Use a spiral as a connector for other components (such as to join together two links holding beads) to make an earring, a charm, or a dangle.

To make a spiral:

1. Start by forming a tiny loop at one end of the wire with the tips of the round nose pliers.

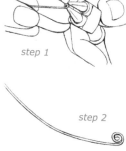

step 1

2. Switch to a chain nose pliers and hold across the loop, while using your opposite thumb to wrap the wire around the loop. Rotate it until the spiral is the size that you want.

step 2

3. Bend the excess wire so it forms a 90-degree angle, or is centered over the spiral.

4. Make a loop at the end to hang the spiral as a charm, or finish as desired.

step 4

To make a hanging bead:

1. Make a spiral, as instructed above through step 2.

2. Add a bead.

3. Bend the spiral up against the lower part of the bead.

4. Add a loop for hanging.

. . . .

Q Is it possible to make my own earring findings from regular wire?

A It's not difficult to make basic ear wires using 20-gauge half-hard or dead-soft round wire.

1. Cut 3" of wire for each finding.

2. Make a small, simple loop *(see page 238)* at one end of one wire and center it.

3. Grab the wire just above the loop with the tips of the round nose pliers and bend it nearly to a 90-degree angle.

4. Hold the loop in your nondominant hand and a round ball-point pen in your other hand about ½" from the bend,

step 2

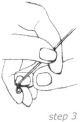

step 3

step 4

and use your thumb to bend the wire around the pen until the new loop is centered over the small loop.

5. Cut the long end to the length desired.

6. Bend a slight angle away from the loop about ⅜" from the end.

7. Use the hammer and block to flatten the front of the ear wire, but don't flatten the part that goes through your ear.

step 7

PROTECT YOUR EARLOBES

It's important to smooth and polish the cut end of the wire so it doesn't scratch and irritate the holes in your ears. Use a small jewelry file or emery board flat across the cut, filing in one direction only; do not use a sawing motion. Then, file the edges on a 45-degree angle, all the way around, for a smoothly rounded tip. Or if you have an electric tool with a small cup burr attachment, you can quickly smooth the points of the ear wires. Choose a cup burr that's a couple of gauges larger than your wire so it's easier to use.

CHAPTER 8

Off-Loom Weaving with Beads

Bead Weaving Defined

Q I thought weaving was about making cloth. What does it mean to weave with beads?

A Weaving, or stitching, with beads creates a flexible beaded fabric in which the beads are held together almost invisibly with thread. Depending on the stitch used, the beaded piece can be soft and drapey or stiff enough to stand alone, like a fabric made of glass. All you need is a needle, thread, and some beads. You can weave with just these materials, called off-loom weaving (covered in this chapter), or you can weave on a beading loom. *(See chapter 9.)*

Weaving can take several forms:

▶ Weaving back and forth in rows to make a flat piece

▶ Weaving around in circular or tubular rows to create a flat circular or a cylindrical piece

▶ Creating shape by adding easy increases or decreases

Q What's the best way to learn these stitches?

A It's a great idea to walk through each stitch with needle, thread, and beads to familiarize yourself with it. Each sample takes only a few minutes to make, and will help you see how simple the stitches really are. When taped into a spiral notebook, the samples become an invaluable reference tool if you want to use one of these stitches later on a project.

Peyote Stitch

Q **I want to be able to do all different kinds of beading stitches. Which one should I learn first?**

A The answer to your question really depends on who you ask! For many expert beaders, their favorite stitch is the first one they used and loved, so each person may give you a different answer. But since you're asking me, my answer is peyote stitch. *(See* Stitch Overview *on the next page.)*

I love peyote stitch because it is easy to do and amazingly versatile. It can be used in so many different ways, and I believe this is one reason why new beaders often (wrongly) think peyote stitch is difficult to learn. Seeing the wide variety of projects that all use the same stitch can seem overwhelming at first, but the stitch itself is amazingly simple.

The simplest type is the flat, even-count, one-drop peyote stitch.

▶ "Flat" means working back-and-forth in rows.

▶ "Even count" means working with an even number of beads across the row.

▶ "One-drop" means adding one bead at a time.

Peyote stitch can also be worked in two-drop and three-drop, which work up more quickly.

SEE ALSO: Peyote Stitch Variations, page 262.

STITCH OVERVIEW

For off-loom weaving, there are many different stitches or ways to hitch beads together with thread, each with its own unique thread path. The various weaving stitches are useful for different purposes. Some bead weavers use and love all the stitches, while others strongly prefer one particular stitch and use it to the near-exclusion of the others. There's no right or wrong way, here; it's just a matter of preference.

Peyote stitch. Stair-step rows that alternate up beads and down beads, like a zipper.

Square stitch. Built in straight rows.

Brick stitch. Looks like peyote stitch, except that it's worked the other way (sideways) with the zigzag on the edges.

Ndebele or herringbone stitch. Beads are added in pairs that create vertical columns; the pairs lean toward each other like the V-shapes in woven fabric, which is why the stitch is also called herringbone.

Right-angle weave. Built in open squares and created in a circular path containing four beads, or a multiple of four. Consecutive beads sit perpendicular to each other.

Netting. An odd number of beads is added each time, in either horizontal or vertical rows, so the fabric develops in open-diamond shapes; the larger the number of beads in each stitch, the more open the diamonds will be.

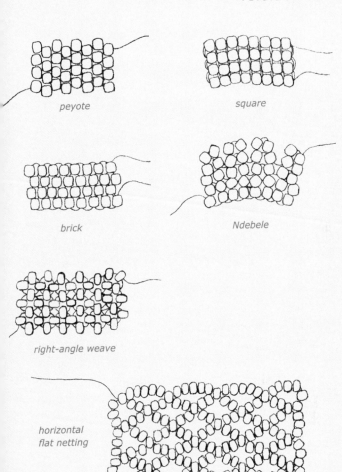

peyote

square

brick

Ndebele

right-angle weave

*horizontal
flat netting*

Q So, how do I work peyote stitch?

A Follow the steps below. As you weave, pay attention to your thread tension. For some stitches, you can snug the work up later, but usually this is not the case. It's important to use firm, even tension from the beginning of your piece.

1. Single-thread a beading needle with about 1 yard of thread and condition the thread with wax, if necessary. (The better you become at working any stitch, the more thread you may want to begin with to lessen the number of times you'll have to stop and add thread as you stitch. Beginners, however, should start by practicing with a short thread length to reduce tangles.)

2. Pick up the first bead with the needle, passing through it once, looping around, and passing through the bead again in the same direction. Slide the bead down the thread to leave the length of tail you want (usually 6" to 12"). This is called the stopper bead, and it keeps the first beads from falling off the thread.

3. String on an even number of beads (including the stopper bead), enough to make the width of the strip you want (try 8 or 10 beads to start). This first group will become rows 1 and 2 of your piece.

4. Pick up one new bead, then pass the needle through the second-to-last bead of the original group.

5. Pick up another new bead, skip one bead in the original group, then pass through the next strung bead (the fourth bead from the end of the original group).

6. Continue to add one bead at a time, skipping every other bead across the row, until you reach the other side.

7. Pull on the thread firmly to snug up the row. At this point, you can remove the extra wrap of thread around the stopper bead, or wait another row or two.

8. To be ready to start a new row, flip the work so the thread is at the top right corner again (or, if you're left-handed, position the thread at the top left).

9. Pick up a new bead and pass through the last bead added in the previous row, which will be easy to identify as an "up" bead in the staggered row.

10. Continue stitching across the row, adding one new bead at a time and then entering the next "up" bead of the previous row.

11. Repeat steps 8 through 10, adding rows until you reach your desired length.

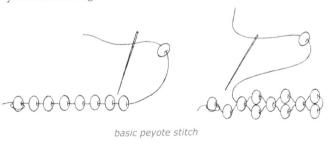

basic peyote stitch

Q How do I keep the first few rows from twisting?

A Be aware that the first few rows of any project are always the trickiest part. Once you've completed ½" or so, suddenly there's a little nub to hold onto, and everything becomes much easier. At this point my students almost always say, "You mean, this is all I have to do now — the same thing over and over?" Suddenly it's easy. So be patient and take your time getting started on those first few rows. Soon the work will progress much more quickly.

In the meantime, if you have problems with twisting, try this trick to get your piece started:

1. Single-thread your needle, add a stopper bead, and thread on enough beads to make an even number, as described in answer to the previous question.

2. Insert a long needle, headpin, or piece of fine wire through the last strung bead and every alternate bead across the thread. These are the beads of the first row. Now, the "up" beads of the second row will pop up and be more obvious.

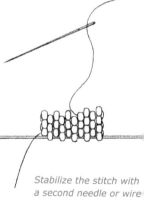

Stabilize the stitch with a second needle or wire

3. Add one bead at a time across the row, picking up a bead and going through the next "up" bead. The needle gives you something to hold onto and helps keep the first few rows in shape.

4. Leave the needle in place until you've worked four or five rows successfully.

....

Q **What does the term "zipping up" mean when applied to peyote stitch?**

A After weaving a flat strip of peyote with an even number of rows, you can fold it in half and join the ends together to make a tube. This is often referred to as zipping up, because the zigzag ends of peyote stitch fit together neatly, like a zipper. To join the ends:

1. Stitch back and forth between each "up" bead.

2. Pull the thread to snug the edges together.

3. Pass the thread back through the beads again for extra security before tying off.

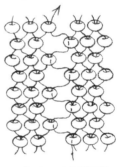

zipping up a peyote stitch into a tube

....

EASY PEYOTE STITCH BRACELET

Let's stop here and make a beautiful little bracelet that will be a reminder of why everyone wants to learn peyote stitch.

Materials

Try three colors of 8° seed beads to mix randomly for this bracelet and one contrasting color for the edges. I chose three greens for the mix (often called "bead soup") to create the piece shown. (I also tossed in one color of 11° seed beads to create additional texture. It's fine to omit it, especially if this is your first peyote stitch project.)

▶ 5 grams silver-lined chartreuse 8° seed beads

▶ 5 grams olive green luster 8° seed beads

▶ 5 grams purple-lined chartreuse 8° seed beads

▶ 5 grams copper-lined chartreuse 11° seed beads, optional

▶ 5 grams hot pink-lined chartreuse 8° hex-cut seed beads (edge beads)

▶ D-weight beading thread in coordinating color

▶ Thread conditioner

▶ Size 10 sharp or beading needle

▶ Toggle or snap clasp

▶ Scissors

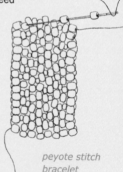

peyote stitch bracelet

Directions

1. Thread the needle with 1½ yards of thread, and wax the thread.

2. Dump out small amounts of the first 3 or 4 beads and mix them together. Keep the edge beads in a separate pile.

3. Pick up one edge bead and pass through it again to make a stopper bead. Slide it down the thread, leaving a 12" tail of thread.

4. Pick up seven more edge beads for an eight-bead-wide bracelet, which will be about ¾" wide, or choose another even number to make your bracelet narrower or wider, as you wish.

5. Pick up an edge bead and pass through the second bead from the end of the first group.

6. Continue beading across the row, using beads randomly from the bead soup. This is row 3.

7. Flip the work so the working thread is at the top right (or top left if you're left-handed).

8. Pick up an edge bead for the first stitch, and then use bead soup across the row. Remove the extra wrap for the stopper bead.

9. Continue working rows, using edge beads at each edge and colors randomly from the bead soup for the center.

10. Add thread when your working thread becomes short, around 5". *(See Threading Techniques on page 288.)*

11. Work the peyote stitch until the bracelet is the length you want (about your wrist size plus ½", minus the width of the clasp).

12. Stitch on a toggle or snap clasp at the center of each end of the bracelet, using the starting tail and ending thread. Weave through beads to reach the center without thread showing, and alternate stitching through the clasp and through the beads of the bracelet until the clasp is secure. After sewing on the clasp, pass through the beads of the first and last two rows to reinforce and strengthen them.

13. Weave in all thread ends, tying three or four slip knots for each one *(see page 18)*, pass through more beads, and trim the thread close to the work.

Peyote Stitch Variations

Q **How do I work a two-drop peyote stitch?**

A This stitch is done in the same way as basic (one-drop) peyote stitch, except that you pick up two beads for each stitch, instead of one. (Peyote stitch can also be worked three-drop, with three beads in each stitch.) Here's how you make the two-drop stitch:

1. Begin in the same manner as steps 1 and 2 of the one-drop peyote stitch instructions *(see page 256),* threading the needle, conditioning the thread, and adding a stopper bead.

2. String a number of beads that is divisible by four, including the stopper bead (for rows 1 and 2).

3. Pick up two more beads and pass through the third- and fourth-to-last beads of the original group.

4. Pick up two more beads and skip two on the row, passing through the seventh and eighth beads of the original group.

5. Continue to add two beads at a time, skipping over every other pair in the previous row, to the end of the row.

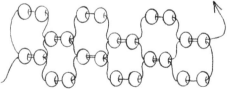

two-drop peyote stitch

6. Flip the work so the thread is at the top right corner (or top left if you're left-handed) and work across the next row as in steps 4 and 5 above.

SEE ALSO: *Peyote Stitch, page 253.*

Q **What is flat, odd-count peyote stitch?**

A Don't bother with this variation until you need it. It's not difficult, but is slower to work because you have to do a fancy little turn at the end of every other row. From working even-count peyote, you see that it takes two beads to work one stitch (a "down" bead to place the new bead on top of, and an "up" bead to pass through). With odd-count peyote, there's always an odd bead left over at the end of the row, with no "up" bead to pass through. So you have to do a couple of stitches to anchor the last bead and turn to start the new row. There are several ways to stitch for this turn; find the one that seems easiest for you.

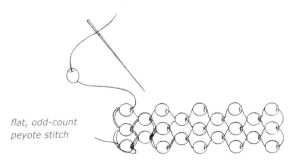

flat, odd-count
peyote stitch

Q What on earth is tubular peyote stitch?

A Most bead-weaving stitches can be worked in the round to create a cylinder or tube. The work seems a little different to start, but right away you'll notice the basic similarity with working the stitch flat. For tubular peyote, you can work around something like a pencil or a removable cardboard tube, if you want. I usually prefer to work without a form, holding the work around a finger of my nondominant hand. Here's how to make a simple tube:

1. Thread a needle and condition the thread. *(See page 118.)*

2. Pick up an even number of beads. The number of beads needed depends on the width of the tube you want. Just as for flat peyote, these first beads will become rows 1 and 2.

3. Tie the tail to the working thread to make a circle of beads, leaving at least an 8" tail, as well as a little extra thread in the circle.

4. Slip the beaded thread ring over a tube or a finger, and pass the needle through the first bead to the left of the knot. (This is the beginning of row 3.)

5. Pick up a bead, skip a bead on the ring, and go through the next bead.

6. Continue adding beads around, until you reach the beginning of the round.

7. End row 3 by passing the needle through the first bead of row 2 and the first bead of row 3. This is called "stepping up" to the next row. Pull firmly on the thread to start forming the tube shape.

8. Repeat steps 5 through 7 until you reach the desired length of your stitched tube.

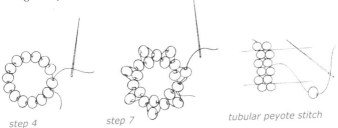

step 4   *step 7*   *tubular peyote stitch*

You can also make a peyote stitch tube with an odd number of beads. This creates a spiral, with no need to step up at the end of the row. When you reach the end of row 3, pass the needle through the first bead of row 3, and you're ready to continue with row 4.

SEE ALSO: Peyote Stitch, page 253.

Q **When using peyote stitch, can I make the piece wider or narrower?**

A To **increase** the width of a piece, add an extra bead by picking up two beads instead of one. On the following row, you can increase more quickly by adding a bead between these two, or more slowly by passing through the two beads together without adding a bead. *(See the next page.)* If you want a flat piece to get wider evenly, work an increase near each side. For a tubular peyote piece, you may want to space several increases evenly around the tube.

After increasing, pull firmly on the thread to seat the next beads.

increasing width

To **decrease** the width of a piece, skip a space without adding a bead. Pull the thread firmly to narrow the gap between beads (a). On the following row, work a single bead above the decrease (b). Again, you can space these to create the shape you want (c).

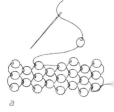

a

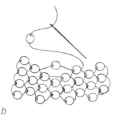

b

c

decreasing width

Q I want to weave a bowl in peyote stitch. How do I start?

A One way to start is with a circular flat peyote base. To make the circle grow and remain flat, you'll work increases spaced evenly around the circle. Here's how:

1. Start at the center with three beads, as shown, and pass through the three beads again. (You can start with four or five beads, but you will have a larger hole at the center. Experiment to see which you prefer.)

2. For round 2, work increases *(see page 265)* by adding two beads in every stitch.

3. Work a plain row (no increases) with six stitches.

4. Continue alternating increase rows with plain rows, and count stitches. As the disk gets larger, either work increases less frequently around the circle (for example, every second or third stitch) or work more plain rows between increase rows.

You don't have to follow a formula exactly. If you increase too little, the disk won't stay flat, but will start to cup. If you increase too frequently, the edges will get too long and start to ruffle. When the base is large enough and you're ready to begin forming the sides of the bowl, continue without increasing. Pull the thread snugly to encourage a crisp turn, if you want a flat base with straight sides. Or work increases less frequently to create a bowl with gradually sloping sides.

circular flat peyote stitch

Q How do I make a ruffled peyote stitch edge?

A Ruffles can add a wonderful decorative effect at the edge of a piece. As hinted in the last question, you can use increases in peyote stitch to create ruffles. Here are two ways to do it:

To begin a ruffle:

1. Add two beads in each stitch across the row.

2. Work two beads into each stitch of the next row and pass through two beads. (The beads will bunch up and be difficult to see, so work carefully and make sure you have good light.)

step 1   step 2

making a ruffle in peyote stitch

You can also start a ruffle more gradually:

1. Alternate one increase stitch with one regular stitch across the row.

2. Work a single bead into each space on the following row, including the space between the two beads of the increase.

3. Work alternating increases again on row 3.

4. Repeat steps 2 and 3 until the ruffle is as full as you like.

Square Stitch

Q **What about other weaving stitches? I've seen one that lies in straight rows.**

A The square stitch is a strong, stable stitch that looks like loomwork, but is easy to create with just a needle and thread. It's similar to peyote stitch, except that the beads form in straight rows, instead of up-and-down rows. *(See* Stitch Overview *on pages 254–255.)*

Pros and cons

▶ One benefit of the straight horizontal and vertical lines is that you can use regular graph paper to draw a design. You can create geometric shapes or work charted designs created for loom weaving and other stitch work.

▶ One disadvantage of square stitch is that adding each bead requires two stitches, or passes, of the needle, instead of one for peyote stitch.

Q **So, how is the square stitch done?**

A To work the square stitch:

1. Single-thread a beading needle with at least 1½ yards of thread and condition the thread with wax, if desired.

2. Pick up the first bead with the needle, passing through it once, looping around, and passing through the bead again

in the same direction. Slide this bead — the stopper bead — down the thread, leaving a thread tail of at least 6" to 12".

3. Pick up the remaining beads needed for row 1, or for the width of the piece you want to weave. (Try five more beads for a narrow bracelet.)

step 4

4. Begin row 2 by picking up one bead and passing the needle down through the last bead of the first row, as shown, and then up through the bead just added.

5. Pick up another bead and continue as in step 4, passing down through the second-to-last bead of the first row and up through the new bead added.

6. Repeat the process of picking up a new bead, passing through the adjacent bead of the previous row, and then passing through the new bead to the end of row 2.

7. At the end of each new row, pass the needle down through the entire previous row and back up through the new row to stabilize and add strength to the piece.

8. Flip the piece so the working thread is at the bottom again, and begin the next row.

step 8

KEEPING TRACK

To make it easy to count completed rows in square stitch
or loom weaving, use a beading needle as a marker. Slide a
long beading needle through row 10. When you've completed
10 more rows, move the needle to row 20. Continue in this way,
keeping track of how many times you move the needle, and
you'll always know what row you're on.

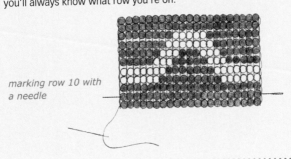

*marking row 10 with
a needle*

Q **Can I do a tubular version of square stitch?**

A Yes, square stitch also can be worked in the round,
either around a cylinder or held on a finger of the nondominant hand.

1. Single-thread the needle with 1½ yards of thread and
condition the thread with wax, if desired.

2. String enough beads to fit around the cylinder or for the
diameter desired.

3. Tie a knot to join the beads into a circle, and pass through a bead to hide the knot.

4. Work square stitch around the row in the same way as instructed for flat square stitch. *(See page 269.)*

5. Pass through the entire row again after working the last bead in that row.

6. Work the next row in the opposite direction.

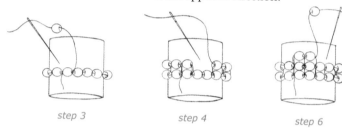

step 3

step 4

tubular square stitch

step 6

SEE ALSO: Square Stitch, page 269.

Ladder Stitch

Q **What is ladder stitch?**

A A ladder makes a stable foundation row for many other stitches, such as the brick stitch and Ndebele or herringbone stitch. It can also be used alone to make a narrow beaded cord. Here are three methods for making a ladder.

Method 1

1. Single-thread a beading needle with 1½ yards of thread and condition the thread with wax, if desired.

step 3

2. Pick up two beads, leaving at least a 6" to 10" tail.

3. Go through the beads again in the same direction and pull both ends of the thread so the beads sit side by side, with the thread exiting the bottom of the second bead.

step 4

method 1

4. String a third bead, pass back through the second bead from top to bottom, and then come back up the third bead.

5. String a fourth bead, pass back through the previous bead from bottom to top, and then come back down through the new bead from top to bottom. Pull firmly to eliminate extra thread between stitches.

6. Continue adding beads, as in steps 4 and 5, until you have the length or number needed for the base row.

7. Pass back through all the beads to strengthen and stabilize the row, or wait until later and use the tail to do it.

A WIDER LADDER

If you want a two-bead-tall ladder, follow any of the ladder methods, but use twice as many beads. For example, start Method 1 with four beads instead of two, and then pick up two beads each time.

Method 2

1. Thread a beading needle on each end of 1½ yards of thread and condition the thread with wax, if desired.

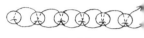

method 2

2. Pick up one bead on one needle.

3. String another bead on the needle from left to right, and pass the other needle through the bead from right to left.

4. Continue to add one bead at a time, passing both needles through the bead in opposite directions.

Method 3

1. Single-thread a beading needle with 1½ yards of thread and condition the thread with wax, if desired.

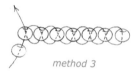

method 3

2. String the number of beads you need for your ladder, or first row.

3. Pass through the second bead from the needle in the same direction the beads were strung.

4. Pull both threads so the two beads sit side-by-side with their holes parallel.

5. Pass through the next bead in the same direction, and snug it up to sit next to the others.

6. Repeat across the row.

Q My ladder stitch row looks wobbly. How can I make it more even?

A My guess is that you're not pulling each stitch tightly enough before moving on to the next one. The beads need to be seated firmly against each other, with no extra thread visible. When the ladder is done, you can still tighten it. Here's how:

1. Position your thumbnail above the ladder and index finger below it.

2. Wiggle and work each ladder bead, or pair of beads, to snug it up against the previous bead, tugging so there's no space or extra thread between beads.

3. Repeat step 2 down the ladder.

4. Pull the needle to remove the excess thread.

. . . .

Q Whenever I try to build a base row using ladder stitch, I can see my thread. Isn't it supposed to be hidden?

A When the ladder stitch is done correctly, the neat stitches of thread show only at the edges, between bead holes. If you're seeing a wrap of thread lying across a bead, you probably crossed over the ladder and stitched into the opposite edge. To prevent these carried threads, always insert the needle into the next bead on the same edge as the thread that is emerging from the last stitch.

The same idea applies to different stitches. Each woven beading stitch has its own thread path that you need to follow so the thread will be as invisible as possible. Following thread paths is important not only when working the stitch correctly, but also when adding new thread and when weaving in thread ends. Watch closely. If something doesn't look right, investigate and fix it now.

Brick Stitch

Q **How do I work brick stitch?**

A The brick stitch looks like the peyote stitch turned sideways, but it's actually worked in a completely different way, with the needle passing under a loop of the thread instead of through a bead. Like square stitch, brick stitch requires two needle passes for each bead added. *(See* Stitch Overview *on pages 254–255.)*

Any brick stitch chart can be beaded using peyote stitch by rotating the chart 90 degrees, and vice versa. However, this refers to the orientation of the chart. You'll follow the instructions for the stitch you want to use.

Here's how to work brick stitch:

1. Single-thread a beading needle with 1½ yards of thread and condition the thread with wax, if desired.

2. Make a ladder *(see page 272)* to serve as the base row.

3. String two beads and pass the needle under the thread between the first and second beads of the ladder, from back to front.

4. Pull the thread snug and pass up through the second bead added. For additional stability, pass down the first bead and up the second bead again.

5. Pick up one bead and pass the needle under the next thread loop on the row below, from back to front.

6. Pull the thread snugly and pass it back through the new bead.

7. Repeat steps 5 and 6 along the row.

8. Turn at the end of the row and pick up two beads for the first stitch.

9. Work single beads across the row again, as in steps 5 and 6.

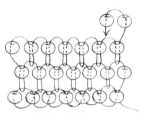

brick stitch

Q **What is tubular brick stitch good for?**

A Tubular brick stitch is often used to make a cylinder or the sides for beaded bowls. Here's how:

1. Single-thread a beading needle with 1½ yards of thread and condition the thread with wax, if desired.

2. Make a ladder *(see page 272)* of the length desired to serve as the base row.

3. Join it into a ring by passing through the end beads twice.

4. Place the ladder-stitched piece around a cylinder, if desired, or hold the ring of beads.

5. Pick up a bead, pass the needle under the next thread between beads on the ladder, and up through the bead added.

6. Pick up one bead and pass the needle under the next thread loop on the ladder base row.

7. Pull the thread snug and pass back through the new bead.

8. Work around the ring, adding one bead at a time, as in steps 6 and 7.

9. Finish the row by passing down through the first bead of the row and up through the last bead added.

10. Repeat steps 5 through 9, adding rows until you reach the desired length.

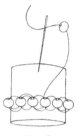

step 5

steps 6, 7

tubular brick stitch

step 10

SEE ALSO: Ladder Stitch, page 272.

Ndebele Stitch

Q **How is Ndebele stitch constructed?**

A The Ndebele stitch, which Western beaders learned from the Ndebele people of South Africa, is often called herringbone stitch. The name comes from the fact that it's worked in pairs of beads that lean away from each other in V's, like a herringbone weave in fabric. Although it's probably an ancient stitch in Africa, Ndebele is relatively new to the American beading scene. Here's how:

1. Single-thread a beading needle with 1½ yards of thread and condition the thread with wax, if desired.

2. Make a ladder *(see page 272)* of the length desired to serve as the base row, using an even number of beads. Hold the ladder with the thread exiting from the top of the far-right bead.

3. Pick up two beads and pass the needle down through the second bead in the base row and up through the third bead in the base row.

4. Continue in this manner across the row, always picking up two beads at a time.

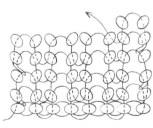

Ndebele stitch

5. Finish the row by adding the last pair of beads, passing the needle under the thread loop of the row below, as in brick stitch, and back up through the last bead added.

6. Turn the piece so the thread is at the top right.

7. Repeat steps 3 through 6 to work subsequent rows.

SEE ALSO: Ladder Stitch, page 272, and Brick Stitch, page 276.

Q **Does Ndebele stitch work as a tubular stitch?**

A Ndebele or herringbone stitch works beautifully in the round. You can make a wonderful beaded cord or chain using four or six beads around (two or three pairs of beads). Here's how:

1. Single-thread a beading needle with 1½ yards of thread and condition the thread with wax, if desired.

2. Make a ladder *(see page 272)* of the length desired and join the ends into a circle by passing through the end beads twice.

3. Be sure the working thread is emerging from the top of the circle and pick up two beads.

4. Pass down through the next bead to the left on the row below and up through the following bead, as shown on page 279.

5. Repeat steps 3 and 4 around the circle.

6. When you reach the first bead of the round, "step up" to begin the next row, by passing the needle through to the top of the stack.

7. Repeat steps 3 through 6 to add rows.

tubular Ndebele stitch

Q **Are beaders using any other African stitches?**

A There are a number of other unique African stitches that work well to make straps, chains, and cords. These same African stitches also can be adapted for other projects. For example, Zulu Tri-Leg makes a beautiful three-winged cord. By varying the design, it also works beautifully for pagoda-shaped earrings *(see page 11)*. For more information on a number of basic Zulu stitches, check out Diane Fitzgerald's books on Zulu beadwork. *(See* Resources.)

Right-Angle Weave

Q **What does RAW stand for?**

A The right-angle weave (RAW) carries its name because it's worked in circular groups of four beads, with the beads sitting at right-angles to each other. It also can be worked with more than one bead on each side. This stitch is more fluid than other off-loom stitches. RAW can be worked with either two needles or one needle. Here's how with one needle:

1. Single-thread a beading needle with 1½ yards of thread and condition the thread with wax, if desired.

2. Pick up four beads and use a square knot to tie the thread and tail together to form a circle. Do not snug the beads too tightly in this circle, as you will need some room to work.

3. Pass the needle through beads 1 and 2.

4. Pick up three beads and pass the needle through beads 2, 5, and 6. Notice that the circles are made in alternating directions, first clockwise and then counterclockwise.

step 4

5. Repeat 4 until the strip is the desired length.

6. Begin a second row by passing the needle through beads 9 and 11, pick up three beads, and pass back through bead 11.

7. Go through the three new beads, and then through bead 10.

8. Pick up two beads and pass through beads 16, 10, and 17.

9. Continue to add rows in the same manner as steps 6 through 8.

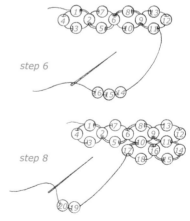

step 6

step 8

SEE ALSO: Basic Knots, page 15.

Netting

Q **How is netting different from RAW?**

A Netting can resemble RAW, but is formed in horizontal or vertical rows, rather than circular groups of beads. Vertical netting can be used to make beautifully draping netted fringe, worked off an edge of fabric such as a scarf or from another piece of beading such as peyote stitch. Horizontal netting also creates a beaded fabric with a diamond pattern. For both horizontal and vertical netting, the openness of the diamonds is determined by how many beads are added in each group, which is always an odd number.

Q **How do I make horizontal netting?**

A Horizontal netting is worked off a base row of beads, and can be worked either flat or tubularly. For a necklace that combines both stringing and weaving, try stringing beads on flexible beading wire and then working flat horizontal netting off this base. Tubular horizontal netting is often used to make delicate beaded holiday ornaments. To work flat horizontal netting *(pictured on page 285)*, you'll pick up groups of beads and work back and forth in rows.

Each group of beads contains an odd number ranging from three beads (for a close, firmly netted fabric) to seven beads (for a more open, fluid piece). It can be beautiful to use a contrasting color for the center (or joining) bead of each group, which also makes the netting easier to follow.

Horizontal Netting with Five Beads

Let's make a sample of five-bead netting with A as the main color and B as the contrasting color:

1. Single-thread a beading needle with 1½ yards of thread and condition the thread with wax, if desired.

2. String 22 seed beads as follows: B, 2A, repeat, ending in B.

3. To turn and start the next row, pick up 3A, B, 2A (you'll always pick up an extra bead when turning at the end of a row) and pass through the second B from the end.

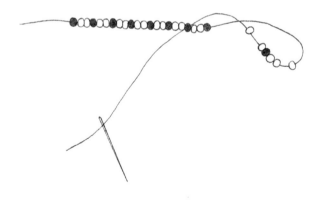

4. Pick up 2A, B, 2A, and pass through the second B bead. Repeat across the row.

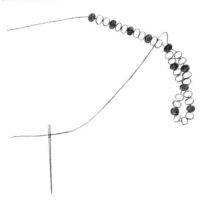

5. Repeat steps 3 and 4 to the desired length.

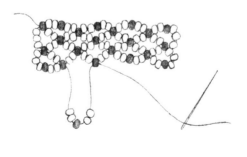

Q How do I make vertical netting?

A This is the stitch to use if you want to work beautiful, drippy fringe off the ends of a velvet scarf. The number of beads in the initial row determines the length and design of the netting. The main bead is A. As for horizontal netting, a contrasting color B looks great for the joining beads, and makes the netting easier to work, especially at first. Let's do 7-bead netting. I've worked the netting off a base of peyote stitch (*see page 253*), but it can also be worked from a few rows of picot stitch (*see page 380*) sewn on an edge of fabric.

1. Single-thread a beading needle with 1½ yards of thread and join the thread to the base row, passing through beads and tying several knots. (*See* Threading Techniques *on page 288.*)

2. Pick up beads for the first vertical row as shown, using B for the first bead and every fourth bead after that. Always add an even number of netting groups. (I've used 20 beads for the first row.)

3. Pass back through the fourth bead from the end (bead 17, the last B added), to form a three-bead picot at the bottom of the netting.

4. Pick up 3A-1B-3A, skip the next B bead on the first row, and pass through the second B bead on the first row (bead 9). Repeat once through bead 1 at the top.

steps 2–4

5. Pass through the base row to skip a bead and pass through the next "down" bead. Pick up 1B-3A, and pass through the second B of the previous row. Pick up 3A-1B-3A as in step 4, skip a B on the previous row and pass through the next B.

6. Repeat, alternating rows to the width desired. End at the top and secure the thread by passing through beads in the base row and tying several knots.

To form a dangle at the bottom of each netted fringe, use a drop bead or a crystal or other decorative bead, followed by a seed bead, to add weight and an elegant touch at the bottom of the fringe. Or alternate a drop on one fringe with a 3-bead picot on the next.

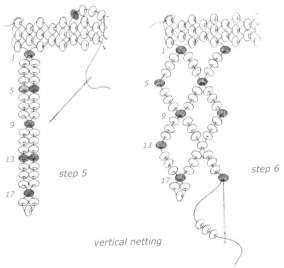

step 5

step 6

vertical netting

Threading Techniques

Q A lot of bead-weaving instructions seem to gloss over the job of adding thread by saying, "Tie a knot and continue beading." What's the best way to add new thread when weaving with beads?

A You're right that a knot or two is not enough to anchor a new thread securely. We know that our favorite jewelry pieces will be subjected to years of gravity, tugging by small children, and general wear-and-tear. The weakest part of a woven piece tends to be the area where a new thread is added, and that's usually where it will break first. I prefer to build my jewelry so it will last for years. Here's my method of adding thread, which I use for all the weaving techniques.

1. Work stitch until the thread is 4" to 5" long, and leave the old needle hanging while you prepare a new length of thread on a second needle.

2. Pass the new needle through two or three beads, starting several rows below the old working thread. Hold onto the thread tail firmly with the thumb of your nondominant hand. Don't let it slip when you tie the first knot, or you'll have to start again.

3. Insert the needle between beads, catching a strand of thread only, and pull the needle until just a loop of the new thread remains.

4. Insert the needle through that loop and pull to tighten the knot. This completes one knot, which is technically called a half-hitch.

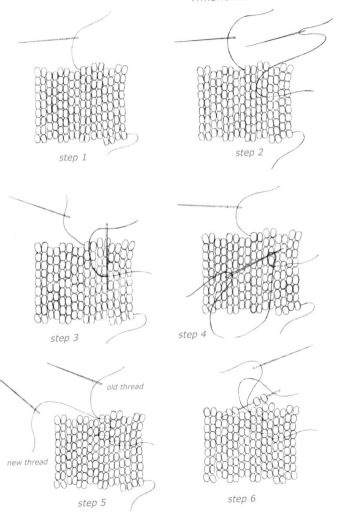

step 1

step 2

step 3

step 4

old thread

new thread

step 5

step 6

5. Pass through another two or three beads and repeat steps 3 and 4, again making sure that the thread doesn't show. Tie a total of three to four knots with the new thread, zigzagging through the piece until the new needle emerges from the same bead as the old needle.

6. Use a square knot or surgeon's knot to tie the old and new threads together securely. *(See Basic Knots on page 15.)* Continue working with the new thread, or weave in the old thread first.

7. Weave the old, short thread back into the work in the same manner as steps 3 and 4, tying three or four knots as you go down the piece. If your beads have small holes, follow a different path so the beads don't fill with thread.

8. Pass through two or three more beads after the last knot and snip the thread. You can also snip the starting end of the new thread, since it's been thoroughly knotted.

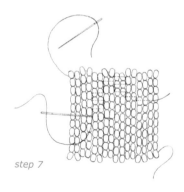

step 7

THREADING TIP

If you have trouble picking up a thread between beads, bend the beaded fabric slightly to expose the thread, and use the point of your needle to take just a small "bite" of thread.

9. Continue working with the new thread. (Whew! Now you know why beaders often work with yards of thread. It's so they won't have to add new thread very often.)

The goal is to make the addition invisible, so the thread doesn't show. The path you take depends on the stitch you're doing: for example, for peyote stitch, you follow a path of diagonal zigzags. For square stitch, you can work in straight rows. For Ndebele, follow one of the vertical lines up the piece.

ALTERNATE ENDING

There's another way to end a thread in peyote stitch without using knots. (It works the same on all stitches.) Here's how:

1. Pass the needle through five beads on the diagonal, and then jog through one bead in the opposite direction.

2. Reverse direction and go diagonally down five beads, over one, and back through five more beads. As long as you reverse directions a few times, the thread should be secure without tying knots.

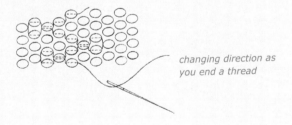

changing direction as you end a thread

Q I'm trying to weave in the ends after adding new thread, and find that I can't get through some of the beads again. Help! What can I do?

A First, don't panic. And don't try to force your needle through a bead, because it may break — especially if it's a thin-walled cylinder bead. Try one of these options:

▶ Follow a different path to weave in the thread (where the beads aren't full of thread already).

▶ Work a few rows with the new thread and then weave the thread into those new rows.

▶ Switch to a smaller needle and vow to only use beads with larger holes in the future.

....

Q When making fringe, I need to pick up several beads of one color. Is there a faster way than picking up one bead at a time?

A There is a nifty technique for scooping up several beads with your needle at once. It works basically the same way as the bead spinner on page 134. You'll need a shallow box; a shoebox lid works well. Place enough seed beads in the box lid to fill a corner when the lid is tipped.

Using a long, threaded beading needle, scoop into the beads repeatedly until you have the right number on your needle. Basically, you're just scooping up the beads whose holes are pointing in your needle's direction. The more you practice this trick, the better you'll get at picking up the number you want.

Q **When I've made a mistake in bead weaving, how do I undo a row to correct it?**

A It's true that we build our beadwork so sturdily that it often seems impossible to undo it! If you do need to rip out a few stitches, try the following:

1. Remove the needle from the thread.

2. Use the needle point to pick gently at the thread between the beads of the last stitch to see which thread is loosest.

3. Poke and lift the loosest strand of thread until you can get your finger in the loop and remove the stitch. If you're having trouble finding it, you can also tug gently on the working thread, and closely observe which thread wiggles in the previous stitch. This is the thread that you want to lift and pull in order to undo the stitch.

4. Repeat this process to unstitch as many beads or stitches as needed to reach the mistake, correct it, and then continue beading.

Bead Weaving in Action

Q **Is there a way to make an easy woven necklace?**

A I know an elegant woven necklace design that works up quickly. This may seem to belong in the chapter on stringing, but technically it's a simple type of weave. I don't know where it came from, because I learned it while doing a repair. This piece works well in 5mm to 6mm pearls (designated as the "A" bead) and 3mm beads such as 8° charlottes or a 3mm Czech FP bead (designated as the "B" bead). For thread, I suggest using one of the stronger options. *(See* Threads: Multiple Choice *on pages 112–113.)* Here are the instructions:

1. Single-thread a beading needle with 1½ yards of thread and condition the thread with wax, if desired.

2. String a simple strand of A-B-A-B-B-B, repeating this pattern for longer than the desired length.

3. Secure the ends with transparent tape or a pair of stopper clips.

4. Thread a second needle with another 1½ yard length of thread and condition the thread with wax, if desired.

5. Pick up one "A" bead and one "B" bead and begin weaving the second strand into the first strand, entering the first "B" bead on the original strand in the "wrong" direction (back toward the beginning of the strand).

6. Pick up a "B" bead and an "A" bead and pass through the middle "B" bead on the first three-B repeat of the original strand, always in the "wrong" direction.

7. Continue in the same manner as steps 5 and 6, weaving in and out of the original strand and adding beads as shown.

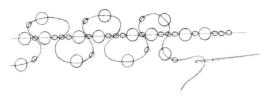

8. Pull snugly as you work the second strand so you don't see the thread and the work forms into a graceful serpentine curve.

9. Add transparent tape or a stopper clip to secure the strands when you reach the desired necklace length.

10. Finish each end as described in the next answer.

. . . .

Q **What's the best way to finish the necklace you describe?**

A I'm usually not a fan of clamshells *(see page 142)*, but they're the best choice for finishing the ends of this necklace. Here's how:

1. Remove the tape/clip on one end and bring both strands of thread through the bottom of the clamshell.

2. String an 11° seed bead and tie the strands securely using a surgeon's knot (or two, if needed).

3. Dot the knot with glue, allow it to dry, and trim the thread close to the knot.

4. Close the clamshell.

5. Use round nose pliers to curve the arm of the clamshell around one end of the clasp, so it's secure but can still move freely.

6. Repeat steps 1 through 5 on the other end.

. . . .

Q **What's another good small project for off-loom weaving?**

A My favorite quick and gorgeous off-loom weaving projects are earrings! They tend to be much faster to make than a bracelet, are light and comfortable to wear, and are a great way to play with colors and complement your wardrobe. I have sensitive ears, so I love the fact that woven earrings are so lightweight.

Because they're both quick to make and impressive-looking, woven earrings make the perfect gift. And because they're small, you can splurge for the really expensive, gorgeous beads that you wouldn't want to buy for a larger project.

Most of the beading magazines include interesting patterns for woven earrings. If you're willing to be a sleuth, you also can find earrings hidden in other patterns. For example, if there's a great pattern for a bracelet that requires six or seven woven medallions or other components that will be joined together, try making just two of them, and use them as pendants for earrings. Also, many slinky woven chain and cord patterns are perfect for earrings. Just weave a short piece, the length of the earring you want, and hang it from an earring finding.

example of woven earrings

Q **The woven earrings I've made so far seem stiff hanging from my ears. How do I make earrings with a fluid, swingy movement?**

A To make an earring more fluid, don't use the weaving thread to stitch the woven piece to the earring finding. Instead use it to sew a small soldered jump ring to the top of the woven piece, carefully open the loop on the finding, insert the ring, and close the loop.

Also, you can add other beads like Swarovski crystals, Czech glass, or Bali silver or vermeil beads to complement the colors of the woven piece. One, two, or three of these beads can either swing from the bottom of the woven piece or sit between the woven component and the finding. Here are some suggestions:

▶ To add a bead or beads at the bottom, string them on a plain or decorative headpin, make a small wrapped loop above the beads, and then stitch this loop to the bottom of the woven piece.

▶ To add beads at the top, you'll need to stitch one soldered jump ring to the top of the woven piece, and knot and bury the thread. With a new thread, stitch the additional beads to the jump ring, adding a second jump ring on top. Tie a square or surgeon's knot, dot the knot with glue, and use your needle to pull the knot inside the little stack of beads. To obtain tiny soldered jump rings, I often cut rings from a piece of chain, which work perfectly to join the various sections. This will make your earrings very fluid.

SEE ALSO: Wire Findings, page 222.

Q Can I use weaving techniques to create a clasp?

A Yes, it's possible to weave a clasp using the same or similar beads and the weaving technique used for the necklace or bracelet, so the clasp blends with the piece or virtually disappears. Or you can use a different weaving technique, if it works better. The book *Findings & Finishings* by Sharon Bateman includes several of these woven clasp designs, including several that resemble a toggle clasp, with a woven post and ring. (*See* Resources.) You'll occasionally find others in current beading magazines. These tend to be slightly more advanced projects, more suited for an intermediate bead weaver.

woven bracelet clasp

Beaded Objects

Q **I've always wondered how to cover an object with beads. How do I weave around a vase, lamp, or bicycle to make a layer of beads that spiral around it?**

A Well, it depends on how long you want to spend and the effect you want. One method is to cover a lamp base with a thin layer of glue and then throw beads at it until it's covered, or lay strands of seed beads into the glue in close spirals and patterns. Another technique is to spread a layer of a softened beeswax mixture onto a surface, and then press beads firmly into the wax to create a design.

To cover a shape with woven beadwork, though, you can use peyote stitch like the Native Americans did. In fact, they called it gourd stitch because they used it to cover gourds. Our tubular peyote stitch will work quite well, if you have the patience for a larger project. The work will progress more quickly if you use tubular 3-drop peyote stitch (start with a multiple of 6 beads and add three beads in each stitch), instead of adding beads one at a time.

I'm not so sure about the bicycle, though. Unless you have a lot of patience, that might work best as a glue project.

....

Q **I'd like to make a beaded purse. What are the different ways of making one?**

A Making beaded purses is a huge topic. You can make beaded fabric for a purse using just about any beading stitch technique we've talked about or can dream up. Probably the easiest beaded purse to make is an embroidered one. *(See chapter 11.)* You could either start with a completed fabric or soft leather purse and embellish it with beads, or bead a design on the cut-out purse sections, before the purse is assembled. Some purses are beaded all over with one type of bead, while others have borders that are filled in with embroidered designs. It's a good idea to sketch your design on paper and assemble the bead colors and shapes needed, before you begin.

You could also make a beaded purse using peyote stitch. It can be constructed as a tube, with the front and back of the purse beaded in one piece. To form the tube into a bag, stitch across the bottom of the tube to close it, add a beaded chain or strap at the top, and then perhaps work some fringe across the lower edge. This type of small purse can include a wide variety of images or designs, from a simple geometric design to a complicated pictorial one. It is often constructed from Delicas or another Japanese cylinder bead. Either way, you'll probably want to plan the design in advance, using colored pencils and graph paper or design graphing software. *A Beader's Reference* by Jane Davis is an excellent book resource to use, too. There are hundreds of graphed patterns in various off-loom stitches to choose from. (*See* Resources.)

CHAPTER 9

On-Loom Weaving with Beads

Loom Weaving Defined

Q What sorts of things can be woven with beads on a loom? Those little plastic looms make me think of something we did in Girl Scouts.

A Actually, there's a rich textile history of bead weaving on a loom. Some of the earliest surviving beaded purses, from the early eighteenth century, were made in France and Austria woven on looms using silk thread and tiny faceted metal beads with enameled color finishes.

Even earlier, Native Americans were weaving wampum belts on simple looms. A crucial moment in Native American cultures came with their exposure to European glass beads in the seventeenth century.

Some of the best works by today's bead loom artists resemble masterful paintings. Each bead is like a pixel of color in the overall design, which can have a painterly or almost photographic quality. Check out the pieces woven by Virginia Blakelock, Doug Johnson, Jeanette Ahlgren, and Laura Willits, to name just a few. You'll find photos of them in many good beading books and on the Internet. (*See* Resources.)

Q Why would I want to try weaving on a loom? It looks complicated.

A If you enjoy working with beads and color, loom weaving is another interesting place to explore and experiment. The technique allows you to create smooth, symmetric beaded fabric with rich design possibilities. Some people feel that weaving on a loom is even easier than off-loom weaving. Again, it depends on what you make, so start with something simple. For beaded fabric woven on a loom, you'll use thread as the "warp," or lengthwise structure, and thread strung with beads as the "weft," or horizontal part of the fabric. By changing the bead style and color, you can execute a simple or intricate design, add texture, and create beautiful effects.

Beaded loomwork is often used to create relatively narrow strips for bracelets, hatbands, belts, or decorative borders for drums. But you can also weave wider sections for purses or framed wall pieces, or even shaped designs, which can be used as neck pieces.

. . . .

Q How do I work out a design?

A You can weave from a preplanned chart, or make up the design as you go along. If you'd like to bead a charted design, you can plan your own on regular graph paper or on the computer using graphing software. (*See* Resources.) You can also work from a charted design in a book or one that you purchase online. For loom weaving, you can use most any chart drawn on graph paper or designed for square stitch.

. . . .

About the Loom

Q **Are looms expensive?**

A To get started with weaving beads on a loom, you don't need a lot of equipment or an expensive loom. Simple is good. In fact, a basic loom can be easier to learn and use. The loom holds the warp (lengthwise threads) under tension while you weave across them with the weft thread and beads. On some looms, you can adjust the length of the warp to match the size of the piece you want to weave, which saves warp thread. The loom may sit on a flat surface, or stand vertically or at an angle.

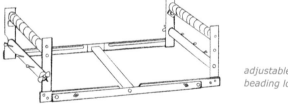

adjustable metal beading loom

Q **If I want to do bead weaving, how do I decide what type of loom to use?**

A You can choose from a variety of loom types and sizes that work well for different projects. There's not one single loom style that adapts to the needs of every design. For example, if you'd like to weave a 7"-long rectangular bracelet, you'll need a simple loom that's longer than you might think. It will need to hold at least a 19" warp, which includes 7" for the bracelet and 6" of thread at each end for finishing. On some looms, the length is adjustable, while on others, part of the warp can be wound onto a spool, so a longer piece can be woven.

For a basic loom, one good option is to build a loom yourself from fiberboard or wood. An Internet search will lead to instructions for a simple loom made from heavy cardboard, which works fine for a narrow woven piece such as a bracelet or headband.

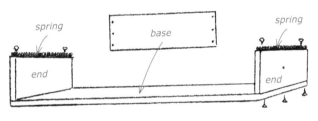

a simple loom design you can make yourself

If you'd rather buy a loom, a simple style that's readily available has a wire frame. This loom works fine for small projects. Be aware that if you warp the loom too tightly, you may distort the frame, which can make it difficult or impossible to achieve an evenly taut warp. This loom, which often retails for less than $10, is preferable to the plastic looms available in the same price range.

Q How do I get started?

A For your first project, I suggest starting with a relatively narrow woven band. This allows you to practice warping the loom and working the design with one pass of the needle. Save the wider, more challenging projects for after you've learned the basics.

If you do get hooked on bead weaving and/or love fine tools and equipment, you may find yourself attracted to a family of well-made looms available in sizes from small to large. (*See* Resources.) They have excellent tension adjustment capability, and some models offer the option of a shedding device, so weaving a row is completed in one pass instead of two. On the largest loom, you can weave a piece nearly a yard wide. They're generally considered to be the Mercedes of bead-weaving looms, so if you're just starting out, you may want to hold off until you fully know what you are doing and feel comfortable that you love bead weaving on a loom.

Using the Loom

Q How do the threads go on the loom?

A On a basic loom, a sturdy spring across each end spaces the warp threads and holds them firmly in place while the warp threads are being strung at the beginning of the project (called warping the loom). Another way to space the warp threads correctly is to string some of the beads you'll be weaving on wire or thread, and attach one of these wires across each end of the loom. Place a warp thread between each bead, and you'll have perfect spacing a bead-length apart. This spacing method, however, does not provide as deep a groove to grip the thread during warping, and warp threads may tend to pop out of place.

....

Q **What type of thread and needles should I use for weaving on a loom?**

A When it comes to choosing the right threads for weaving, here are some pointers:

▶ Use a strong, smooth thread such as the newer D-weight nylon. Many of the thread types discussed in chapter 4 work well for loomwork. (*See* Threads: Multiple Choice *on pages 112–113.*)

▶ If available, choose threads on larger spools or reels, as they're usually more economical and will wind off the spool with fewer kinks than threads that are wrapped on a small bobbin.

▶ When using thread from a small bobbin on your loom, unwind and pull the length of thread firmly between two hands to stretch it and remove some of the curl before beginning to weave with it. This step will reduce tangling, which is especially helpful for the weft thread.

▶ Select a thin thread that fits easily through the beads at least twice for the weft (crosswise thread). Realistically, most bead weavers use the same thread for both the warp and weft.

As for needles:

▶ Use regular long beading needles or extra-long needles made especially for loomwork.

▶ If you're weaving a wider piece, you may find that the longer needles save time, because they allow you to pass across the width using fewer stitches.

▶ For 11° round or Japanese cylinder beads, start with a size 11 or 12 needle. As you become more experienced, you may want to switch to a smaller size 13 needle, because it will reduce thread fraying and splitting and allow you to pass through each bead more times.

· ·

Q **Okay, so I have a simple loom I can use. How do I set it up for bead weaving?**

A To get started, you first need to string the warp threads onto the loom. I'll assume that your loom has a spring at each end for spacing the warp threads. If not, use a wire strung with your beads. Here's how:

1. Tie the end of the thread to a screw, peg, or other anchor at one end of the loom.

2. Start at one side and guide the thread over the spring at that end of the loom, straight across to the same slot in the opposite spring. Wrap the thread around the screw or peg on

the second end, and back through the next slot on the top spring. Pass the thread down to the corresponding slot in the first spring, keeping the thread tension even, but not too tight.

3. Continue to wrap the thread back and forth between the springs, with each pair of threads spaced a bead length apart. This may mean wrapping into every loop of the spring, or every other one. Test the spacing by picking up a few beads on a beading needle and placing them behind the warp threads. Slightly wide spacing is better than narrow spacing. Because each bead will sit between two warp threads, you'll need one more warp thread than the number of beads in the width of your design.

4. When you have the correct number of threads, tie the last warp thread to a screw or peg on the loom and cut the thread from the spool.

5. Single-thread a beading needle with 1½ yards of thread and condition the thread with wax, if desired.

6. Tie the weft thread around the outside warp thread, using an overhand knot. *(See page 16.)* Leave a 6" tail, which you will weave in later. *(See illustration on next page.)*

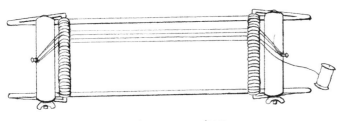

wrapping warp on a loom

Q Which way should my loom be sitting while I work on it?

A The placement of your loom is a matter of personal preference. Hold the loom in the position that feels most natural to you, which may require a little experimenting.

You can place the loom vertically, so you'll be weaving the rows from side to side. From this position, you can begin weaving at the top of the warp threads and work the rows downward, or start at the bottom of the loom (and your chart) and build the rows away from you.

Or, you can try placing the loom horizontally on the table and bead in vertical rows, with the needle pointing perpendicularly away from and toward you, as shown below.

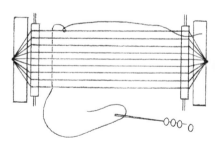

beginning work on a loom

QUALITY CONTROL

One common mistake while bead weaving is missing a warp thread (failing to pass above it). It's a good idea to check each row by pushing up on the warp threads ahead of the row. If you have missed a warp thread, the thread will pop up above the beads, and it's easy to fix it right away. If you don't detect the missed thread until later, you can fix it by running a new weft thread, or a thread tail that you're weaving in, over the missed warp.

Q I'm having a hard time getting the tension right for my warp threads. How tight should it be?

A You want all the warp threads to be under equal tension, wrapped smoothly and evenly, not too droopy and not too tight. Pulling the warp threads too tightly can distort the loom and cause some of the warp threads to be loose and others tight — especially if you're working on a wire frame loom. When you remove it from the loom, your piece may be warped and refuse to lie flat. Some weavers find it easier to control the tension if they warp the loom from the center out to each side.

Q So how do I actually get the beads onto the loom?

A Once the loom is warped and a weft thread is tied on, you're ready to begin adding beads. Here's how:

1. Using the needle, pick up all the beads needed for the first row (following your chart or design) and slide them down to the knot.

2. Bring the needle, weft thread, and beads under the warp threads, and with your free index finger, push the beads up between the warp threads. One bead should appear between each pair of threads, as shown *(in step 2 on the next page)*.

3. Keep the needle above the warp threads and pass it back through all the beads. Try not to pierce the thread inside the beads or the warp thread, which will weaken the thread and make it difficult to adjust the threads later. *(See next page.)*

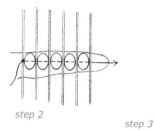

step 2

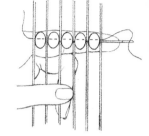

step 3

weaving the first row

4. Repeat, following your chart row by row.

Use an even tension as you work the weft rows. Pulling the thread too tightly can cause the piece to curl after it's removed from the loom. Or, if you use a varying amount of tension from tight to loose, the finished beadwork may buckle.

· ·

Q **Do on-loom pieces always have straight sides?**

A If you want a shaped piece of weaving, you can work increases and decreases to make the rows of beads shorter or longer. You can increase beads only to the number of warp threads on the loom, so you'll need to plan any shaping before warping the loom. Beading books that cover loomwork in-depth, like *Beading on a Loom* by Don Pierce (*see* Resources), include thorough instructions for working increases and decreases.

· ·

Q **What sizes of beads can I use when weaving on a loom?**

A You have a number of choices, because you can use most any size seed bead. The beads most often used for loom weaving are 11° and 10° seed beads or Japanese cylinder beads. You also can use other sizes of seed beads, such as 8°, 6°, or 15°, for different effects.

You want to select beads that are uniform in size, which is why many bead weavers choose to work with Japanese cylinder beads. If your beads are less uniform, like many Czech seed beads, you can end up with gaps in the weaving, and the thread may show. To avoid this problem, separate out the uneven beads, and weave with beads that are the same size.

If you're working a patterned design, smaller 15° beads will allow a greater amount of detail. Planning the design on graph paper will help you decide how much detail to include. It's tricky to create graceful curves in a charted design. Fill in each square of the graph to make curves as smooth as possible.

Troubleshooting

Q **My first loom piece looked really good on the loom, but now that I have taken it off, it bunches up a bit. What did I do wrong and how can I fix it?**

A If a woven piece puckers or buckles when you remove it from the loom, it may mean that the warp thread tension was too tight or uneven. You may be able to remove or relax the puckers by laying the piece flat on a table and gently rolling and massaging the beads around, so the warp threads inside can move and relax the tension. If the piece won't relax, you may have pierced a number of warp threads during weaving, so the threads are unable to move, or your weft threads may have been worked with uneven tension.

If the piece refuses to relax and lie completely flat, you might consider framing the piece or mounting it to a firm backing. Not to worry — in the process you'll have learned a lot about how to make your next piece smoother.

Q How do I add more thread while I'm weaving?

A To add additional weft thread, work to the end of a row and leave a 6" tail. Cut a new weft thread and tie it to the outside warp thread as before, leaving a tail. Then, continue beading. You can bury the thread tails as you go, or weave all the weft tails into the work later, when the weaving is completed.

To keep the weft thread ends out of your way as you continue weaving, pull them toward the completed section and secure them temporarily with small pieces of tape.

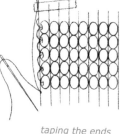

taping the ends out of the way

Q I'm having trouble weaving even edges on my loom-work. How can I make them smoother, less wobbly?

A There are several things you can do to make the edges of loomed pieces look neater.

▶ One factor is your thread tension. When tightening the weft threads on a row, you want the thread to be smooth and snug, but not tight enough to distort the warp threads at the edge.

▶ Another factor is the bead type. In chapter 2, there's a discussion of uniformity in different types of beads. (*See Bead Sizes on page 46.*) Some beads, such as Japanese cylinder beads and Japanese seed beads, are relatively uniform, while a hank of Czech seed beads usually includes a number of misshapen and unusually thin and thick beads.

▶ No matter which beads you choose, there will be at least a few that need to be removed; this is called culling. The misshapen ones should be discarded. The thicker and thinner ones can be saved for fringe or another use, such as working increases or decreases in off-loom weaving.

▶ You can also make some simple edge adjustments while weaving. If a row seems to be ending a little short, try placing a wider bead at the outer edge. With practice, your eye will start to notice any edge variations, and you'll be able to correct them as you go along.

Finishing the Ends

Q **How do I finish off all those thread ends from the warp?**

A There are a variety of different ways to finish a beaded loom-woven piece, depending on the effect you want, how much time you choose to spend, and how the piece will be used. In each case, you'll need to secure all the warp threads, so the piece will be strong and stable. Options include:

▶ Backing the beaded piece with leather or fabric

▶ Making the warp threads into beaded fringe at the top and/or bottom edges

▶ Beading a decorative border along the edges

▶ Leaving the piece unlined with plain edges, with the warp threads woven back into the piece

Method 1

The quickest way to finish the warp threads only works for pieces that will be mounted or backed with leather or fabric, so only one side of the beadwork will show.

1. Remove the beaded piece from the loom by cutting the warp threads as close as possible to the end screws or pegs.

2. Use a smooth overhand knot *(see page 16)* to tie all the warp threads at each end into a tight, secure bundle. Place the knot as close as you can to the beadwork without distorting the edges of the work.

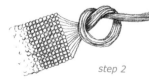

step 2

3. Cut the thread ends about ½" beyond the knot, fold the knot to the wrong side, and stitch it in place. Stitch through nearby beads in several spots to anchor it securely.

step 3

Method 2

This method begins while the piece is still on the loom, by creating a thread-woven band or selvedge that helps to stabilize each end of the beaded work. This method is secure, takes a little more time to complete, and gives a finer finish.

1. Use the remaining weft thread (attaching new thread as needed) to weave across the ends of the piece in rows, without adding any beads. Work over a warp thread on one row and under it on the next.

2. Stop every few rows and use the needle between warp threads to press the woven rows tightly against the beaded work.

3. Complete about ¼" of weaving, tie the weft thread to the outer warp, and slide the thread end into a slot in the spring.

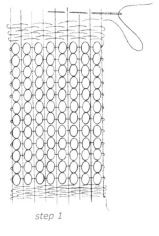

step 1

4. If the wrong side of the piece will be seen, you can finish the ends neatly with a piece of narrow ribbon. Spread tacky glue lightly on one side of the ribbon and place it under the

warp threads, just beyond the woven section. Wrap the ribbon and lap the ends neatly.

5. When it's dry, cut the warp threads flush with the edge of the ribbon, fold the woven section and ribbon onto the bead-work with the ribbon join facing the bead-work, and stitch the end in place.

6. Weave through the ribbon and then through a bead to secure the sides and edges of the ribbon. Repeat for the other end.

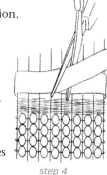

step 4

Method 3

Reweaving the warp threads back into the beaded piece is the finest way to finish the ends of loomwork, especially if both sides of the work will be seen. It also takes the most time.

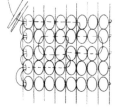

1. Cut the piece off the loom as indicated in step 1 of Method 1, leaving long ends for weaving. About 8" at each end works well, so you'll want to allow extra warp length for this finish when setting up the loom.

2. Thread each warp thread on a needle and weave it back into the beadwork. *Beware:* If you're not careful, the beads on the first few rows will fill up with thread quickly, and you won't be able to use them for other threads. (*See* Thinking Ahead *on the next page.*) If you run into beads filled with thread, weave the thread up between beads, over and under the weft threads, until you reach a clear area to weave it in.

Thinking Ahead

When using Method 3, plan out a path to follow with each thread, preferably one that runs vertically into the piece to distribute the warp thread ends. For the first warp thread, you might pass through two beads on the second row and then back through two beads on the third row, continuing to zig and zag this way for about four rows before cutting the excess warp thread. It's a good idea to tie a knot around a thread intersection at least once while weaving in each thread. Follow this pattern across the row, then reverse it for the last couple of warp threads to avoid the beads filling up with thread.

....

Q Can't I just use glue to hold down all the warp threads on the wrong side?

A Whether you can use glue on your bead weaving depends on the type of piece you're making and the quality of result that you want. If you're weaving a small piece and the ends will be completely enclosed, it may be fine to use some glue. In general, though, glue can add stiffness to the piece, and if you're not careful, the glue can ooze out between beads, which may show on the right side. Try Method 1 *(see page 316)* instead, tying the warp threads into a knot and then stitching them to the wrong side.

If the project will be mounted on a stiff base like a barrette, another alternative is to follow Method 2 *(see page 317)*, creating a woven band on each end. Then apply glue, clear nail polish, or a fray prevention product to add stability to the woven bands only. When the piece is dry, cut the warp threads about 1½" beyond the woven section, twist the thread ends, and fold the woven band and ends under the loomwork. Sew the ends to the back of the beadwork to anchor them.

. . . .

Q **What do I do with the threads still hanging off the sides of the piece?**

A If you didn't weave in the weft thread tails as you went along, you'll need to do it now as part of the finishing process. Some bead weavers prefer to weave in all the weft threads before the piece is cut from the loom, while others choose to leave the weft thread ends hanging until all warp threads have been safely woven in first. Their reasoning is that they may need to stitch through this spot again later, and may accidentally pull the thread tail out of the bead. Here's how you weave in loose weft threads:

1. Untie the knot around the warp thread at the edge of the work, using a T-pin or strong, sharp needle to loosen the knot.

2. Thread a needle onto the tail and pass through beads toward the center of the row.

3. Tie a knot around a warp/weft thread intersection, and continue through the beads in the row. Or you can turn and zigzag through beads in the rows below.

4. Pull the thread snug, tie a knot around a thread intersection, pass through a few more beads, and cut off the excess thread.

Making Fringe

Q **How do I use all those warp threads to make fringe on the ends of a piece?**

A Beaded fringe can be a beautiful way to embellish the top and/or bottom edges of a woven piece, while finishing off the warp thread ends at the same time. There are many different types of fringe you can use, such as branched coral, twisted fringe, and netted fringe designs. To start, though, it's a good idea to stick with simple straight fringe worked without adding thread.

Tips

▶ When setting up the loom, you'll need to take the fringe into account when planning the length of the warp. For 1" to 2" of simple fringe, you'll need 6"- to 8"-long warp ends.

▶ If you plan to add a larger bead or picot at the end of the fringe, you'll probably want to center a strand of fringe under every other bead across the loomwork. This work goes faster and has the added benefit of giving you two warp threads to use for finishing each length of fringe.

▶ It's usually better not to stitch fringe on the outer warp thread. Unless the beads in the fringe are heavy, it generally will not hang straight. Weave in the outer warp thread, and begin the fringe with the second thread.

Technique

1. String the desired number of beads on a warp thread.

2. Skip the last bead strung and pass the needle back through all the other beads, and through the next bead of the loomwork. At the end of the fringe, use a drop, a crystal, a Czech glass bead, or a 3-bead picot for a decorative effect.

3. String the second warp thread on a needle and run it down through the fringe and back up; knot it to the first thread. Using two threads doubles the strength of the fringe.

4. Weave the thread tails on a zigzag path into the loomwork, if there's room in the beads, or back into the fringe.

Fringe Options

▶ A picot is a small loop used to make a decorative edge. To create a picot, string two extra seed beads at the end of the fringe, then skip three beads and pass up through the fringe and into the next base bead.

▶ Another attractive option is to create looped fringe. String beads on the warp thread for the desired length, add a decorative lower bead, and string the same number of beads again. Pass through the next bead in the loomwork.

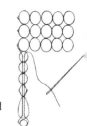

using warp ends to make beaded fringe

▶ For longer fringe, you may need to add new thread. Varying the length of the fringe is another way to reduce crowding and create an interesting finish. Fringe also can be worked off the surface of the loomwork, to create texture as a design element.

Q **I find it difficult to get the beads of the fringe to sit close enough to the beaded piece. Any tips?**

A To tighten the fringe so it's snug against the edge of the piece, hold on to the end bead as you pull firmly on the thread. Doing so allows you to remove any excess slack in the thread so you'll see only beads in the finished piece.

....

Q **What if I don't want fringe? Are there any other nice finishes I can use?**

A As an alternative, you can work a decorative beaded picot stitch to finish the edges of a beaded loom-woven piece. A variation of this stitch is used to embellish the edges of woven or knit garments, as discussed in chapter 11. (*See* Stitching Techniques *on page 376.*)

You also can use warp and weft thread tails to stitch the edging, so you'll be weaving them in at the same time. To work picot stitch on the side of a woven piece:

1. Start with the closest thread tail.

2. Pick up one seed bead, pass the needle under the outer warp thread between rows, and pass back through the bead.

> ### SHORT THREADS
>
> When a thread tail becomes too short, weave it into the work. Zigzag a couple of times, tie a knot, and then pass through a couple of beads. Weave the next warp or weft thread down the work and continue stitching with it. Always use the thread that's closest to the spot where you're stitching. Weave and knot any remaining threads into the piece.

3. Pick up two beads, stitch under the outer warp thread in the next row, and pass back through the second bead.

4. Repeat this two-bead stitch across the edge.

picot edge stitch

CHAPTER 10

Crocheting with Beads

Beads and Fiber Arts

Q I like to knit and love to bead, but I don't understand why anyone would want to add beads to knitting or crochet. Aren't they very different types of work?

A Actually, combining beads with fiber adds a whole new dimension to both! Glass has such a wonderful relationship with light, and can bring some of that light into relatively opaque threads and yarns. The hard, smooth surface of glass provides a beautiful contrast and intriguing texture, while the fiber adds fluidity and drape. These mediums have been combined for centuries, in knitted beaded purses; heavily bead-embroidered wedding costumes; and bead-woven aprons, neck- and arm-rings, and head pieces.

Q Okay, so how does it work?

A The usual method for creating bead crochet or knitting is to prestring beads on thread or yarn. You then slide them into place as you crochet or knit, so each bead (or group of beads) is captured in or sits above a stitch. To combine beads with crochet, you can use a number of different styles.

▶ One very popular technique is the **crocheted rope**, a softly structured tube in which you see very little thread, with the beads stacked neatly on the outside of the crocheted tube. The beads are often arranged in patterns, such as a spiral or other repeating texture, but they also may have a random design or be a single color. *(To make the bracelets shown below, see the bead sequences on pages 350–352.)*

crocheted rope bracelets

Furry Drops   *One-Color Spiral*

▶ Another style of bead crochet is more random, constructed so that the varied colors of the threads and yarns are a more visible part of the design and are combined with beads in a wide variety of colors, shapes, and sizes.

▶ A third method looks more like crocheted fabric, with beads that may slide into place to create a design, or are applied individually as the work progresses.

SEE ALSO: Knitting with Beads, page 364.

Q **My friends all seem to be crazy about bead-crochet ropes. What's so great about this technique?**

A Well, for one thing, the resulting bracelets provide wonderful opportunities to play with color and patterning. They're soft and comfortable to wear, can be worn in

CROCHETED ROPES

When beads are strung on thread and then crocheted in a spiral — with a bead placed in every stitch — the beads form a cylindrical tube or rope. The thread becomes nearly invisible. These supple beaded tubes are certifiably delicious and addictive, both to make and to wear. For examples of this style, look for beadwork by Martha Forsyth and Pat Iverson, as well as books by Judith Bertoglio-Giffin, Carol Wilcox Wells, and many others. (*See* Resources.)

coordinating sets, and make terrific gifts. Sewn with an invisible join, they look seamless and there's no need for a clasp. The bracelets roll over your hand and can fit the way you prefer, either close to the wrist or more loosely like a bangle. The fluid, claspless style is especially comfortable for those of us who bang around on a mouse all day.

Q **I already know how to crochet. Why does everyone act like bead crochet is so hard to learn?**

A Making bead-crochet ropes is one of my favorite beading techniques, but I also think it's one of the more difficult to learn — and teach! Even if you know how to crochet, learning to crochet beaded ropes is different, because the work is small and placing the beads correctly adds another level of skill. Bead crochet requires dexterity in both hands, the ability to control thread tension, good vision, and the patience to work with tiny objects. For beginners learning the technique, the trickiest two areas seem to be starting the rope and learning to make an invisible join in the finished rope.

If you're having trouble learning, stick with it! It's well worth the effort. I'll give you a lot of troubleshooting tips here, which may help you over the hurdle. Or that next class may be the one that makes it all come together for you. These flexible, comfortable bracelets are my daily companions. I don't go anywhere without wearing several of them on my arm.

Q My bead-crochet teacher is insisting that the members of our class make several bracelets in multicolor spiral patterns with opaque beads that are all the same size. This seems boring and so restrictive. Why can't I make the crocheted ropes I want?

A Don't worry, you'll be making the ones you want soon enough! It's a good idea to trust your teacher, who has probably taught bead crochet to quite a few others before you and knows some of the tricks that make it easier to learn the technique. A few people seem to pick it up easily, but for many students, crocheted ropes can be difficult to learn. When first learning to crochet a beaded tube, a recent student called it "horrifying," which is quite a strong word for a really fun beading technique, but it's the way a lot of students feel while they're learning. She can laugh about it now.

POINTERS FOR BEAD CROCHET

▶ String the beads on the thread in a pattern. If you're a beginner at bead crochet, stick with a simple, repeating pattern in all-one-size beads.

▶ Use 8° or 11° seed beads in six different bright, contrasting, opaque colors. *(To figure out how many beads you need, see page 338.)* Some people find the larger 8° seed beads easier to see, but they don't lie as neatly in a six-bead circle, so it's easier to lose your place. Try both sizes and see which works better for you.

▶ Start with a light color of thread, which is easier to see. Choose size 10 cotton thread or button-and-carpet polyester/cotton thread that is soft and resists splitting. *(See* Resources.)

▶ Try a steel crochet hook size 11/12 (1mm) to start, but realize the best size for you can vary, depending on your tension. Many people tend to crochet too tightly while learning, which can result in a stiff, inflexible rope. Switching to a slightly larger size 10 (1.15mm) steel hook can help in forming looser stitches and a more supple rope.

▶ Make sure your thread contrasts with your bead colors, so it's easy to see. **Do not** cut the thread off the spool; you'll need about 10 times as much thread as the length of your beads.

▶ Remember that 6" of strung beads crocheted with six beads around *(for a definition of this term, see page 336)* will make about 1" of rope. So, for a bracelet that's about 7" long (for an average wrist), string 42" of beads. This measurement is approximate, because each crocheter has her own unique tension.

Try not to be too impatient. After you've made a few simple crocheted ropes with spiral designs, you'll have the confidence to try incorporating other sizes of seed beads, drops, small Czech glass donuts, pearls, or crystals, and to attempt more elaborate patterns. Making a solid color rope is probably the most difficult of all, because there's no pattern to follow as you crochet the beads. It can be relatively easy to "lose" a bead, which means suddenly finding you don't have the correct number of beads in your round.

Some bead-crochet students learn the technique in a class or two, while others come back for 10 or more classes before they feel completely confident to crochet a rope from start to finish on their own. Take your time, practice, and enjoy the process. If you're determined to master the technique, you will.

Q If I want to learn bead crochet on my own, what's the best way to start?

A Of all the various types of beading that you might want to learn, I think bead crochet benefits most from learning with a teacher. Many local bead stores offer group classes or individual coaching sessions, which will help you identify mistakes quickly and get you started with good technique. But, of course, it's fine to try it first on your own. First read Pointers for Bead Crochet *(see opposite page),* and let's see if I can get you started.

Note: These instructions assume that you are right-handed. If you work left-handed, you'll hold the hook in your left

Getting Started

One of the easiest ways to learn is to have an experienced bead-crochet friend or teacher begin the rope by crocheting 1" of the tube for you, so you'll have something to hold onto. It's much easier to take over and practice the beaded slipstitch until you feel comfortable with it, matching a red bead over a red bead of the previous row, a white bead over a white. That's why we use six different colors to learn, so you can see the pattern and know it's correct. Once you're comfortable with the crochet technique, it's easier to go back and learn how to start the tube. But if you don't have a crochet friend handy, it's okay to start at the beginning. Learning this way, the process may seem slower. Be patient with yourself.

hand and carry the thread in your right, just the mirror-image of these directions. You'll be crocheting in a clockwise direction, but the rest of the directions remain the same.

String the Beads

1. String a large-eyed needle onto the end of the spool of thread. You want to keep the thread attached to the spool so you can use as much thread as you need for the bracelet.

2. Dump out a small pile of each color bead onto your beading surface, and pick up one bead of each color in sequence: A-B-C-D-E-F.

3. Repeat this pattern until you have enough beads strung to make a bracelet. (*See* Pointers for Bead Crochet *on page 330.*)

step 3: string six colors in an A-B-C-D-E-F pattern.

Make a Slipknot

4. With beads strung on the thread, make a slipknot about 8" from the end of the thread. (*See* Basic Knots, *page 15.*)

5. Place the slipknot loop on the crochet hook. Hold the hook in your dominant hand, as shown in the box below, and hold the beaded thread in the other hand.

step 4: make a slipknot

CROCHET TIP

Find a comfortable way to provide tension on the thread to keep it from slipping. One way is to wrap the thread around your left pinky finger a couple of times and then over the index finger. Another method is to wrap the thread around the ring finger and then twice around your index finger.

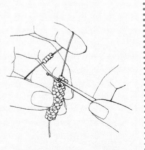

how to hold a crochet hook and thread

---

6. Scoot most of the beads down the thread toward the spool and out of your way, leaving ½" to 1" of beads between your finger and the slipknot to begin working with.

Start the First Row

7. Slide one bead down to the hook and make a chain stitch to capture it. For a chain stitch, grab the thread on the far side of the bead and pull it through the loop on the hook.

step 7: making a chain stitch around a bead

8. Repeat step 7 for the next five beads. Notice that you are working the beads in the reverse order from the way they were strung. You will end up with a chain of six beads, each captured in a chain stitch, which will become the first row of the bracelet.

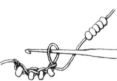

step 8: chain stitch with beads captured inside

9. Close the circle for the first row by inserting the hook into the thread loop at the left side of the first bead, flipping the bead to the right side of the hook or away from you, and slide a new bead close to the hook (bead 7).

10. Make sure that bead 7 stays above bead 1 and work a slipstitch by wrapping the thread over the hook and pulling it through the two loops on the hook. At

step 10: closing the circle

first, it's fine to pull through these loops one at a time. This is the first stitch in the second round.

Continue Working Rounds

11. Working in a counterclockwise direction, insert the hook into the thread loop at the left side of the second bead, and flip the bead to the right side of the hook (away from you), slide a new bead close to the hook (bead 8), and make a slipstitch.

12. Repeat step 11 four more times for a total of six slipstitches to complete round 2.

13. Continue working in rounds, as in steps 11 and 12, until the bracelet is the desired length and you've finished the last entire sequence of the pattern. If you don't finish the sequence, the design won't match up correctly when it's joined. (You don't have to think about this on your first bracelet, but it's a good idea to work the first and last couple of rows a little more snugly than usual, which will give you a neater join.)

step 13: working the second round

SMOOTH AND STEADY

To make it easier to pull the thread through the loops on the hook, slide the loops up the hook to make the loops larger. Then grab the thread, pull it through, and rotate the hook down toward you so it doesn't catch on the loops as it passes through. Maintain even tension on the thread. If you pull too hard, the work will be too tight; too loose and the loop will flop off the hook.

14. Cut the working thread about 9" from the final stitch and bind off by pulling the thread end through the last loop.

LOOK AND LEARN

Notice that for each stitch, you'll work a yellow bead on top of the previous yellow bead, a red bead on top of the red, and so on. When you move to a more complicated stitch pattern, this will no longer be true, but for now it can help you stay on track. Also notice that the beads in the top row are standing up sideways, while beads that have been crocheted and flipped into place are sitting down flat on their holes, so the holes are vertical. If you ever fail to flip a bead correctly and keep the new bead above it, you'll get a visible mistake, with a "loose" bead that's not sitting correctly.

Q **What does it mean when you refer to "six-around?"**

A The number of beads "around" refers to the number of beads worked in each round of the rope, with one bead in each slipstitch. It determines the diameter of your rope. Various patterns require differing numbers of beads per round, to create the design.

Q **How many beads do I need to string to make a rope?**

A A rough guideline is that 42" of strung beads will make a 7" bracelet, when crocheted six around. This equals 6" of beads for 1" of finished rope. From here, you can calculate quantities based on the size bead you are using. For example, if you're using 11° beads, which run 19 beads per inch, multiply 19 times 6 to determine that you need 114 beads per inch of rope. For a 7" bracelet, multiply times 7 for a total of 798 beads. Now divide by 6 to find that you need 133 beads (1.21g) of each color.

A different number of beads crocheted around will create a difference in the number of beads that need to be strung:

▶ For six-around, string 6" of beads to make 1" of rope.
▶ For five-around, string 5" of beads to make 1" of rope.
▶ For four-around, string 4" of beads to make 1" of rope.
▶ For three-around, string 3" of beads to make 1" of rope.

As you plan your rope, keep the following in mind:
▶ Amounts will vary somewhat depending on bead size and crochet tension, so it's better to string a little extra and then stop crocheting when your bracelet is the correct

GUIDELINES FOR LARGER BEADS

To crochet a bracelet 7" to 7½" long, here's a guide to approximately how many beads you'll need.

bead size	number of beads	hook size	weight/ rows	number of beads
8° seed beads	four-around	1.25mm hook	.4 ounces	400 beads
8° seed beads	five-around	1.25mm hook	.45 ounces	500 beads
6° seed beads	four-around	1.25mm hook	.75 ounces	275 beads
6° seed beads	five-around	1.25mm hook	.9 ounces	360 beads
4mm rondelles or wafers	three-around	1.15mm hook	93 rows	280 beads
6mm rondelles or wafers	three-around	1.15mm hook	73 rows	220 beads
2mm × 3mm FP donuts	four-around	1.25mm hook	70 rows	280 beads
3mm × 5mm FP donuts	three-around	1.25mm hook	69 rows	210 beads
3mm FP round	four-around	1.15mm hook	70 rows	280 beads
4mm FP round	three-around	1.15mm hook	58 rows	175 beads
3mm to 6mm pearls, mixed	three-around	1.25mm hook	65 rows	200 beads
6mm FP roller beads	three-around	1.25mm hook	43 rows	140 beads

length (but always stop at the end of a pattern repeat, so the pattern will line up when joined).

▶ To allow for differences in beads and crochet tension, it's a good idea to have a small amount of extra beads.

▶ Remember that larger beads or a fatter rope will require a longer bracelet in order to fit the same way, with the same inside diameter. (*See* Bracelets and Necklaces *on page 161.*)

Making Bracelets

Q Okay, so now I have a bead-crochet rope. How do I join it into a bracelet?

A The invisible join is a beautiful thing, like fitting tiles neatly together. Here's how:

1. String a tapestry (blunt) needle (size 26 or 28) on the starting thread and weave it inside the tube. (I usually zigzag around a couple of times before cutting the thread, which is probably not necessary, but feels more secure.)

2. String the needle onto the ending thread and arrange the bracelet with the ending thread on top and the starting edge on bottom.

step 3: stitching the ends together

3. Stitch to the left (clockwise), inserting the needle from the inside of the tube to the outside, and alternating stitches from the top edge and bottom

MATCHING COLORS

For the bracelet with six colors around and most other spiral repeat patterns, you'll notice that the colors match up when you're sewing the ends; red on bottom sewn to red on top, yellow on bottom sewn to yellow on top, and so on. Color-matching can be a big help when learning to join, a reassuring check that you're aligning the bracelet ends correctly.

edge, all the way around. The beads are numbered from each end, so bead 1 is the highest on each end and beads 2, 3, and 4 stair-step down. The beads on the lower (starting) edge of the bracelet should already be lying flat with vertical holes, while the last row of beads worked (on top) will need to be flipped into position as you sew the ends together. Be sure to flip them to the right; otherwise, they won't line up correctly when stitched.

4. Insert the needle into the thread loop of bead 7 on the top, from the inside of the tube out. This is the last loop you crocheted into.

5. Make sure the thread doesn't wrap around a bead and stitch into the thread coming out of bead 1 on the bottom.

6. Go back to the top edge, flip bead 6 to the right, and stitch into the thread loop below it.

7. Continue alternating a stitch on the top and a stitch on the bottom. After completing the first few stitches, you can pull the thread snug, and continue to tighten it as you stitch.

8. Stitch all the way around, finishing with bead 1 on the top (which may tend to hide inside the tube) and then bead 7 on the bottom.

9. Check to see that the design lines up correctly. If not, you can carefully unpick the stitches and try again. (Believe me, we've all done it — many times!)

10. Make sure all stitches are snug, and continue to work a couple more stitches.

11. Weave the thread back and forth through the tube several times, tying a slipknot after each stitch, if desired. (Some people don't tie knots, so do whatever feels secure to you.)

12. Insert the needle into the tube and out one more time, and cut off the excess thread.

. . . .

Q I just strung a whole length of seed beads in a complicated pattern to make a bracelet. Now I see that there's an extra bead in the pattern, way back near the beginning. I don't think I can stand to string it all over again! What should I do?

A If you picked up an extra bead by accident, you can break it so your pattern will be correct. The trick is to break the bead without cutting or damaging the thread inside it. If you simply break the bead with pliers or wire cutters, the sharp edges of glass can easily slice the thread. Here are two possible solutions, either of which is a lot faster than restringing the entire design:

breaking an extra bead with a T-pin

▶ **Option 1:** Place the bead on top of a phone book or thick magazine and gently press a pushpin, T-pin, or large-size chenille needle into the bead until you feel it pop. Because the pin is larger than the bead hole, it breaks the bead from the inside out, so the thread will be safe. Cup your other hand over the bead so the tiny pieces don't fly around the room.

▶ **Option 2:** If your pin/needle is not thick enough to break the bead, use chain nose pliers or nail clippers to break it. With the pin or a sturdy needle inserted into the bead, grab and break the bead on the side away from the thread so it doesn't come near the sharp edges.

Q **What if I missed a bead?**

A If you've left out a bead in the pattern, mark the spot with a small safety pin, or tie on a piece of contrasting thread. When you reach that part of the design, crochet a chain with no bead at

correcting for a missing bead

that spot. On the next round, be sure to work into this stitch so your pattern will be right. Later, sew a bead of the correct color in place using sewing thread.

Q **Help! I'm running out of thread in the middle of crocheting a bracelet!**

A It's not difficult to join a new spool of thread securely. Make sure it's the same color, though, or it can have a dramatic effect on the look of the bracelet. There are a number of ways to add thread; this is how I do it.

1. Transfer the remaining beads from the old thread by tying a knot and sliding the beads to the new thread. Make sure you transfer them in the same direction (that is, from the end of the old thread to the beginning of the new thread), so you haven't reversed the order of the beads in your pattern. If the knotted thread doesn't fit through your beads, use a long needle on the new thread and transfer groups of beads to the new thread.

2. Secure the working loop by making a chain stitch, cutting the old thread, and pulling the tail through the loop, leaving about 2" of thread.

3. Insert the crochet hook into the last loop where you made a stitch, wrap a loop of the new thread 2" from the end, and pull it through.

4. Hold both strands of the new thread and make a chain stitch (no bead) by wrapping both strands over the hook and pulling them through the loop on the hook.

5. Continue to pull until the tail comes through the loop. Pull on the new thread to adjust the loop size, and pull on the tail to snug up the knot. You're now ready to continue crocheting with the new thread.

step 4: adding new thread

6. Crochet around the tails so they're hidden inside the tube, or leave them sticking out and work them in later.

Q Sometimes I have a bead in the tube that doesn't look quite right; it's looser and sits sideways, instead of horizontally, on the tube. How can I fix that?

A You're describing a common error made in bead crochet, especially by beginners. When you crochet through a loop and flip the old bead away from you, the thread must travel straight up from the row below, without wrapping around a bead. The new bead you're adding must remain on top of the flipped bead. If the new bead slips below it, you'll get a strange, floating bead in that row.

To avoid this mistake, make sure the old bead is pushed down firmly after flipping, with the thread coming straight up beside it and the new bead sitting on top.

Once the tube has been completed, this is not an easy problem to fix. You can try turning the bead into the correct position and anchoring it with a couple of hand-sewn stitches, which may look fine if the pattern is relatively busy.

The best solution, to quote expert crochet instructor Ann Feeley of Boston, is to "stop and admire your work" often while crocheting, and rip out any row that doesn't look quite right. The top row of beads should all be standing up sideways, while the previous rows should all be seated neatly with vertical holes. If you check your work often, you'll learn to catch these problems before you continue crocheting.

Design and Technique

Q **What about thread color? Does the thread really matter, since it doesn't show very much?**

A Even though the thread seems to nearly disappear between the beads, the choice of thread color actually has a significant effect on the design and look of the finished rope. It can be a lot of fun to play around with the thread color as an additional design element. If you're using transparent beads in your design, be aware that the thread color will show through and affect the bead color. A lot of bead crocheters always use thread that matches their beads. This is one good option, but it is certainly not the only choice.

Let's say you want to crochet a summertime rope using opaque aqua beads. You can play it safe and try to match the thread as closely as possible, or break out of the box and try bright orange thread. The orange thread may make the piece really pop!

One of my favorite bracelets uses chrome yellow thread with olive luster beads and chardonnay-mix drops. You don't really see the yellow thread, but it makes the bracelet appear to be lit from within. Made with olive thread, it's a completely different bracelet.

For another interesting effect, try using light gray thread for crocheting pale pink transparent 8° seed beads. String a silver-lined light gray 3mm square bead every 43 beads, and crochet six-around. The result is delicate and not too sweet, like an antique piece.

So go ahead and have fun with the thread color. It can be an interesting experiment to make the same bracelet twice, using the identical beads and stringing pattern but with two different thread colors. See how much difference the choice of thread can make. And remember: The difference will be even greater if you're crocheting with larger beads or tend to crochet more loosely.

. . . .

Q **I've learned how to do crocheted ropes, and my work usually looks good. Sometimes, though, the rope seems a little too stiff or the beads too loose, so the pattern doesn't look quite right. Do you have any ideas to help me with that?**

A Your question is really about crochet tension. If you crochet too tightly, you'll end up with a stiff, inflexible rope. At the extreme, it may not even want to curve enough to fit around the wrist!

One solution is to relax more while crocheting, which often happens naturally as a person becomes more comfortable with the process. Even smiling and relaxing your mouth can cause your stitching to relax. (I could draw some parallels to labor and giving birth, but I won't.)

Another solution is to adjust the size of the crochet hook. A larger shaft will create looser stitches.

For those times when your rope seems too loose, the beads flop out of their assigned places a bit so the design looks wrong, or you feel you're seeing too much of the thread, try using a hook one size smaller to give a slightly firmer, more stable result. Larger-diameter ropes, such as those crocheted eight-around, are more susceptible to a looser look.

Each person has her own unique crochet tension, so it's a matter of trial-and-error to determine the best-sized hook for the project you're making. Most experienced bead crocheters are accustomed to tinkering with the size of the crochet hook to get the results they want. Even if you always use 11° beads, some of them run smaller (such as Czech 11°), while other 11° beads are relatively large (such as the French ones). Be willing to experiment. But in general, when you crochet with larger beads, you'll probably want to change to a larger hook.

Q If I don't always want to make an invisible join, what are some other ways to finish crocheted ropes?

A As an alternative to the invisible join, a crocheted rope bracelet or necklace can include a normal clasp, much like any other bracelet or necklace.

For a smooth finish at the ends, try adding a decorative Bali silver bead cap over each end of the rope before joining the clasp. The clasp can be sewn in place using the ends of the crochet thread, or a length of flexible beading wire can be strung through the center of the rope, through the bead cap, and then crimped around the clasp, as for any other strung bracelet or necklace.

For another finish that works beautifully on a crocheted rope necklace, try a Bali magnetic clasp as both the clasp and the focal point of the necklace. Use the end of the crochet thread to alternately stitch through a bead on the rope, the clasp loop, and the opposite bead until all beads are secured and the clasp fits snugly.

If you're crocheting a skinny little rope with 2mm sterling silver beads *(see* Sterling Rope *on next page),* create a polished finish by sewing a matching 6° seed bead at each end as a transition to the clasp. Or, for a virtually invisible clasp, stitch half of a small, ordinary sewing snap onto each end of a crocheted rope necklace. It practically disappears when fastened.

Branching Out

Q **I've made a lot of bracelets. Can I crochet a piece that's long enough for a necklace?**

A Crocheted ropes make beautiful necklaces and lariats. A lariat is a longer clasp-free style that's worn with the ends draped over each other, or with one end looped through a ring at the other end. Be aware that as your rope becomes longer, it becomes more difficult to slide all the beads down the thread each time you need more thread to continue crocheting.

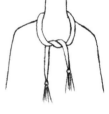

two lariat styles

For a shorter necklace of 16" or less, you can string all the beads at once and crochet it in one piece. For longer necklaces, many crochet pros create the rope in sections, and then join the sections with invisible joins *(see page 339)*. The sections can be all the same, or you can use a subtle or bold pattern variation in each section to create texture and variety.

> ## STERLING ROPE
>
> For a beautiful, plain sterling silver necklace, string 2mm round sterling silver beads on light gray thread and crochet five-around.

Q I've made a few basic ropes, but now I want to try some new patterns. Can you suggest a few?

A The sky is the limit. Once you start doing bead crochet, you'll notice others wearing and making these ropes, and meet other crocheters in classes. Crochet friends often swap favorite patterns, color combinations, and design ideas.

You can find other patterns in books and on the Internet, from simple to complex. Judith Bertoglio-Giffin's first book, *Bead Crochet Ropes,* includes the Basketweave bracelet with an 84-bead repeat! (*See* Resources.) The chart of Bead-Crochet Patterns *(see pages 350–352)* shows the bead sequencing for several more basic crocheted rope designs, to get you started.

It can be difficult to imagine how these patterns will look when completed — and impossible to show effectively in this book. Varying the bead size, shape, and color will dramatically change the effect.

BEAD-CROCHET PATTERNS

To make any of these ropes, you'll first decide on a pattern, select the beads, prestring the beads in the pattern for the length you want, and then crochet it using the correct number of beads around. All of these are six-around patterns except for the last one; repeat each bead sequence for 42" or the desired length.

Furry Drops. Use 3.4mm drops (A) and one color of 11° seed beads (B). The drops come in many amazing colors and mixes, including metallic-lined drops that have a wonderful, magnified, watery look when viewed through the wide end. For a fun variation, substitute 10° triangle seed beads for the 11° round seed beads. *(See the finished Furry Drops bracelet on page 327, left.)*

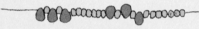

A, B, A, B, A, 7B / shows two repeats

Textured Stripe. Use two colors of 11° (A and B) for some stripes, Delicas (C) for others, and 8° hex-cut beads (D) for another repeating stripe. Varying the bead shape and size adds an interesting texture to this simple bracelet. The extra bead (13 beads in each color instead of 12 that would typically be used in a six-around design) will create a little jog between colors. You can also make a Textured Stripe bracelet using random lengths of each color.

13A, 13B, 13C, 13A, 13D / shows one repeat

Dotty. Use 8° seed beads (A) and 11° beads (B). The larger beads will pop up off the background.

1A, 8B / shows two repeats

Scattered Crystal. As a variation to the Dotty pattern, try using 3mm crystals (A) and 11° seed beads (B). The crystals can be all one color, or alternate between three complementary colors. Slightly larger 4mm crystals look nice, too, but are a bit more difficult to crochet. My favorite bracelet in this style uses 11° beads in matte metallic dark green iris and crystals in citrine, olivine, and Indian red.

1A, 8B, 1C, 8B, 1D / shows two repeats plus one bead

Classic Raised Spiral. Use one color of 11° beads (A), one color of 8° beads (B), and one color of 6° beads or 4mm crystal or Czech glass (C). This pattern makes a great texture.

3A, 1B, 1C, 1B / shows two repeats

Bumpy Spiral. Another interesting variation of this design adds a larger bead as every fourth bead at the center of the spiral. One of my favorites uses an 11° bead (A), 8° (B), slightly larger 8° hex-cut (C), and 2mm × 3mm Czech FP donuts (D). The bracelet has texture and sparkle, with the donuts poking out at interesting angles. Round 4mm Czech FP also works well as the pop-out bead.

3A, BCB, 3A, BCB, 3A, BCB, 3A, BDB / shows one full repeat

One-Color Spiral. Try using 11° beads (A) and the same color beads in 8° (B). The larger bead creates a raised spiral. My favorite is in matte metallic dark green iris with burnt orange thread. Also try using variegated thread with transparent beads. The thread creates the color changes, from subtle to bright. *(See the finished bracelet on page 327, right.)*

3A, 3B / shows 2 repeats

Crystal Flowers. It's fun to make a set of skinny bracelets with 2mm round sterling silver beads (A), with flowers made of 3mm Swarovski crystal bicones (B and C). The flowers can zigzag evenly around the bracelet, or you can place three or four flowers on the top of the bracelet and leave the rest of the rope plain. Then, make a few that include just a single flower — adorable!

6A, 2B, 4A, BCB, 4A, 2B, 6A / shows one flower repeat

Tiny cord. For another delicate rope that makes a great necklace for a focal bead, use 13° charlottes (one-cuts) or 15° Japanese seed beads in a single color. If you use topstitching thread, the thread shows between beads and its color can become an interesting design element. To see only beads and no thread, use finer sewing thread (which will not provide as much strength). Use a headpin or wire to make a pendant with the focal bead, creating a wrapped loop at the top that's large enough to slide along the rope. *(See page 191.)* The finished rope size is ³⁄₁₆" diameter. For an even thinner rope, try crocheting three-around.

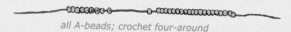

all A-beads; crochet four-around

Q About the crystal flower pattern: Isn't it tricky to get the flowers to line up correctly?

A There are a number of different flower patterns in crocheted ropes. But if you'd like to place several crystal flowers *(see facing page)* on a single rope, it's fun for the flowers to line up along the top of the rope. So, spacing becomes important.

For crocheting six-around, string as follows, repeating for the desired number of flowers.

- ▶ 71 2mm round sterling silver (SS) beads (A)
- ▶ 2 3mm crystals (B)
- ▶ 4 2mm SS beads (A)
- ▶ 1 3mm crystal (B)
- ▶ 1 3mm center crystal (C)
- ▶ 1 3mm crystal (B)
- ▶ 4 2mm SS beads (A)
- ▶ 2 3mm crystals (B)

To make a rope with a single flower:

1. String 20" of 2mm SS beads.
2. String one flower pattern repeat in 3mm crystals.
3. Finish with 2mm SS beads to the desired length.

Q Is it possible to make a crocheted rope ring? I saw one that looked crocheted, and I need a pattern.

A You can make a crocheted rope ring using small beads such as 2mm sterling silver beads or 11° seed beads, crocheted three-around. One fun ring design has a flounce of larger beads at the top; either daggers or drops work well for the flounce.

To make an average-sized ring (the rope has some give):

1. String 45 11° beads.

2. String three daggers or drops alternating with two size 11° beads for eight repeats.

3. End with 45 11° beads.

4. Crochet three-around for the plain rope.

5. Increase to five-around through the dagger area by crocheting two stitches in one loop, crochet one stitch plain, and increase once more.

6. Return to three-around after working the daggers by inserting the hook through two stitches at once, work one stitch plain, and decrease once again.

7. Stitch an invisible join *(see page 339),* which will sit at the center back of the ring.

Using Larger Beads

Q **What about working with larger beads? How can they be used for crocheted ropes?**

A My favorite crocheted ropes are simple one-color designs made with larger Czech glass or semiprecious stones. They have a bold, chunky look when worn stacked in threes. And they work up very quickly! I use a size 9 steel hook with larger beads. Test to see which hook works best for you.

If you decide to crochet with large or irregularly shaped beads, I suggest working with doubled thread for added strength. To string and crochet with double thread, hold the two strands together and use them as one. I use doubled thread whenever working with beads larger than 8° seed beads.

Here are some juicy pattern ideas for larger beads. For stringing amounts, see Guidelines for Larger Beads on page 338.

▶ **Pinecone.** Try 6mm rondelles (all the same size and color) crocheted three-around. The result has neat, overlapping scales like a pinecone, and looks great with contrasting thread to set off the scales. I also love 6mm faceted roller beads crocheted three-around.

*pinecone pattern
with larger beads*

▶ **Donuts.** Another favorite solid-color or random-mix design uses smaller 2mm × 3mm or medium 3mm × 5mm Czech FP donuts crocheted four-around. Many of the new varieties of these beads look like semiprecious stones.

▶ **Squares.** For another fun chunky crocheted rope, try using Miyuki 4mm squares as the primary bead (A) with 6° seed bead accents (B), in the Furry Drops pattern. *(See Bead-Crochet Patterns on pages 350–352.)* To make the bracelet fluid enough to curve around the wrist, I use a much larger crochet hook (steel size 3) and crochet loosely.

▶ **Squares variation.** For another bracelet in this style, I randomly mixed two colors of squares — terra-cotta matte and hot pink-lined lime green — and used matte transparent pink for the 6°. Spring had finally come to

Boston (sort of), so I had been yearning for more color, and this one has a fresh orange-coral-pink effect. Another beautiful classic combination combines matte bronze squares with brown iris 6° beads. The finished bracelet has an elegant metallic look.

▶ **Random seed.** You can also make a chunky bracelet with 6° seed beads crocheted five-around. For these, it's fun to use a random mix of colors, such as black, grays, and white, or copper, greens, and matte ivory. To create interesting "elbows" at intervals around the bracelet, mix in an occasional 4mm square bead by stringing a square every 36 beads. Of course, you also can work repeating patterns in 6° beads. I use a size 9 steel crochet hook and double-thread when crocheting 6° seed beads. You can crochet the same types of mixes with 8° beads crocheted six-around. One of my favorites uses a random mix of turquoise beads and charlottes with a 3mm matte green-gold square added every 42 beads.

▶ **Random pearls.** One of the most elegant crocheted bracelets is one made entirely with freshwater pearls, crocheted 3 or 4 around. You can use creamy white pearls in a random mix of sizes and shapes,

---

PRACTICE, PRACTICE

It's a good idea not to attempt a solid color bracelet until you are confident with working patterned designs. Using several colors helps you as you crochet each repeat by providing a natural reference point to the other beads in the pattern and allows you to notice more quickly when you have made a mistake.

---

or combine bronze, gold, taupe, and olive pearls for a rich, lustrous effect. Or, create your own color combination from the pearls in your bead box! The varied pearl shapes give the bracelet an interesting, organic texture. I finished this one by stitching on a toggle, so it fits my wrist more snugly.

▶ **Flat look.** Pearls also look great mixed into other rope styles, such as the classic flat caterpillar design from Judith Bertoglio-Giffin's book, *Bead Crochet Ropes.* (*See* Resources.) I like to use 11° seed beads in two colors for the body (colors A and B, one on each side, so it's reversible), then alternate a 3mm × 5mm pearl drop (C) with a 8° seed bead (D) along the edges. (*See sequence below.*) Or, to create an interesting ruffled effect, try using all pearls at the edges. The slight crowding will cause the edge beads to ruffle. This pattern is crocheted six-around.

3A, 3B, 3A, C, 2B, C, 3A, 3B, 3A, D, 2B, D / shows one repeat

flat look with pearl drops

Personal Favorites

I made the Squares bracelet *(see page 355)* in matte metallic dark green iris squares with pine green transparent 6° seed beads. Can you tell that I love this rich dark green? I also love to make bracelets in interesting sets, since I never wear just one bracelet at a time. If I'm wearing smaller 11° ropes, I may pile five or six on my wrist. With the chunky beads, a set of three coordinating bracelets looks good. So think of sets when choosing bead colors, and build around a color or two that you love and wear often.

Working with Patterns

Q I feel like I've already explored so many of the patterns for 11° beads. Is it possible to make these wider by working more beads around?

A Yes, you can crochet 11° seed beads with eight-around, which opens up a whole new range of pattern possibilities. If you work with a number higher than eight in each round, the tube may start to collapse (although you can try filling the tube with fabric cording or plastic tubing, if you want). When you crochet with eight-around, you may find that changing to a hook one size larger gives a smoother result.

Some people prefer to string and work from a charted pattern, while others are happy to follow a list of beads to string. As the pattern becomes more complicated, it's probably easier to follow a chart. In this chapter I've presented patterns both ways, so you can try them both.

Here is a gorgeous diamond pattern developed by Barbara Bush of Boston for 11° beads worked eight-around. It's designed for four colors (A, B, C, X), but can easily be adapted to more or fewer colors after you've made one and learn how the colors are placed.

Diamond Twist

To understand this pattern, note that each line is a row, and each line adds up to 8. You can string them in order, then crochet it like any other pattern, but with 8 beads in each round.

Row	Pattern	Row	Pattern
1	1A 4B 3X	9	4C 1A 3X
2	2A 3B 3X	10	5C 3X
3	3A 2B 3X	11	1B 4C 3X
4	4A 1B 3X	12	2B 3C 3X
5	5A 3X	13	3B 2C 3X
6	1C 4A 3X	14	4B 1C 3X
7	2C 3A 3X	15	5B 3X
8	3C 2A 3X		

The Diamond Twist pattern looks beautifully luminous in four closely coordinating colors, such as silver-lined gold, copper, light brown, and medium brown, or silver-lined crystal, amethyst, and two soft shades of blue.

. . . .

Q **What if I'd like to make up some of my own patterns?**

A Developing your own bead-crochet patterns can be a lot of fun. The process requires a certain amount of trial-and-error to make the parts of the design end up where you want them on the rope, but the results will be worth it. One way to begin is by varying an existing design that you like. Another method goes as follows:

1. String and crochet a short tube, about 3" long, of opaque white beads using the size and number of beads around that you want for your design.

2. Use colored markers to place dots on the beads, marking where you'd like to see certain colors fall in your pattern.

3. Settle on the design and then unravel at least one pattern repeat and write down the stringing pattern. Remember that you'll string it in the reverse order that you want to crochet it, so write down the stringing pattern from the end, back to the beginning of the repeat.

4. Try stringing and crocheting 2" to 3" of the design idea, using the actual bead colors and sizes you want, to see how it works and whether you like the design. If necessary, make adjustments to the pattern and test it again.

To design original patterns, some crocheters have adapted graphing software to meet their needs. Others chart their designs on diagonal strips of bead-crochet graph paper and then wrap the paper around a pencil or other cylinder to test it. Be aware that the diameter of the cylinder will affect the way the beads line up, and some patterns twist more than others. Also remember that changing the number of beads around the rope will alter the pattern.

RECYCLING TEST BEADS

If you use water-soluble markers, you may be able to wipe the dots off the white beads and reuse the test piece a few times. Shiny white beads are easier to wipe clean than matte white ones.

Q **I've seen a different type of bead crochet that looks artsy and organic. Do you know how this is done?**

A There's another style of bead crochet that tends to be much less symmetric and more free-form. Often worked in single-crochet instead of slipstitch, it can include:

▶ A range of bead colors and sizes in a piece

▶ The insertion of multiple beads in a single stitch (often 3)

▶ Various fibers, textures, and colors, with the fibers sometimes forming a major component of the design

Rather than the regular repeats of crocheted ropes, this random style often includes a wide variety of bead shapes, sizes, and colors combined in a more organic fashion, which may be crocheted in a tube or back and forth in rows.

Selecting and arranging the beads can be very playful and creative. This style includes the work of Bethany Barry, as seen in her book *Bead Crochet: A Beadwork How-To Book,* as well as some designs of Lydia Borin (search for her work on the Internet).

For more organic bead crochet, such as a rectangular bracelet, you'll prestring beads on the thread just as for bead-crochet ropes, using a mix of 8° and 6° seed beads, drops, squares, triangles, crystals, Czech glass beads (daggers, ovals, rondelles, and rounds), Bali silver beads, and small lampwork and furnace glass beads. For strength and to provide a sturdy fiber base, you'll want to string the beads on a heavier nylon cord or nylon upholstery thread. (*See* Resources.)

This random style of bead mixing is often referred to as "bead soup." Adding three beads to each single-crochet will create a short, beaded drop in each stitch.

THREAD PAINTING

If you have difficulty fitting the thread with a large-eyed needle through some of your beads, you can stiffen the end of the thread by cutting the end on an angle and painting about ¾" of thread with nail polish, fray reducer, or correction fluid; roll it between finger and thumb and allow it to dry. Now use the stiffened end of the thread as a needle to pick up the beads.

CHAPTER 11

Other Fiber Techniques

Knitting with Beads

Q I've heard that you can combine beads with knitting. Is that true?

A Yes, beads can add a gorgeously subtle accent to a knitted garment, or they can become a predominant feature of the design. Here are two different ways to incorporate beads into knitting.

▶ In the first and most popular method, you string the beads onto the yarn ahead of time and then slide them into place, one at a time or in groups, at the correct location as you knit. As with bead-crocheted ropes, when stringing the beads onto yarn for bead knitting, the last bead strung becomes the first bead you will knit. This creates less of a problem in knitting when the beads are all the same.

▶ In the second method, you add beads to individual stitches while knitting. This is done by placing a bead onto a small crochet hook, hooking an individual stitch, and then sliding the bead over the stitch. The stitch can be either knitted or slipped. This style of bead knitting works with any stitch pattern, doesn't have to be preplanned or prestrung, and the added bead sits neatly atop the stitch.

You can also use the second method to add shank buttons to the button bands of a sweater. Lily Chin's book, *Knit and Crochet with Beads,* includes a wealth of information about combining knitting and beads, as well as adding beads to crocheted fabric. The Rowan pattern books also include beautiful knitting patterns that incorporate beads. (*See* Resources.)

Knitting Designers, Take Notice!

As a bead knitter, my major complaint is that a lot of knitting patterns leave us hanging when it comes to the beads. It's as if the beads were an afterthought, or as if bead stores only sell one type of bead. I just hate a great-looking knitting pattern that says only that I'll need 600 beads. Wait, what type? Size? Color? At least tell us what **you** used, because the photos are never clear enough for us to see the bead details. Not to mention that the beads must have holes large enough to fit on the yarn. So please, knitting designers, tell us exactly what beads you used in the sample garment, so that we bead knitters will at least have a starting point for purchasing appropriate beads.

Q **What's a good smaller project for adding beads to knitting?**

A One frequently suggested project for knitting with beads is a pendant bag, with curved loops of beads between knitted stitches. These are lovely, fluid objects, but I rarely see them being worn. For something you'll wear often, you can use similar techniques to make a beautiful bead-knitted bracelet. Soft and comfortable, the beads add sensuous weight and drape.

I knitted one with chocolate-brown size-8 pearl cotton and acid green 11° charlottes (any 11° seed bead will work), using tiny size 0000 steel knitting needles. Yes, the needles are small — but so is the bracelet, and the project goes quickly. As with bead-crocheted ropes, you'll prestring the beads onto the thread before you begin. This type of bead knitting is actually much easier than making crocheted ropes: Instead of capturing a bead in each stitch, you'll slide small groups of beads between knitting stitches.

A hank or ounce of seed beads is more than enough for most bracelets. On my knitted bracelet I added groups of 4 and 5 beads across each row, and used two small sewing snaps for the closure. The snap closure is smooth and practically invisible, and the bracelet feels wonderful to wear. Here's how you make one:

1. Cast on 10 stitches.

2. Rows 1–10: Knit in garter stitch (knit every row) to make a flat strip where you can later sew the snaps.

3. Row 11: K2, slide 1 bead down to the work, K3, slide 1 bead, K3, slide 1 bead, K2.

4. Row 12: Repeat Row 11.

5. Rows 13–14: For the next 2 rows, repeat Row 11 but slide 2 beads into place above each bead.

6. Subsequent rows: Repeat, increasing the number of beads every 2 rows until you're adding 4 beads at each side and 5 beads at the center. Continue adding 4 and 5 beads until the bracelet is nearly the correct length, about ¼" longer than your wrist.

7. Now decrease the number of beads added, until you're back to adding 1 bead, as at the beginning.

8. End with ten rows in plain garter stitch. Cast off.

9. Sew half of each snap at each end of the bracelet (on the top of one flap, and on the bottom of the other), so the ends overlap by ⅜" or so. Weave in yarn ends.

(For books and Web sites with bead-knitting supplies and infor-mation, see Resources.*)*

. . . .

Q I want to include beads in my knitting, but the beads that fit easily on my yarn seem too big and clunky. How can I incorporate smaller, more delicate beads for a subtle look?

A I agree that proportion is really important when com-bining beads with yarn. Since knitting patterns often neglect to tell us what size beads to use, it falls on the individ-ual bead knitter to determine which beads will fit on the yarn and look great for a given project. If you bring a ball of your yarn to the local bead store, most bead store employees will be happy to advise you about different beads and help you come up with a solution.

To get the smallest beads onto your yarn, the trick is to use beads with relatively large holes. In general, Japanese seed beads have larger holes than Czech seed beads. I've tested a lot of these larger-hole beads with different weights of yarn to help get you started.

When shopping for beads, always bring your yarn and stringing needle with you so you can test the beads for fit. If you're having trouble stringing the beads on your yarn, realize

MATCHING BEAD SIZE TO YARN

▶ On lace weight, fingering, and sock weight yarns and pearl cotton size 8 thread, you can string most Czech glass beads; 11° Delicas; Japanese seed beads including 11°, 8°, and 6°; and 3mm and 4mm squares. Many Czech 11° seed beads also will fit on these thinner yarns. Such small beads would be beautiful knitted into an airy mohair scarf.

▶ On the next larger weights of yarn, such as sport and DK weight, you can string 6° seed beads and 3mm and 4mm squares. Heavier worsted and bulky yarns also work with all these beads except the 3mm squares. The Czech glass bead called a faceted roller bead (see page 52) has a cylindrical shape, large hole, and faceted sides and will also fit on thicker yarns up to bulky weight.

that part of the problem may lie with the needle, rather than the bead hole itself. In most instances, you can use a large-eyed needle or a dental floss threader to string beads onto the yarn. A twisted wire needle is another option for thin yarns, because they're available in a variety of sizes, including fine size 12. The thinnest needle option is to add a loop of beading thread to a size 12 beading needle and string the yarn through this loop, so that the needle and yarn do not pass through the bead hole at the same time. (See page 110.)

SEE ALSO: Bead Sizes, page 46, and Beading Needles, page 105.

Q Are there any tricks to fitting smaller beads onto my yarn?

A One problem is that when stringing, a doubled strand of yarn has to fit through the bead, just after the needle. There are some beads that would slide easily onto a single strand of your yarn, but a doubled strand won't fit through. To eliminate this double-strand problem, you can try:

▶ Wrapping the end of one strand of yarn with thread and hand-sewing to anchor it, then passing the thinner needle and thread through the beads

▶ Dipping the end of the yarn in glue or nail polish as discussed on pages 210–211 to stiffen it so you can use the yarn end as a needle to string the beads

Finding a viable solution is certainly worth a try, especially if you'd really like to try knitting with smaller beads.

· ·

Q How many beads should I string onto each ball?

A Most knitting patterns will instruct you on how many beads to string onto each ball of yarn. You'll be pushing the beads along the yarn until you're ready to knit them, so the yarn needs to be relatively smooth and strong enough to withstand the abrasion.

One way to reduce abrasion, especially good for delicate yarns, is to knit with a plain ball of yarn until you reach a row that includes beads, and then switch to a ball that has beads strung on it. Depending on the design, you can carry the unused yarn along the edge, twisting the two yarns together every few rows so you don't have long floats at the edge.

Another way to avoid scooting so many beads along the yarn is to prestring about three-quarters of the beads you'll need for that ball before you begin knitting with it, and then string the last one-quarter of beads onto the other end as you near the end of the ball.

Q Is there any other way to use a smaller-hole bead with bigger yarn?

A Yes, if you're using a thicker yarn and would like to incorporate beads into the design that just will not fit onto your yarn, there is another option that allows you to use any size bead.

▶ You can string the correct number of beads onto a strand of finer yarn or thread, and knit with the two strands held together (your fashion yarn plus the finer one).

▶ You can substitute a strong beading thread that's available in a wide range of colors for the finer strand. *(See* Threads: Multiple Choice *on pages 112–113.)* Coordinate the thinner beading thread with the color of your fashion yarn, and the thread will practically disappear into the finished knitting.

▶ When you're ready to place a bead into a stitch, you can separate the beaded strand, bring it to the front of the knitting, and knit the stitch with the fashion yarn. Slide a bead down into position in front of the stitch, and then return the thinner strand to the back. (Or, if you're adding a longer bead such as a bugle or rectangle, you can knit two stitches before returning the thinner strand to the back.) Continue knitting with both strands held together until you're ready to place another bead.

▶ You can use bead embroidery stitches to sew smaller-hole beads to the knitted fabric when it's finished, as described in the Bead Embroidery section that follows.

Bead Embroidery

Q Is bead embroidery a new technique?

A Although bead embroidery is enjoying new popularity these days, it's actually one of the most ancient forms of beading, next to stringing. Bead-embroidered garments play a significant role in the traditions of nearly every culture throughout the history of the world, from Africa to Thailand to Hungary.

Embroidering with beads is one of the most versatile types of beading. It's easy to learn, with just a few basic stitches to master, and you can sew beads onto just about any garment or object. When embroidering a fabric with beads, you have virtually unlimited options: you can scatter a bead here and there, sew beads just along the edges, or completely cover a fabric with beads.

You'll want to consider the strength of the fabric when planning bead embroidery, especially if the beading will be dense. The fabric must be sturdy enough to support the weight of the beads in the finished piece. When hung or worn, gravity exerts a continuous pull on the fabric.

Although I'll explain a few of the basic stitches, there are others you can learn and many interesting variations to explore. You can combine a wide variety of bead sizes and types. Try couching a line of beads in place, or use backstitch to get a similar result.

If you'd like to learn more about bead embroidery, check out two wonderful books: Amy Clarke and Robin Atkins' *Beaded Embellishment: Techniques & Designs for Embroidering on Cloth* and Yukiko Ogura's *Bead Embroidery*. (*See* Resources.)

Q **I'm just getting started with bead embroidery. What sorts of fabric work well?**

A You can embroider with beads on many different types of fabric, from sheer chiffon to velvet to heavy tapestry fabric. But when you're first getting started, it's a good idea to choose a medium-weight, stable fabric such as woven cotton, denim, or wool.

Printed or jacquard-woven fabrics can add another interesting element. The print or woven design can either dictate the embroidery colors or design, or complement a design you have in mind.

Q When I'm sewing beads in a design onto fabric, how do I keep the fabric from puckering or gathering up?

A Stiff fabric, such as heavy denim, will probably be fine, but to create smooth bead embroidery on most other fabrics, you'll need to do something to stabilize the fabric before beading. Options include:

▶ Working over a paper backing

▶ Adding a layer of nonwoven interfacing

▶ Adding a layer of water-soluble stabilizer

▶ Working with your fabric stretched taut in an embroidery hoop

The best method for stabilizing depends on the weight of your fabric, the density of the embroidery, and the final use of the piece. For example, you probably won't want a layer of paper lining a beaded garment, but it may be the perfect choice for a beaded wall piece or other nonwearable project.

Q How do I work with a paper backing?

A You can baste the paper to the wrong side of the area to be embroidered, or if the piece will be densely beaded, you can draw a design on paper and baste it on top of the fabric, so you're able to follow the design while beading. The paper will seem stiff at first, but it will soften as you work. Once you've completed your design, you can carefully tear away the paper from the perforated holes created by your needle going in and out to create the beaded design, or leave it in place. If you're using interfacing or stabilizer, baste it to the wrong side of the fabric before beginning to bead.

. . . .

Q Is there a trick to working with a hoop?

A If you decide to use an embroidery hoop when sewing beads onto fabric, try to use one that's larger than the embroidery area. If this is not possible, you'll need to pad the hoop by wrapping the inner ring with strips of fabric and making a few stitches to anchor the strips in place. The padding will help keep the piece from slipping while you work, as well as cushion any beads that lie between the hoops after you reposition the work. Work with the fabric taut, but avoid overstretching it in the hoop, which may cause the design to pucker or distort after the hoop has been removed.

. . . .

Q Do I need special needles for bead embroidery?

A Needles for bead embroidery have similar requirements as needles for bead weaving; they need to fit through glass bead holes, which do not stretch or give. For most bead embroidery, you can use size 11, 12, or 13 beading needles (long) or sharps (short).

SEE ALSO: Beading Needles, page 105.

Q **What threads should I use? And how can I tie a secure knot that won't pull through the fabric?**

A For bead embroidery, especially if you'll be embroidering a garment that will be worn and tugged, use strong thread that can hold up to wear. Use any of the strong synthetic beading threads discussed in chapter 4, not regular sewing thread. *(See pages 112–113.)* Since it's easier to add thread when embroidering than when weaving, you can start with a shorter thread of 1 yard or less, if desired.

Before starting to stitch, tie a knot at the end of the thread. Here's how:

1. Lick the tip of your index finger.

2. Wrap the thread around your finger, so the cut end overlaps the thread.

3. Roll the loop with your thumb, so the end spirals inside the loop.

4. Slide the loop down the thread to tighten it.

This knot takes a little practice. If it's not happening easily for you, try making a loop near the end of the thread, passing the cut end through the loop twice, and then tighten it (a double overhand knot).

To make the knot more secure, especially on more loosely woven fabrics, it's a good idea to sew a backstitch or two before you begin to embroider. Take a couple of small stitches in place, and then bring the needle to the right side to begin work. Hide these stitches with the first couple of beads.

SEE ALSO: Basic Knots, page 15.

Stitching Techniques

Q What stitch can I use to make an outline or write someone's name?

A My favorite stitch for making straight or curved lines is the backstitch. It can be worked with different numbers of beads in each stitch, depending on how much heavy use or wear the piece will receive. You can follow a penciled line, work random lines, or use the backstitch to fill in an entire area by working in straight or curved rows. I generally work backstitch with four beads per stitch, but you can also try three, five, or more. Here's how:

1. Thread the needle, knot the thread, and bring the needle up from the wrong side of the fabric.

2. Take a small stitch in the fabric to anchor it.

3. String four beads and slide them down to the fabric.

4. Insert the needle into the fabric, just at the end of the line of beads.

5. Bring the needle up at the center of the group of four, or two beads back from where the needle went down, being careful not to pierce the thread.

6. Pass through the last two beads.

7. Repeat, changing direction as desired.

backstitching with beads

Q What is couching?

A Couching, an embroidery stitch used to tack down items on fabric, is another option for making beaded outlines. It can be worked with one or two needles and threads.

One Needle

To work beaded couching with a single thread:

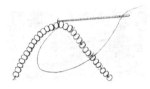

single-needle couching

1. Thread the needle, knot the thread, and bring the needle up from the wrong side of the fabric.

2. String the desired beads on the beading thread.

3. Arrange the beaded strand on the fabric as desired, and pass the needle to the wrong side.

4. Bring the needle up a few beads away from the end and stitch across the stringing thread, passing the needle back to the wrong side.

5. Repeat for the length of the line of beads. Knot and secure end.

Two Needles

To work beaded two-needle couching:

two-needle couching

1. Thread the needle, knot the thread, and bring the needle up from the wrong side of the fabric.

2. String the beads on the first thread and arrange the beaded strand on the fabric.

377

3. Use a second needle and thread to anchor the beads in place.

   a. Knot and bring the second thread to the right side a couple of beads from the end of the line to be couched.

   b. Pass the thread over the stringing thread and back into the fabric on the other side, creating a small straight stitch. Because the couching thread doesn't carry any beads, you can use a contrasting, thicker thread or a more fragile metallic thread to add another color and a design element.

4. Knot and secure all ends on the wrong side.

Q I'd like to scatter beads over a fabric background, like random sprinkles or stars. How do I do that with bead embroidery?

A Working scattered bead embroidery enables you to use the bead color and finish to create additional impact to every stitch. For a single-bead stitch:

1. Knot the thread and bring the needle up through the fabric where you want to place the bead, pulling the thread all the way through the fabric.

2. Pick up a bead with the needle, and slide it down to the fabric.

3. Move the thread in different directions to see where you want to place the stitch, and insert the needle into the fabric next to the bead.

embroidering single scattered beads

4. Pull the thread to the wrong side.

You can make these single-bead stitches in neat rows, or scatter them randomly over the fabric. If you'll be jumping more than 1" between stitches, it's a good idea to go through the bead again, and/or knot the thread between stitches, so the beads are not too loose and floppy.

· ·

Q What is a bead stack?

A You can work the same type of single stitch (described in the previous Q&A) with several beads to create a fringe or stack of beads. This can be used to create interesting texture in the bead embroidery. You can cluster these in groups of the same or different heights, or scatter them evenly over an entire fabric. Here's how:

1. Bring the needle to the right side and pick up several beads, anywhere from two to many. The last bead strung will be the stopper bead to anchor the fringe.

2. Skip the last bead and pass the needle back through the other beads in the stack and back through the fabric a short distance from the first thread.

embroidering a bead stack

3. Be sure to knot after each fringe before moving on to the next one.

· ·

Q What's the best way to add beads to the edge of fabric?

embroidering a beaded picot edge

A You can outline a fabric edge or hem with beads by working a picot stitch. It works equally well at the edge of a picture frame or book or to improve the drape of a lightweight garment.

1. Tie a knot in the thread and bring the needle through a folded edge of fabric.

2. Pick up one bead, stitch through the folded edge, and pass back through the bead.

3. Now pick up two beads, stitch through the folded edge about one-and-a-half bead's distance away, and pass through the second bead.

4. Repeat the two-bead stitch all along the folded edge.

Choosing a Project

Q What's a good idea for a first bead embroidery project?

A One fun way to experiment with bead embroidery is to embellish a few greeting or gift cards. Using a purchased card, you can stitch scattered beads over the design or create an elegant beaded edge. Or start with some medium-weight cardstock and create your own simple design, using one or more of the bead embroidery stitches.

Before you mail the card, add a thin sheet of foam or small piece of bubble wrap so the beads won't be crushed in the sorting equipment at the post office.

....

Q **What if I want to embroider beads onto a T-shirt? How can I be sure the shirt will be washable?**

A Whether you plan to wash or dry-clean a beaded garment, it's a good idea to make sure the beads will come through the cleaning process with colors and finishes intact — before you start beading. Some beads change color and appearance when they are dry-cleaned or washed, while others do not. Silver-lined, galvanized, and dyed beads, for instance, are usually not good choices as well as others that have less-stable finishes. *(See* Finishes *on page 43 and* Choosing Colors That Last *on page 63.)*

The best idea, whichever cleaning method you prefer, is to test the beads before you use them. Stitch a few of each color and type of bead onto a swatch of the fabric, and launder or dry-clean it the way you plan to care for the finished piece.

To launder a washable garment, either hand wash it carefully or place it in a zippered laundry bag and use your washer's gentle cycle, so the hand-applied beads don't get tugged on too much. Lay the piece over a rack or hanger to dry, smoothing and finger-pressing it into shape to reduce wrinkles. If the piece requires ironing, place the beadwork face down on a doubled bath towel and press it gently from the wrong side with low to medium heat.

Q Where can I find ideas for embroidering with beads?

A If you're having trouble coming up with beading designs, here are some thoughts to get you started:

▶ Use a printed fabric you love and embroider outlines and parts of the print, using matching or contrasting colors. Once the piece is underway and you feel more confident, you can always branch off and vary the design.

▶ Embroider a patterned tapestry fabric. You might bead the design fairly solidly in some areas, and just add outlines or no beads in other areas.

▶ Sketch a design on fabric, paint a design with textile paints, or transfer a photo to fabric and then bead over it.

▶ Embroider a beaded patch on a denim jacket or other garment.

Q What if I want to bead a picture or design that's completely covered with beads?

A The more densely you place the beads, the stronger the fabric and beading thread need to be to support the weight of the embroidery. You can work most any bead embroidery stitch close together over an entire fabric, or use a combination of stitches to get the result you want.

Q **Is there a way to make beaded garments less heavy?**

A You can control the weight of a beaded garment by adjusting the size of the beads and the distance between beads. In order to be beautiful and effective, a bead-embroidered garment doesn't have to have wall-to-wall beads. With beads, a little light and sparkle go a long way.

If you're concerned that a garment may be too heavy, use an airier design with more open areas and fewer beads. Also, make sure that the fabric you're embroidering on is strong enough to support the weight of the beads.

Q **I recently heard of a fantastic evening dress. It had an uneven hem with the front at the knees and a floor length "train" (sweeping the floor, not dragging on it). The back tail of the dress was beaded on both sides. How do you suppose that was accomplished?**

A The dress sounds beautiful. I would probably embroider the beads on the right side of the fabric first, and then embellish the inside layer. For each side, it's important to use thread that matches the fabric and short, neat stitches, so the stitches do not show between beads.

Another way to approach this project would be to stitch back and forth between the right and wrong sides, adding beads on both sides as you go.

Q I've seen beads added to skating and dance costumes to add sparkle and movement to the garment. How is this done?

A As a skater glides and twirls, glinting beads and swaying beaded fringe can create subtle but dramatic effects that enhance the skater's movements. To create this type of embellishment, you can try a couple of different methods.

One way is to embroider the beads onto a strip of ribbon or fabric, and then sew or snap the embellished sections onto the costume.

A second method is to sew the beads directly onto the costume. If you use this method, be aware that most skating and dance costumes are made from very stretchy fabrics. When the garment is stretched, the thread carrying the beads can be pulled to the breaking point. To avoid this problem, knot small sections of beading carefully and cut the thread so lengths of thread do not float across the back of the fabric. You may want to use a backing layer or patches of another, nonstretch fabric behind the beaded area. Then you'll be beading through two layers to add extra support for the weight of the beads.

CHAPTER 12

Repairs and Alterations

Broken Strings

Q How much do I need to know about repairing bead-work?

A That depends on how independent you want to be with your jewelry and beaded collection. For me, a large part of working with beads involves repairing old pieces, replacing missing beads, and restringing pieces that have worn out. You can feel free to borrow techniques from any chapter of the book to repair jewelry and garments, as needed.

In this way, I find that beading is somewhat similar to regular sewing. It's great to know how to construct a jacket, but just as often we may end up sewing on buttons and mending popped seams.

....

Q What's the most common beading repair that you come across?

A By far, the most frequent jewelry repairs I see involve a necklace that was strung on thread that has frayed and broken, or a bead tip with a broken arm. Many of these pieces were constructed in the Far East or Africa on whatever string-ing materials were available — often cotton string or fishing line that was meant to be only temporary.

▶ Avoid the temptation to patch the piece up. Take this opportunity to rebuild it so it's even stronger than before.

▶ If all the beads have been found and I can reconstruct the design (the owner has often forgotten), the repair may be a simple job of restringing the necklace on flexible beading wire and fastening it with crimps.

▶ If the original clasp is good-quality and still in decent shape, I often reuse it. Otherwise, this is a good time to upgrade the clasp, so the piece will look even better during its new, longer life.

▶ If the necklace was strung with knots between beads, there are two options. Either it can be repaired in the same way — with silk, knots, and bead tips or French coil — or I can give the piece more longevity by using small seed beads between the larger beads to recreate the color and spacing of the knots, and restring the piece on flexible wire.

> ## WHERE THERE'S A WILL . . .
>
> Stubbornness helps. If you really want to fix something, you'll find a way. By the way, that's how a lot of new beading designs are created. Someone makes a mistake, decides it looks interesting, and has the curiosity and stamina to follow through and figure it out. Voilà — a new design is born.

Clasps and Crimps

Q How can I repair a bracelet clasp if the thread has been "sliced" by glass beads? The clasp is separated from the bracelet, and the beads at the end are already full of thread. How do I attach a new clasp?

A As you might guess, there's not a simple solution. You can try picking out some of the thread from the end beads, but this is usually an exercise in frustration if more than a couple of beads are involved.

▶ See if you are able to pass through the beads with a smaller needle (such as a size 15) and finer thread.

▶ Consider changing to a different type of clasp, or try attaching the clasp with jump rings instead of stitching through the beads.

▶ Consider — as a last resort — cutting off the ends that are full of thread and reweaving these sections. It will probably only involve reworking a few rows.

▶ Be sure to eliminate the sharp beads that cut through the thread last time, and use a strong thread.

Q **What if I've already crimped a piece to finish it, and then I find out it's too long. Is there any way to remove the folded crimp?**

A By tinkering, I developed a way to remove crimps. It can take a couple of minutes, and the work must be done carefully, because you don't want to damage the coating on the wire. But I have found that I can almost always remove a crimp, if necessary. The method basically involves "chewing" off the crimp on a finished piece so that it can be made shorter, or another problem can be fixed without starting all over again with new wire. (*See* Nibbling Off a Crimp *on the facing page.*)

NIBBLING OFF A CRIMP

Here's my tried-and-true method for removing crimps without damaging the wire.

1. Drape the strand over a finger of your nondominant hand, to move the beads out of the way, so you can get at the crimp easily.

2. Use the flat side of a pair of flush cutters to take small slices, or "bites," off all sides of the crimp.

3. Rotate the crimp as you go. Don't be in a hurry, as you don't want to bite into the coating of the wire, or it will be ruined. At some point, the crimp will drop off with no damage to the wire.

4. Shorten the piece or make whatever corrections are needed and then string a new crimp.

good crimp

ready to fall off

Adjusting Length

Q **What if I've finally finished a piece and it's too short?**

A If the too-short piece is a strung bracelet, it's probably easiest to just cut it apart and make it again.

For a necklace, you might consider adding a piece of flexible beading wire at one or both ends to get the extra length you need. You may be able to incorporate the additional crimp(s) into the design in one of these ways: using a decorative twisted crimp, adding a crimp cover that looks like a metal bead, or hiding the folded crimp inside a bead with a larger hole.

Another option for lengthening a necklace is to make a new section using the same or coordinating beads. Attach each end of it to the ends of the original necklace, using the same type of clasp as the necklace. If the original necklace has a button-and-loop closure, you can add a button to one end of the new piece and a loop to the other. A bonus of this solution is that you now have two length options for wearing the necklace, either with or without the new section.

If this seems too complicated, you can always restring the too-short necklace, and salvage the cut piece of wire for a bracelet or two.

new section

adding a section to make a necklace longer

Q How do I lengthen a woven bracelet?

A You may be able to remove one side of the clasp and weave more rows of the design. Another alternative is to change to a longer or larger clasp.

Q Is there a way to make a finished woven bracelet or necklace smaller without taking the whole thing apart?

A If the piece is completely finished, with the threads cut, woven in, and knotted — honestly, the easiest way is to give the piece away to someone you love and make it again in the right size! Whether you can make a necklace or bracelet smaller without taking it all apart depends on a number of factors: the style of the piece, the construction method used, and how much length you would like to remove. Another consideration is how determined you are to fix it! Here are some possible ways to approach the situation.

CREATIVE THINKING

The main difference between a designer and someone who likes to follow instructions is that the designer is willing to try new things, play, and make mistakes. Eventually, this type of person will come up with something wonderful.

1. One quick way to make a piece smaller is to replace the clasp with a smaller/shorter one. This solution often works well with a too-long bracelet. *(See Shortcut on page 393.)* One shorter-than-usual clasp style is the sliding tube clasp.

option 1: a sliding tube clasp

2. Another clasp that takes up very little space and can help shorten a piece is a regular garment snap. You can sew half the snap onto each end of a woven bracelet or necklace, and overlap the ends to fasten it.

3. If the piece is too thick to overlap, try weaving a short plain beaded flap at each end of the piece; square stitch *(see page 269)* works well for this. Sew half a snap onto each flap (on the bottom side of the top flap and on the top side of the lower flap), and overlap them to fasten. This makes a short, nearly invisible closure that's easy to fasten.

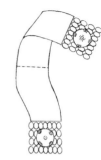

option 3: a square stitch flap

4. Another solution for a necklace is to use a pearl shortener, which clips around the necklace so that it hangs shorter. It can be used in back or in front.

5. For many necklace styles, you may be able to overlap the piece in back and add another closure such as a snap, hook-and-eye, or second lobster claw and ring to close it.

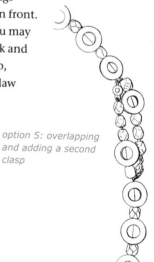

option 5: overlapping and adding a second clasp

option 4: a pearl shortener

Shortcut

Need to shorten a bracelet? If you used a jump ring to attach the clasp originally, it's easy to replace the clasp. You may want to eliminate the jump rings as well, to remove additional length. This solution worked one day for a woman who had spent weeks making a beautiful woven bracelet for her daughter-in-law that ended up being too long. She was getting ready to cut the bracelet apart to make it smaller. Thinking fast, I suggested changing to a narrower clasp, which solved the problem in a flash.

Beaded Bags

Q I have a beaded purse that is missing and/or losing some beads. Can I repair the damaged area so it looks good and is safe to carry?

A Whether the bag can be carried really depends on the condition of its foundation. Glass beads are relatively heavy. If the bag's foundation is shredded or so weak that it can't support the weight of the beads, there is no point in trying to restore it. However, if the base is strong and stable, you may be able to repair the bag so it's usable.

There are many different types of beaded purses: embroidered, knitted, crocheted, peyote-stitched, netted, right-angle-woven, and on and on. In fact, there are probably as many different types of beaded purses as there are methods of beading and beading stitches! In order to repair the bag, you first need to figure out what type of construction was used to make it.

Q **So, how do I figure out how to repair the bag?**

A If you can't readily see what technique was used to construct the bag, go into "gathering data" mode; ask questions, read, and learn everything you can before making any decisions. Study the bag closely, especially the areas where beads are loose or have been lost. Then, search the Internet and beading books to see if you can find anything that resembles your bag or its stitches.

To learn more about your piece, bring the bag into beading or knitting shops, bead shows, groups, or guild meetings — anyplace where someone may recognize the technique and shed some light on its construction. Most people are happy to take a look at your problem and share information on something they know about and that interests them. You don't have to follow all their advice about how to fix it. Just remember that you're gathering data, and stash the information away as an option.

If you've figured out what stitch or technique is used, it may help to take a class to learn the basics of that technique.

Q Once I figure out the technique, what else do I need to know?

A To repair a beaded purse, it's ideal to use the same beads, if you have them. But if beads are missing, it's usually more important to match the color first, and then match the size as closely as possible. Estimate how many beads you need by counting the missing beads, or count how many beads are in a small area (such as a square-inch) and multiply by how many square-inches are missing.

Vintage Repair

Q I have a vintage beaded bag that I'd like to repair. How do I go about matching beads that are probably not made anymore?

A You'll find Web sites that specialize in vintage and very tiny seed beads, and you may be able to find some reasonable substitutes. (*See* Resources.)

The eye tends to notice the broken or missing area first. After the bag is repaired, the new beads tend to blend in, especially if the color matches and the stitches are worked in the same way as the rest of the bag.

Once you determine the construction method and find beads that will work, you are ready to attempt the repair. Start by repairing just a small area and see how it looks. You can draw useful techniques from other parts of this book. Besides replacing missing beads, you'll also want to knot and work in any loose ends so other beads don't continue to fall off. You can also stitch into these loose end beads to stabilize them.

SEE ALSO: Threading Techniques, page 288.

Q The fabric in my vintage bag appears to be silk. Is that a problem?

A Many vintage bags are embroidered on silk. This is usually good news, because silk fabrics tend to be strong, and you can often sew on new beads that will blend in.

If the silk base seems to need more support, however, consider underlining it with a new layer of fabric. Sew each stitch of the repair through both layers. Depending on how perfect you want the finished bag to look inside, you may be able to finish the edges of this layer as the new lining, or reline the bag after the repair has been completed.

Q A lot of the threads in my bag appear to be breaking. Is the situation hopeless?

A If a bag is old and woven or knitted with thread, the thread may have rotted with age. Often, the weight of the beads simply overwhelms the thread. After all, beaders of 100 years ago didn't have access to the high-tech, indestructible threads that we do now. If that's the case, the bag most likely will continue to tear and come apart in different areas, even after you repair it.

If the entire bag is in danger of falling apart, stop and realize that you probably won't be comfortable carrying it. It may be more practical to mount and frame a beautiful bag or other beaded artifact. Framing will also help to keep the bag from deteriorating further. You'll need to make an aesthetic decision whether to repair the piece as much as possible before framing, or to frame it "as is."

Mounting and Framing

Q I know how to frame a flat piece of art, but how would I frame a beaded bag?

A The framing doesn't have to be complicated. You might want to shop for picture frames first to get an idea of the size and frame style that work well with your bag. If the bag is thick, you may need to use a deeper frame design, or even a shadowbox frame, to accommodate the bag's depth without crushing it. If you enjoy shopping in antique stores, you may find an old frame that will work for the project.

Once you decide on a frame size and style, you can either have the frame shop do all the work for you, which can be fairly expensive, or try doing part of the work yourself. For example, you could mount the bag and prepare it for framing, and then have the shop make the frame for you. Doing the mounting yourself is fun and can save quite a bit of the framing cost.

Q How would I go about mounting the bag myself?

A One easy way to mount a purse is to first cut a piece of foam core slightly smaller than the frame opening. Then you can cover it with velvet, linen, pleated silk, or another fabric that complements the bag and the décor of the room where you plan to hang it. If you find the perfect color, but the fabric looks too thin, use a layer of thin batting or interfacing to add cushioning. Wrap the layered fabric around the foam core and pin or tape it at the back, mitering and folding the corners neatly on the reverse side.

Decide on the placement for the bag and pin it in place if necessary. Then use a needle and thread to attach the bag to the fabric-covered foam core, stitching through all layers. Make your stitches neat and nearly invisible on the right side by using short stitches and thread that matches the bag. Support all parts of the bag so gravity won't cause the bag to continue to tear.

When the bag is mounted and ready for framing, bring this assembly to the frame shop. They can now cut and make the frame to fit it exactly, or place it in the antique frame for you. When the work is complete, you'll be able to view and enjoy the beaded bag for many years, without worrying about falling beads or further disintegration.

You also can consider using this same technique to preserve other beautiful old pieces that are too delicate to use, such as a fine lace handkerchief or a fragile silk baby jacket.

Appendixes

Glossary

Aiko. Brand name for precision cylinder seed beads made by the Japanese manufacturer Toho.

Anneal. To heat glass or metal to remove internal stress. Annealing metal wire makes it soft and pliable. Annealing glass makes it tougher and more break-resistant.

Asymmetrical pattern. A pattern that is not the same on either side of a central line. In beading, the term is often used to describe the left and right sides of a necklace or bracelet.

Aurora borealis (AB). A permanent bead treatment or finish that gives a rainbow effect. May be applied to the outside of a bead or to the inside of a transparent bead.

Backstitch. A hand-sewing or bead embroidery stitch formed by taking a short stitch backward followed by a longer stitch forward. Often used to outline a design.

Ball-peen hammer. A hammer with a rounded face on one side of the head and a flat face on the other. Used for shaping, flattening, and hardening wire and other metals.

Bead board. An inexpensive design tool used for laying out beads to create a design, usually before stringing.

Bead cap. A curved cap, usually made of metal, used to frame or embellish a stone or glass bead in a jewelry design.

Bead cone. A cone-shaped jewelry finding, usually metal and generally used in pairs to hide the join at each end of a necklace where several strands of beads come together.

Bead reamer. Hand tool, also called a broach, used to ream out, or enlarge, bead holes. Works best on softer bead materials.

Bead release. Thick claylike liquid used to coat a steel mandrel or rod before a lampworked bead is formed around the rod. Prevents hot glass from sticking to the metal.

Bead soup. A term used to describe a mix of several types and/or colors of beads that will be used randomly in a design.

Bead tip. Small metal finding used to finish ends of a jewelry piece strung on thread. The cup of a bead tip holds the knotted thread end, and the metal arm is bent to attach the strand to the clasp.

Beadwork. The practice of connecting beads to one another or to fabric, using wire or a needle and thread. Term includes stringing, weaving, crochet, knitting, and embroidery done with beads.

Box clasp. A clasp or jewelry fastener constructed like a small box, usually with a metal tongue that slides into the box and stays securely closed until it is released.

Button-and-loop closure. A clasp or jewelry closure made by sewing or forming a button or ball at one end of the jewelry piece and a correctly sized loop of beads at the other. Loop fits over ball securely.

Cabochon (cab). A stone or glass piece without a hole, having a flat back and a curved or domed top, generally without facets. Usually oval or round in shape; often used in jewelry making.

Ceylon. Pearlized or luster coating on an opalescent bead.

Chain mail. A type of wirework in which jump rings are joined together in patterns to create a mesh fabric.

Charlotte (1X). A seed bead that has a single facet ground into its surface to add sparkle.

Chevron. A design that resembles an inverted "V." Used on a traditional style of Venetian beads, where Vs are usually positioned around each end of the bead, near the holes.

Clasp. A fastener, usually metal, used to join the ends of a necklace or bracelet.

Cloisonné. An ancient technique in which enamel (powdered glass) is melted onto a metal base. The base is often divided into sections by thin metal strips to create designs.

Coil crimp end. A wire coil used to finish the end of leather or fabric cording and join it to a clasp or other finding.

Coin. A flat bead shape that resembles a coin. The bead hole may be positioned vertically through the disk or pierced through the top of the disk.

Combed designs. A type of lampwork design often found on traditional Venetian beads, in which a pick or other tool is dragged across hot glass stripes to create a feathered effect.

Couch/couching. A bead embroidery stitch often used for outlining, which can be executed using either one or two needles and threads.

Crocheted rope. A beaded rope formed by stringing beads on thread, often in patterns, then crocheting them in a spiral path, forming a tube.

Culling. Sorting through beads to separate thin, thick, or misshapen beads from other beads before beginning bead-work. Gives work a smoother, more uniform appearance.

Cushion bead. An extra bead placed at each end of a strung piece, after the crimp, to protect the beading wire from the sharp edges of the crimp tube.

Cylinder crimp. Small metal tube used for crimping and securing jewelry designs strung on flexible beading wire.

Dead-soft. Refers to jewelry wire that has been annealed or otherwise treated so it is soft, pliable, and easily bent.

Embroidery. Decorating fabric with designs using a needle and thread or yarn. Beads and sequins may be incorporated into the designs.

Embroidery hoop. A double frame of wood or metal used to stretch and hold fabric taut during embroidery or other handwork.

Eye beads. Ancient handmade bead designs made of layered dots of color that resemble an eye. Traditionally used for protection, especially for babies, these designs are still popular among modern lampwork artists.

Eyepin. A short length of wire with an eye or loop at one end, used for hanging a bead or other small object.

Felted beads. Small spheres made of felted wool that can be strung, embroidered with smaller beads, and worn in jewelry designs or used for embellishment.

Fiber or ribbon beads. Beads made from wrapped or twisted yarn, braid, or ribbon and secured with stitching or glue. Can be strung in jewelry designs or used for embellishment.

Figure-eight clasp. Simple metal jewelry closure made from wire shaped into a nearly closed letter "S," or a slightly open number "8." Used with a ring on each end.

Filigree. Metalwork with delicate, open designs that can resemble lace.

Fire-polished (FP). Type of faceted glass bead made in the Czech Republic. After being machine-faceted, beads are heated in a hot oven to glaze the edges.

Fishhook. Type of oval clasp or jewelry closure with a hook on one end that resembles a fishhook.

Flamework. Also called *lampwork,* a method of wrapping and layering melted glass to form individual beads, using a torch with a flame of fuel, such as propane or natural gas, plus pure oxygen to create a hotter flame.

Focal bead. Larger bead often made of glass, stone, woven beadwork, or metal, used at the center or focal point of a necklace or bracelet design.

French coil. Fine, coiled wire that's cut into short lengths and used to protect the thread or other stringing material where it passes through the clasp or ring.

French ear wire. J-shaped wire finding used in making earrings for pierced ears.

French-beaded flowers. Method of stringing seed beads on wire and shaping the wire to form petals, flowers, leaves, and other naturalized forms.

Galvanized. Electroplated metal or other coating used as a finish on the outside of a bead.

Gross (GR). A group of 12 dozen or 144 pieces.

Gunmetal. Dark gray or nearly black finish often used on base metal findings.

Half-round. Refers to a shape of wire that is semicircular when viewed in cross-section.

Hank. A unit of measurement for Czech seed beads on strands. Usually includes 12 strands, but a hank of special, larger, or expensive beads may contain 10 strands or even 6.

Headpin. A short length of wire with a flat head, ball, or other decorative shape at one end to prevent beads from falling off.

Hook-and-eye clasp. A simple clasp or jewelry closure, usually made of wire or other metal, that has a hook at one end and a loop or eye at the other.

Iris. An iridescent metallic coating used as a finish on glass beads.

Jump ring. A small round or oval loop of wire that's used for joining jewelry clasps and other components together.

Knot cup. *See* Bead tip.

Lampwork. *See* Flamework.

Lariat. A longer necklace style, often without a clasp, that is typically worn wrapped around the neck with the ends looped over one another, or with one end passed through a loop on the other end.

Lever-back. A style of metal earring finding for pierced ears often made of sterling silver or gold-filled, with a spring-loaded back that folds open and closes securely.

Lobster claw. A type of simple metal clasp with a spring-loaded arm that opens and shuts securely.

Loom weaving. Creating fabric using warp threads strung on a loom, and passing alternately through them with weft threads. When beads are strung on the weft threads, beaded fabric is created. One bead sits between each warp thread, and the second pass of the needle locks each bead in place.

Loomwork. Weaving on a loom, which can include seed beads strung on the warp threads and woven into the fabric, as described above.

Luster/lustre. A high-gloss bead finish.

Mandrel. A metal object or rod used to shape a piece. Often used in wirework and to create the hole in a lampworked bead.

Mass (MA). A group of 1,200 pieces. Often used in wholesale packaging of Czech glass beads.

Memory wire. Steel wire that has been hardened so it has a "memory" or retains its shape. Available in loops of various diameters for jewelry making.

Micro-crimps. Tiny 1mm crimps used to hold beads in place in floating or illusion jewelry designs.

Mille. A group of 1,000 pieces; from the Latin word for the number 1,000.

Nacre. The iridescent inner layer of certain mollusk shells. When built up in layers around a tiny object or irritant, nacre forms a pearl.

Niobium. A rare gray metal sometimes used in jewelry making. Can be heated and anodized to create a range of bright colors. Desirable for those allergic to other metals.

Pewter. Metal alloy of tin that can include other metals such as antimony, copper, and lead.

Picots. A series of decorative loops along the edge of a fabric or ribbon, which can be woven or embroidered with thread or beads.

Planish. To create a smooth or shaped finish on metal by striking it lightly with a hammer.

Polymer clay. A malleable material that can be shaped into beads, pendants, and other decorative objects, and then heated in an oven to cure and harden it.

Pounding block/bench block. A small, smooth block of steel that supports wire and other metalwork during hammering, flattening, and shaping.

Puntil (punty). A metal or glass rod used during glassmaking for supporting and manipulating hot glass.

Rocaille. Refers to the Rococo period (French, eighteenth century). Often used to describe silver-lined transparent seed beads.

Sharps. General sewing needles with a sharp point, medium length, and relatively narrow eye that are often used for beading.

Single-crochet (SC). A basic crochet stitch formed by holding the working loop on the hook, inserting the hook into the next loop or stitch, wrapping the yarn over the hook, pulling a loop through it, wrapping yarn over the hook again, and pulling it through both loops on the hook. In the UK, this stitch is called a double-crochet.

Sliding tube clasp. A metal clasp or jewelry closure that consists of two tubes, one that slides inside the other, with a pressure fit. Often designed as a multistrand clasp with two to six rings on each side, or with a bar on each side.

Slipknot. A simple knot formed by making a loop, passing the top end of the loop behind it, and pulling it through to form another loop. The size of the second loop can be adjusted by pulling on the end of the cord or thread.

Slipstitch. A basic crochet stitch formed by holding the working loop on the hook, inserting the hook into the next loop or stitch, wrapping the yarn over the hook, and pulling a loop through both loops on the hook.

Snap clasp. A type of metal clasp or jewelry closure with a ring on one end and a ball protrusion on the other. The ring is placed over the ball and snapped into place, held by a patented, spring-loaded inner ring. Also called a ball-and-socket or a trailer-hitch clasp.

Spacers. Beads that are wider than they are tall from hole to hole, so they work well when strung between larger beads, adding narrow slices of color and pattern.

Split ring. A small, round or oval wire loop that's formed from two wraps of thin wire, like a tiny key ring. Used for joining jewelry clasps and other components together securely.

Split ring pliers. A special tool designed to hold a split ring securely open while a ring or other jewelry component is inserted into it.

Spring-ring. A simple jewelry clasp that is opened by pushing back on a small, spring-loaded lever that slides along the circle and is generally used with a jump ring or split ring. When the lever is released, the opening springs shut.

Temper. Refers to the relative hardness and strength of metal. In glasswork, refers to a heat treatment that toughens the glass by reducing internal stress.

Tigertail. Generic name for inexpensive beading wire made from three to seven strands of steel.

Toggle. A jewelry clasp, usually made of metal but also can be beaded, that consists of a ring or other open shape at one end and a strong post at the other. The clasp is fastened by inserting the post through the ring.

Toho. Japanese seed bead manufacturer.

Troy weight. An ancient system of measurement. In the present day, the troy ounce is still used in the pricing of precious metals, and is about 10 percent heavier than the standard avoirdupois ounce.

Tube crimps. *See* Cylinder crimp.

Tumbler. Piece of electric equipment used for polishing and hardening metal and smoothing stone.

Vermeil. Sterling silver plated with gold.

Warp. The vertical threads in a woven fabric, which are the threads strung on the loom.

Weft. The horizontal threads in a woven fabric, which are woven back and forth across the warp. In bead weaving, the beads are strung on the weft thread.

Wire guard/wire protector. A small metal horseshoe-shaped finding strung at each end of a piece of jewelry where the beading wire passes through the clasp. Protects the wire from wear and ensures that the loop is the correct size.

Zipping up. Slang term that refers to the process of joining the two ends of a strip or section of peyote stitch using needle and thread. The "up-beads" of one end fit into the down spaces of the other, like a zipper.

Resources

BEADING BOOKS

There are thousands of beading books to choose from today. Learn more about beading by exploring topics that interest you.

All-Around Useful Books

Bateman, Sharon. *Findings & Finishings: A Beadwork How-To Book.* Interweave Press, 2003.

Blakelock, Virginia L. *Those Bad, Bad Beads.* Virginia L. Blakelock, 1988.

Dairy Barn Cultural Arts Center. *The Best in Contemporary Beadwork: Bead International 2002.* Dairy Barn Cultural Arts Center, 2002.

Deeb, Margie. *The Beader's Guide to Color.* Watson-Guptill Publications, 2004.

Dubin, Lois Sherr. *The History of Beads: From 30,000 B.C. to the Present.* Harry N. Abrams, 2004.

Durant, Judith and Jean Campbell. *The New! Beader's Companion.* Interweave Press, 2005.

Fischer, Sandi (Ruby). *Beading with Ruby.* Ruby's Jewelry Design & Beadwork, 2002.

Lark Books, eds. *500 Beaded Objects: New Dimensions in Contemporary Beadwork.* Lark Books, 2004.

Mann, Elise. *The Bead Directory: The Complete Guide to Choosing and Using More Than 600 Beautiful Beads.* Interweave Press, 2006.

Samejima, Takako. *Bead Fantasies: Beautiful, Easy-to-Make Jewelry.* Japan Publications Trading, 2003.

———. *Bead Fantasies II: More Beautiful, Easy-to-Make Jewelry.* Japan Publications Trading, 2005.

———. *Bead Fantasies III: Still More Beautiful, Easy-to-Make Jewelry.* Japan Publications Trading, 2006.

———. *Bead Fantasies IV: The Ultimate Collection of Beautiful, Easy-to-Make Jewelry.* Japan Publications Trading, 2006.

Stringing
Campbell, Jean. *Getting Started Stringing Beads.* Interweave Press, 2005.
Hogsett, Jamie. *Stringing Style: 50+ Fresh Bead Designs for Jewelry.* Interweave Press, 2006.

Off-Loom Weaving
Barsky, Galina, and Varvara Konstantinov. *Netting All the Way.* Jewelry by Varvara, 2004.
Benson, Ann. *Classic Beadweaving: New Needle Techniques & Original Designs.* Sterling Publishing, 2004.
———. *The New Beadweaving: Great Projects with Innovative Materials.* Sterling Publishing, 2005.
Campbell, Jean. *The Art of Beaded Beads: Exploring Design, Color & Technique.* Lark Books, 2006.
Campbell, Jean, ed. *Beadwork Creates Beaded Bags: 30 Designs.* Interweave Press, 2003.
———. *Beadwork Creates Beaded Rings: 30 Designs.* Interweave Press, 2004.
———. *Beadwork Creates Bracelets: 30 Designs.* Interweave Press, 2002.
———. *Beadwork Creates Earrings: 30 Designs.* Interweave Press, 2005.
———. *Beadwork Creates Necklaces: 30 Designs.* Interweave Press, 2002.
Campbell-Harding, Valerie. *Beaded Tassels, Braids & Fringes.* Sterling Publishing, 2001.
Cook, Jeannette, and Vicki Star. *Beading with Peyote Stitch: A Beadwork How-To Book.* Interweave Press, 2000.

Cypher, Carol Huber. *Mastering Beadwork: A Comprehensive Guide to Off-Loom Techniques.* Interweave Press, 2007.

Davis, Jane. *A Beader's Reference.* Krause Publications, 2003.

Elbe, Barbara. *Forever in Beads: Memories & Nature Transformed into Beads.* BEE Publishing, 2002.

Fitzgerald, Diane. *The Beaded Garden: Creating Flowers with Beads and Thread.* Interweave Press, 2005.

———. *Beading with Brick Stitch.* Interweave Press, 2001.

———. *More Zulu Beadwork.* Beautiful Beads Press, 1999.

———. *Netted Beadwork: A Beadwork How-To Book.* Interweave Press, 2003.

———. *Zulu-Inspired Beadwork: Weaving Techniques and Projects.* Interweave Press, 2007.

Hector, Valerie. *The Art of Beadwork: Historic Inspiration, Contemporary Design.* Watson-Guptill Publications, 2005.

Konstantinov, Varvara. *Coraling Technique: Step-by-Step Instructions for Making Ten Original Design Necklaces, Bracelets and Earrings in the Most Popular Russian Beading Technique.* Jewelry by Varvara, 2003.

Loh-Kupser, Amy. *Patterns for the Beadfuddled Beader, Volume 1: Peyote Beading Patterns; also Volumes 2, 3, and 4.* Amy Loh-Kupser, 2000–2001.

Prussing, Christine. *Beading with Right-Angle Weave: A Beadwork How-To Book.* Interweave Press, 2004.

Star, Vicki. *Beading with Herringbone Stitch: A Beadwork How-To Book.* Interweave Press, 2001.

Wells, Carol Wilcox. *The Art & Elegance of Bead Weaving.* Lark Books, 2002.

———. *Creative Bead Weaving: A Contemporary Guide to Classic Off-Loom Stitches.* Lark Books, 1998.

Loom Weaving

Pierce, Don. *Beading on a Loom.* Interweave Press, 1999.

———. *Designs for Beading on a Loom.* Donald Pierce, 2001.

Knitting, Crochet, and Embroidery with Beads

Barry, Bethany. *Bead Crochet: A Beadwork How-To Book.* Interweave Press, 2004.

Benson, Ann. *Designer Beadwork: Beaded Crochet Designs.* Sterling Publishing Co., 2005.

Bertoglio-Giffin, Judith. *Bead Crochet Ropes.* Bead Line Press, 2002.

———. *Patterns & Graphing for Bead Crochet Ropes.* Bead Line Press, 2004.

Chin, Lily. *Knit and Crochet with Beads.* Interweave Press, 2004.

Clarke, Amy C., and Robin Atkins. *Beaded Embellishment: Techniques & Designs for Embroidering on Cloth.* Interweave Press, 2002.

Cypher, Carol Huber. *Hand Felted Jewelry and Beads: 25 Artful Designs.* Interweave Press, 2006.

Davis, Jane. *Bead Embroidery: The Complete Guide.* Krause Publications, 2005.

Lehman, Linda, and Shelley Grant. *Bead Crochet Jewelry: Tools, Tips, and 15 Beautiful Projects.* Schiffer Publishing, 2004.

Neiman, Mary Libby. *Bead Crochet Basics: Beaded Bracelets, Necklaces, Jewelry and More!* Design Originals, 2004.

Ogura, Yukiko. *Bead Embroidery.* Japan Publications Trading, 2007.

Wirework and French-Beaded Flowers

Chandler, Linda L., and Christine R. Ritchey. *Getting Started Making Wire Jewelry and More.* Interweave Press, 2005.

———. *Woven Wire Jewelry: Contemporary Designs and Creative Techniques.* Interweave Press, 2004.

Fisch, Arline. *Textile Techniques in Metal: For Jewelers, Textile Artists & Sculptors.* Lark Books, 2003.

Jones, Linda. *Making Colorful Wire & Beaded Jewelry: 35 Fabulous Designs*. Interweave Press, 2006.

Lareau, Mark. *All Wired Up: Wire Techniques for the Beadworker and Jewelry Maker*. Interweave Press, 2000.

Nathanson, Virginia. *Making Bead Flowers and Bouquets*. Dover Publications, 2002.

Peterson, Irene. *Silver Wire Jewelry: Projects to Coil, Braid & Knit*. Lark Books, 2005.

Ryan, M. T. *Glamorous Beaded Jewelry: Bracelets, Necklaces, Earrings, and Rings*. Dover Publications, 2006.

Wiseman, Nancie M. *Crochet with Wire*. Interweave Press, 2005.

———. *Knitting with Wire*. Interweave Press, 2003.

BEADING AND RELATED MAGAZINES

Art Jewelry, http://art.jewelrymakingmagazines.com
Bead & Button, http://bnd.jewelrymakingmagazines.com
Bead Style, http://bds.jewelrymakingmagazines.com
Beadwork, www.interweave.com
Lapidary Journal Jewelry Artist, www.lapidaryjournal.com
Ornament, www.ornamentmagazine.com
Step by Step Beads, www.stepbystepbeads.com
Step by Step Wire Jewelry, www.stepbystepwire.com
Stringing, www.stringingmagazine.com

NATIONAL SHOWS

Bead & Button Show, www.beadandbuttonshow.com
Bead Fest, www.beadfest.com
Tucson Show Guide, www.tucsonshowguide.com
The Whole Bead Show, www.wholebead.com

BEADERS OF INTEREST

Jeanette Ahlgren, *www.mobilia-gallery.com/artists/jahlgren*

Judith Bertoglio-Griffin, *www.beadline.com*

Ingrid Goldbloom Bloch, *http://ingridgoldbloombloch.com*

Ruby Fischer, *www.rubysbeadwork.com*

Douglas W. Johnson, *www.douglaswjohnson.com*

Jennifer Maestre, *www.jennifermaestre.com*

Kate Fowle Meleney, *www.katefowle.com*

Laura Willits, *www.laurawillits.com*

BEAD SHOPS AND SUPPLIERS

Before ordering by mail, be sure to support your local bead shops! We list just a few of the many, with city locations in parentheses.

Ands Silver, *www.andssilver.com,* Bali and Thai beads

Anne Choi, *www.annechoi.com,* handmade sterling silver beads

Antelope Beads, *www.antelopebeads.com,* ceramic beads, Kenya

Armour Products, *www.armourproducts.com,* Armour Etch Bath Kit

Artbeads, *www.artbeads.com,* Griffin German silk cord

Auntie's Beads (Grapevine, TX), *www.auntiesbeads.com*

Austin Gem and Bead, *www.austingemandbead.com*

Ayla's Originals (Evanston, IL), *www.aylasoriginals.com*

Barking Rock Farm, *www.barkingrock.com,* vintage seed beads

Bead Cats (aka Universal Synergetics), *www.beadcats.com,* beads and supplies selected by artists Virginia Blakelock and Carol Perrenoud

Bead Gallery (Salem, NH), *www.beadgalleryinc.com*

The Bead Monkey (Minneapolis, MN), *www.thebeadmonkey.com*

The Bead Shop (Palo Alto, CA), *www.beadshop.com*

Bead Spinner Lady, *www.beadspinnerlady.com*

Bead Stopper, *www.beadstopper.com*

Beadalon, *www.beadalon.com,* flexible beading wire

Beadazzled (Baltimore, MD), *www.beadazzled.net*

Beaded Images, *www.beadedimages.com,* designs and patterns by Barbara Elbe

Beaded Impressions, *www.abeadstore.com*

beadFX (Toronto, ON), *www.beadfx.com*

BeaDivine.com, *www.beadivine.com*

Beads East (Manchester, CT), *www.beadseast.com*

The Beadsmith, *www.helby.com*

Beadworks (nine shops in the U.S.), *www.beadworks.com*

Beadwrangler, *www.7beads.com,* bead spinner, pearl cotton, Jean Stitch thread for crochet, size 0000 knitting needles, Big Eye Needle

Beautiful Bead, *www.dianefitzgerald.com,* Diane Fitzgerald

Bella Venetian Beads, *www.bellavenetianbeads.com*

Bobby Bead (Minneapolis, MN), *www.bobbybead.com,* Toho Aiko cylinder beads

Canada Beading Supply (Ottawa, ON), *www.canbead.com*

Caravan Beads (Portland, ME), *www.caravanbeads.com,* Miyuki beads, C-Flex beading wire, BeadCreatorPro design software, C-Lon thread and cord

Cochenille Design Studio, *www.cochenille.com,* Stitch Painter software for beading, knitting, and weaving

Corina Beads, *www.corinabeads.com,* books, videos, tools

Cynthia Rutledge, *www.cynthiarutledge.net,* kits

Design Originals, *www.d-originals.com,* crafts books

Diana Friedberg, *www.worldonastringproject.com,* DVD series on beads

Don Pierce, *www.larrytheloom.com,* Larry the Loom

Donegan Optical Company, *www.doneganoptical.com,* Optivisor headband magnifier

Dremel, *www.dremel.com,* Dremel rotary tool

Empyrean Beads, *www.empyreanbeads.com,* vintage seed beads

FindingKing (eBay supplier), jump ring opening tool

Fire Mountain Gems, *www.firemountaingems.com,* Accu-Flex beading wire, Wide-Eye Needle

Foxden Designs (Franksville, WI), *www.foxdendesigns.com*

Fusion Beads (Seattle, WA), *www.fusionbeads.com*

General Bead (San Francisco, CA), *www.genbead.com*

Green Girl Studios, *www.greengirlstudios.com*

i-bead, *www.i-bead.com,* kits and patterns by Amy Loh-Kupser

Intercal, *www.intercaltg.com,* Mastex nylon upholstery thread

James Smirich, *www.smirich.com,* handmade lampwork beads

Jewelry Supply, Inc., *www.jewelrysupply.com,* Tool Magic

Just Beads, *www.justbeads.com,* auction site for lampwork beads

Kimdoly (Vancouver, B.C.), *www.kimdoly.com*

Knitty, *www.knitty.com,* online knitting magazine with bead-knitting projects

Land of Odds (Nashville, TN), *www.landofodds.com,* Griffin and Gudebrod silk cords

Liliana Bead, *www.lilianabead.com,* handmade artwork, glass beads, and jewelry

Lilly's Bead Box (Knoxville, TN), *www.lillysbeadbox.com*

Lima Beads, *www.limabeads.com*

Marcia Katz, *www.festoonery.com,* loom

Mill Hill, *www.millhillbeads.com,* Magnifica Japanese cylinder beads

Mirrix Tapestry and Bead Loom, *www.mirrixlooms.com,* high-quality looms

Miyuki Beads, *www.miyuki-beads.co.jp/english,* Delica Color & Durability chart

Moondance Designs, *www.moondancedesigns.com*

Nina Designs, *www.ninadesigns.com,* Bali and Thai silver findings

Nordic Needle (Fargo, ND), *www.nordicneedle.com,* pearl cotton, 0000 knitting needles

Northampton Beadery (Northampton, MA), *www.northamptonbeadery.com*

Ornamentea (Raleigh, NC), *www.ornamentea.com*

Ott-Lite, *www.ott-lite.com,* specialized natural light craft lamps

Out On A Whim (Cotati, CA), *www.whimbeads.com,* Vellux mats

Paramount Wire, *www.parawire.com,* copper wire in 30 colors from 12 to 32 gauge, memory wire

Pellon Consumer Products, *www.pellonideas.com,* stabilizer, interfacing

Pema Arts, *http://tibetanbeads.com*

Rio Grande, *www.riogrande.com*

Rishashay, *www.rishashay.com,* Bali silver findings

Roessler Glass, *www.roesslerglass.com,* furnace glass

School of Beadwork, *www.schoolofbeadwork.com,* retreats, workshops

Shepherdess (San Diego, CA) *www.shepherdessbeads.com*
Shiana, *www.shiana.com,* Bali, Thai, vermeil findings
Shipwreck Beads (Lacey, WA) *www.shipwreckbeads.com*
SoftFlex Co., *www.softflexcompany.com,* beading wire, flush cutter
Toho, *www.tohobeads.net,* Aiko and Treasure seed beads
ToolGS, *www.gshypocement.com,* G-S Hypo Cement
U Bead It (Sacramento, CA), *www.ubeaditsacramento.com*
Urban Maille Chain Works, *http://urbanmaille.com*
U.S. Bead Warehouse, Sweet Creek Creations,
    www.usbeadwarehouse.com
Via Murano, *www.viamurano.com,* Twisted Tornado Crimp
Vintaj Natural Brass Co., *www.vintaj.com,* brass findings

Acknowledgments

Thanks to the wonderful people at Storey Publishing, especially Deborah Balmuth and Nancy Wood. I appreciate Lisa Wolf of Crystal Blue Beading Company, formerly of Watertown, Massachusetts, for suggesting me for this project, and for allowing me to play in her store for years while I soaked up as much beading knowledge as possible. Warm thanks to my fellow beaders who helped by reading chapters, including Terry Kwan, Ann Feeley, Ann Tremelling, and Carole Stratton. Gratitude goes to Nancy Tauber, Barbara Bush, and Linda Linebaugh for contributing their designs and expertise. And special thanks to Karen Mahon for getting so excited about the ideas for this book, on that first day, that I couldn't even entertain the notion of not writing it!

Index

Page numbers in *italics* refer to illustrations; page numbers in **bold** refer to charts.

Other Storey Titles You Will Enjoy

Beaded Jewelry: Knotting Techniques
by Carson Eddy, Rachael Evans, and Kate Feld
Whether you're working with pearls, gemstones, or other beads,
this concise guide leads you step-by-step through the techniques
of knotting between each bead.
88 pages. Paper. ISBN 978-1-61212-486-5.

Beaded Jewelry: Stringing Techniques
by Carson Eddy, Rachael Evans, and Kate Feld
This illustrated guide introduces you to types of beads, stringing
materials, findings and clasps, and the tools you'll need to make
your own beautiful beaded necklaces and bracelets.
88 pages. Paper. ISBN 978-1-61212-482-7.

Beaded Jewelry: Wirework Techniques
by Carson Eddy, Rachael Evans, and Kate Feld
Learn how to make your own handmade beaded wire jewelry
with this carefully illustrated guide, including chapters on
wire types, chain materials, tools, techniques, and more.
88 pages. Paper. ISBN 978-1-61212-484-1.

***The Knitting Answer Book*, 2ⁿᵈ Edition** by Margaret Radcliffe
Fully updated essential reference with answers to every knitting
quandary, for knitters of all levels and all types of projects.
440 pages. Flexibind. ISBN 978-1-61212-404-9.

Knit One, Bead Too by Judith Durant
With these step-by-step instructions for five easy techniques
and sixteen original patterns, transform simple bags and
clothing into stunning creations.
160 pages. Hardcover with concealed wire-o. ISBN 978-1-60342-149-2.

***The Handmade Marketplace*, 2ⁿᵈ Edition** by Kari Chapin
The must-have marketing guide for motivated artisans, fully
updated and expanded to include new online developments,
revised trends, crafter profiles, and more!
256 pages. Paper. ISBN 978-1-61212-335-6.

These and other books from Storey Publishing are available
wherever quality books are sold or by calling 1-800-441-5700.
Visit us at *www.storey.com* or sign up for our newsletter
at *www.storey.com/signup*.